THE FOREIGN POLICY

RESEARCH INSTITUTE SERIES

The Foreign Policy Research Institute

University of Pennsylvania

NUMBER 10

THE FOREIGN POLICY RESEARCH INSTITUTE

University of Pennsylvania

SUN YAT-SEN
AND COMMUNISM

by

Shao Chuan Leng

and

Norman D. Palmer

FREDERICK A. PRAEGER, *Publishers*

New York

BOOKS THAT MATTER

First published in the United States of America in 1960
by Frederick A. Praeger, Inc., Publishers
64 University Place, New York 3, N. Y.

© 1960 by Frederick A. Praeger, Inc.

Library of Congress catalog card number 60-16426

Manufactured in the United States of America

This book is Number 91 in the series
of *Praeger Publications in Russian History
and World Communism*

This is the tenth in a series of studies to be published by Frederick A. Praeger, Publishers, under the auspices of the Foreign Policy Research Institute at the University of Pennsylvania, established under a grant of the Richardson Foundation, Greensboro, North Carolina. The views expressed in SUN YAT-SEN AND COMMUNISM are those of the authors.

To David and Pat

Preface

This book is an attempt to examine in depth the relations between Sun Yat-sen and Communism in the hope of casting new light on this complicated subject and of providing useful perspective on the history of modern China. The volume begins with a review of Sun's early contacts with the West and the process of his ideological development. Then it proceeds to analyze the reasons for Sun's Russian orientation and the effects of the Canton-Moscow alliance. To answer the question whether Communism is the logical climax of the work of Sun Yat-sen, the last part of the book not only examines the Communists' interpretations of his doctrine but compares the similarities and differences between Sun Yat-senism and Chinese Communism.

In preparing this book, the authors have received generous assistance from many quarters. We should particularly like to express our appreciation to the University of Virginia's Institute for Research in the Social Sciences, whose two summer grants and splendid secretarial help made the writing of this volume possible. We are also grateful to the Richmond Area University Research Center and the Old Dominion Foundation for their respective grants, and to the Foreign Policy Research Institute of the University of Pennsylvania for assistance in arranging the publication of the book. For valuable Chinese sources, our thanks go to the Division of Orientalia of the Library of Congress, the Chinese-Japanese Library of the Harvard-Yenching Institute of Harvard University, and the Library of the Humanistic Science Institute of Kyoto University.

A number of friends and colleagues have been kind enough to read the manuscript in whole or in part and to give us the benefit of their comments. In this connection we owe a special debt to Professor Paul M. A. Linebarger and to the late Dr. Tsui Shu-chi for their helpful suggestions and criticisms. The responsibility for all the facts and opinions in this volume rests, of course, solely with the authors.

SHAO CHUAN LENG
NORMAN D. PALMER

Contents

SUN YAT-SEN AND COMMUNISM

Chapter 1

Introduction

The Chinese revolution of the twentieth century did not begin with the Chinese Communists, nor did it end with their accession to power on the mainland of China in 1949. China is clearly still in a process of transition. The exact pattern of the "New China" is not yet clear; and the clash between the old China and the new, between foreign and indigenous influences, is still a prominent feature of the Chinese scene. That clash is taking place in the ideological as well as in the physical arena; it is a struggle for the minds of men, as well as for their support of some particular government. Although the Chinese people, and Chinese society, are being forced into a new mold, it is not yet certain whether the goal is the usual Communist mold, or whether it is a new pattern of regimentation shaped by the adaptation of Communist principles to Chinese conditions. If Maoism is different from Marxism-Leninism, are the differences those of doctrine or of tactics? Does Maoism belong

1

at the end of the other "isms" which are collectively associated with Communism, or is it *sui generis,* either a radically new departure in Communist ideology or a new addition to the world's excess supply of ideologies? In short, what is Maoism, and what is its place in the ideological history of mankind?

Another question of almost equal importance arises. What is the connection between Maoism and previous doctrines or ideologies that have shaped Chinese society and patterns of life and thought over the centuries—particularly within the last century? Is it essentially a foreign importation, with some adaptation to Chinese conditions, or is it basically indigenous? To the extent that it is a product of Chinese thought and conditions, how is it related to other patterns of thought and conduct in China? In particular, what is its relation to Confucianism [1] and to Sun Yat-senism? Many of the leaders of the New China, Communist version, were themselves trained in the Confucian tradition, but they have consciously and openly repudiated Confucianism. On the other hand, they have not attempted to cut themselves off from China's past, and they have often claimed to find support for their own policies in the traditions of their country. In his famous essay, "On New Democracy," Mao Tse-tung wrote: "As China's present new politics and new economy have developed out of her old politics and old economy, and China's new culture has also developed out of her old culture, we must respect our own history and should not cut ourselves adrift from it." At the same time Mao stressed the necessity of separating "all the rotten things of the ancient feudal ruling class from the fine ancient popular culture that is more or less democratic and revolutionary in character." [2] The new generation in China is not being taught to ignore China's past; instead, it is being exposed to a heavy dose of reinterpretation which serves the purposes of the present regime. In other words, the Chinese Communists do not deny the past; rather they rewrite it to suit their purposes.

With respect to Sun Yat-sen and Sun Yat-senism—i.e., the political thought of Dr. Sun—the Chinese Communists seem to act indiscriminately as heirs, reinterpreters, and critics.

Ever since the death of Dr. Sun in 1925, they have claimed to be the rightful inheritors of his mantle. This claim has been strengthened by the fact of Sun's own alliance with the Soviet Union, the equivocal nature of his own statements on Communism, the eventual failure of the Nationalists under Chiang Kai-shek to justify their claim to the "mandate of heaven" and to the legacy of Dr. Sun, and by the increasingly successful efforts of the Communists to gain mass support, to win the civil war, and to consolidate political power. Their claims have also been supported by Madame Sun Yat-sen, who, ever since the split of 1927, has been pro-Communist in orientation and who has held important posts in the People's Republic of China, including that of a Vice-Chairman of the Central People's Government. On many occasions Madame Sun has referred to her husband's advice to his people to "walk hand in hand with the Soviet Union," and has insisted that the Chinese Communists, and they alone, are following in the footsteps of her illustrious husband, the Father of Modern China. The Chinese Communists, in their turn, have often made the same claim; but, as has been suggested, their attitude toward Dr. Sun has been a somewhat equivocal one. While they have preserved the memory of the great Chinese revolutionary, they have pictured him as a leader of the bourgeois, and not of the socialist, revolution who, however, was sympathetic with Communism and who left certain teachings which were of value in ushering in the "New Democracy."

Mao Tse-tung himself, and many other theoreticians of Chinese Communism, have discussed the relationship between Sun Yat-senism and their principles, in a manner which suits their own ends. Generally speaking, they pay a certain amount of lip service to Sun's principles, but they interpret them according to their own lights, and they boast that their own infallible doctrine represents a far more advanced stage of political and theoretical development. In a section of "On New Democracy," Mao Tse-tung commented on the differences and similarities between the Three People's Principles and Communism.[3] According to him, the political programs of the two doctrines during the stage of democratic revolution were basically consistent with each other; but he made it clear that the consistency was between "the minimum program of Communism" and the Three People's Principles, and that it was based on an alleged reinterpretation by Dr. Sun of his own principles, as they were expressed in the Manifesto of the First National Congress of the Kuomintang in January 1924. In this Manifesto and at several later periods, Sun was alleged to have emphasized the three policies of alliance with the Soviet Union, alliance with the Communists, and alliance with the workers and peasants. Mao called these "the revolutionary, new, and genuine Three People's Principles." These are the aspects of Dr. Sun's teachings which the Chinese Communists have chosen to emphasize, and which in their view save him from becoming just another bourgeois social reformer.

It is this interpretation that helps to clarify such a classic of Maoist dialectic as Mao's statement that "the Three People's Principles with the three cardinal policies are the revolutionary, new, and genuine Three People's Principles—the Three People's Principles of New Democracy." But even Mao, who has been less critical of Sun Yat-senism than some Communist spokesmen, pointed to certain basic differences between the Three Principles of Sun Yat-sen and Communism. They differed, he declared, in their programs for the stage of democratic revolution, in the question of socialist revolution, in world outlook, and in revolutionary thoroughness. These differences, concluded Mao, "distinguish Communists from the followers of the Three People's Principles. It is undoubtedly quite wrong to overlook this fact, to see only the side of unity and not the side of contradiction." [4] Since Mao wrote these words in 1940, the Chinese Communists have emerged from a limited area of the hinterland of north and northwest China to become the masters of all of mainland China; and, apparently, their confidence in themselves and in the uniqueness and validity of their ideology has grown with their success. While they have less need to take shelter behind the mantle of the Father of the Chinese revolution, they still find it expedient at times to use Sun's name to gain respectability for their regime before the eyes of the outside world. Each year, some kind of commemorative service is held in Communist China to mark the anniversary of Dr. Sun's death or birth. Communist spokesmen frequently take the occasion to picture Sun as a link between the New China and the old democratic revolution, and to appeal to his "true followers" in Taiwan to reunite with the fatherland.

From the standpoint of both historical and contemporary interest, a study of Sun Yat-sen and Communism is as timely as it is badly needed. All of the many studies of Dr. Sun, the greatest figure in modern China—Mao Tse-tung not excepted —throw some light upon this subject. But none treats it systematically, and the reader is left with a feeling of bewilderment. The question therefore remains unanswered: exactly what is the connection between Sun Yat-senism and Communism? Why did Dr. Sun conclude an alliance with Soviet Russia, thus providing international Communism with the first great opportunity to experiment with its united front strategy? To what extent was Sun influenced by the doctrines of Communism, and to what extent have the Chinese Communists been influenced by his doctrines? We must recognize frankly that the present confusion on this subject (a clear picture of which is so important for an understanding of the course of the Chinese revolution and for what W. W. Rostow has called "the prospects for Communist China") is by no means due solely to the lack of systematic studies of this difficult problem. Indeed, the difficulties in the path of a clear understanding of the nuances of this topic are manifold and bewildering. At least three may be itemized:

(1) There is, first of all, the difficulty of determining what Sun's own views were, on Communism or on almost any other subject. Sun Yat-senism is by no means an integrated or coherent body of doctrine. Sun was not a very systematic thinker, and his ideas and policies changed with the success or failure of his own efforts and with the course of events affecting China. His contacts with Communism and the Communists came during the years of disillusionment which followed the attainment of what had been his main objective

during many years of exile and sacrifice—namely, the overthrow of the Manchu Dynasty and the establishment of a
republic in China. The last sentence of his "Autobiography"
(a brief tract which appeared soon after the revolution of
1911-1912) describes Sun's rather premature rejoicing at
the success of the Chinese revolution. Referring to his inauguration on January 1, 1912, as provisional president of China,
he wrote: "Thus after thirty years of struggle, I finally saw the
successful realization of my long-cherished aim—the creation
of the Chinese Republic." [5] Sun soon realized, however, that
the revolution was far from won, and that, in fact, it had been
arrested in mid-passage and was being betrayed. Hence, his
last years were no more successful than the earlier period of
struggle. Only after he turned to the Soviet Union for assistance and after he reorganized the Kuomintang along Communist lines, was he in a position to take up again the work of
consolidation and national unity, or even to escape the intrigues
of cabals within and without the ranks of his Party. His premature death in March 1925 spared him the agony of witness-
ing the fatal split within the ranks of his supporters in 1927—
a split that left rival claimants to his mantle, that seriously
retarded the work of national development, and that eventually,
through civil war and global conflict, paved the way for the
Communist victory in China. But although Sun did not have
to witness the tragedies of the past generation, he realized
quite clearly that, as he stated in his final will and testament,
"the work of the revolution is not yet done." The revolution
which he thought had been accomplished in 1912 was in fact
far from complete in 1925. More than thirty-five years later the
same statement can be made with almost equal truth.

In these last years of disillusionment, Sun reacted against
the Western powers, and his anti-foreign and anti-imperialist
sentiments became markedly stronger. At the same time, he
came under the influence of Communism, and made his historic alliance with the Soviet Union. More and more, he
emphasized the necessity for a social as well as a political
revolution in his country. His ideas, as well as his policies,
were already a hodgepodge, drawn from many sources and

experiences. In his later years, instead of sorting these ideas out and developing a coherent pattern of political and social philosophy, he came under other ideological influences. Thus, he never had an opportunity to funnel these various, and often conflicting, ideas and impressions into a systematic and coherent pattern. Since he was not a very systematic theorizer, perhaps he could not have clarified his thinking and resolved the many inconsistencies in his views and policies, even if he had had the time. He was a magnetic personality and a great leader of men, but he was not one of those persons, like Lenin, who are equally at home in theory and in action.

It has been said that Sun Yat-senism was at one time an ideology that had influenced far more people than the ideologies of Communism and of Fascism combined. This statement is probably no longer true, if it ever was, but it does indicate the importance of trying to understand precisely what Sun Yat-senism was. It has been suggested that it was not a consistent or coherent body of doctrine; therefore, to refer to it as an "ism" may be in itself misleading. It was not, in essence, an authoritarian creed, but neither was it a wholly democratic one. It was a strange blend of many doctrines, modified by Dr. Sun's own mental processes and adapted to the peculiar conditions of China in the first quarter of the twentieth century. "With Sun Yat-sen, in short," states R. R. Palmer, "democracy easily shaded off into a theory of benevolent and constructive dictatorship, and Marxism, communism, socialism, 'livelihood,' the planned society, welfare economics, and anti-foreign and anti-imperialism sentiment were all mixed together." [6]

(2) Sun Yat-sen, like Marx, has been the victim of his alleged followers and interpreters, who have tended to push the man, the human being, into the background and to give prominence to their own versions of the ideas of the master. The legacy of Dr. Sun was a divided one; and neither the Communists nor the Nationalists—nor those Chinese who have tried to find another way for their country—have had any difficulty whatever in finding support for their ideas in the teachings of Sun Yat-sen. The apotheosis of Dr. Sun, which

began immediately after his death—in fact, even before his death—made a realistic appraisal of his life and teachings almost impossible. Every day, during the heyday of Nationalist China, in schools, government offices, and elsewhere, obeisance was made to the memory of Dr. Sun, and his famous will was read as if it embodied the final truth. Sun's splendid mausoleum on the Purple Mountain outside of Nanking became a great national shrine. Thus, the man was buried in the legend, and those who sought power and influence in China did so in the name of Sun Yat-sen. Even the victory of Communism in China has not changed the picture. The Nationalist government on Formosa has repeatedly vowed its determination to return to the mainland and to carry Sun's *San Min Chu I* revolution to its successful completion. The Chinese Communists, on the other hand, have insisted that they are the rightful successors of Dr. Sun and that their revolution is the logical development of his "new" Three People's Principles. All this has contributed, in no small measure, to the general confusion about Sun Yat-senism.

(3) A particularly baffling problem is that of determining the relative effect of foreign and of indigenous influences upon Sun Yat-sen. Brought up in the Confucian tradition, Sun always tried to interpret and to identify himself with those features of Chinese history and philosophy which most appealed to him. He also reacted strongly against foreign influences and pressures, and sought to give his countrymen a greater sense of dignity and of human worth, and a faith in their own country and civilization. The changes in Chinese life and politics, for which he labored in the face of incredible odds for many years, were designed to free the Chinese from the shackles of superstition and autocracy and corrupt rule at home, and from foreign domination of all kinds. In a sense, he was the first true Chinese nationalist; he urged his people to identify themselves with China as a nation, as a means to gain independence from internal and external foes.

On the other hand, throughout most of his life he was subjected to foreign influence, and most of his life, in fact, was spent outside his own country. The two longest periods that

he spent in his native country were during the first twelve and
the last nine years of his life. He lived for several years in
Hawaii, Europe, and Japan. He made at least four trips to
the United States. Even though he developed marked anti-
Western attitudes after the failure of the revolution of 1911-
1912 and of his efforts to obtain substantial assistance from
the West, he continued to maintain his contacts and his
correspondence with Westerners of many walks of life. Indeed,
he was himself one of the most Westernized of Chinese. There
can be no doubt that his studies, contacts, and foreign experiences profoundly influenced his total cast of mind and his
approach to the problems of his own country.

Sun wanted to bring China into the modern world and to
gain for her an equal and honored place in the family of
nations. Even during his long periods of exile and frustration,
and disappointment with the lack of support from his own
countrymen, his thoughts were primarily on China. He was
first and foremost a Chinese. His life span covered a troubled
and eventful period of China's history. It was marked by such
events as the last years of the decadent Manchu Dynasty, the
ascendancy of the Dowager Empress, Tzu Hsi, the defeat of
China by Japan in the war of 1894-1895, foreign inroads on
China which threatened the extinction of Chinese independence, the Boxer uprising of 1900, the end of the examination
system, the overthrow of the Manchus and the varied fortunes
of the Chinese "Republic" after 1911, the internecine strife
between warlords and rival regimes, China's humiliation during and after World War I, the virtual collapse of Sun's
own revolutionary Party, the Kuomintang, the alliance between this Party and the Communists which led to the first
so-called "United Front," the beginnings of the literary renaissance in China, and many other momentous developments.
Dr. Sun followed all of these events with absorbed interest,
and he did much to shape many of them. Certainly, they all
had some effect upon him. Whether their total impact was
greater than that of his foreign experience and study is a
question which cannot be precisely answered.

To what extent did the Communists really influence Sun

Yat-sen? Clearly, he was impressed by the Russian revolution, and he was attracted to many aspects of theoretical Communism. At a dark hour in the history of China and of his own revolutionary movement, he allied himself with the Communists. He asked for and welcomed Soviet advisers, and he allowed Chinese Communists to join the Kuomintang. For several years, he worked closely with these dangerous allies. He has been called "the first of many world statesmen to fall victim to the fallacy of the 'popular front'." In the opinion of K. M. Panikkar, "The transformation of Sun Yat-sen, the original champion of Westernization, the product of a missionary school, from liberalism to open support of Leninism contains in itself the history of China's reawakening and the failure of its liberal renaissance." [7]

Sun's reaction against the Western powers and his alliance with the Soviet Union had obvious effects upon his policies and actions, but it is difficult to appraise the effects of this orientation upon his fundamental beliefs. Some of his statements in the years 1923-1925 seemed to reflect a real change in his thinking, whereas others seemed to be all of a piece with ideas which he had voiced repeatedly during a generation of revolutionary activity. Most of the views which he enunciated in his lectures in 1924 on the Three People's Principles had been expressed in fairly specific form as early as 1905. Occasionally, however, in these famous lectures he seemed to show evidence of his Communist associations and of the influence upon him of the Russian revolution and of Communist dialectics. During the years of his Soviet alliance, he still expressed, both by word and by deed, serious reservations about Communism as an ideology and about its applicability to the Chinese scene. But, at the same time, in his formation of the three major policies, in his letter to the Central Executive Committee of the Communist Party of the Soviet Union, and in other ways, he also manifested a strong pro-Russian leaning and a tolerant attitude toward Communism.

To what extent is Communism the logical climax to the work of Sun Yat-sen? To be sure, the great Chinese revolu-

tionary gave a powerful boost to the Communist cause by his
open alliance and sympathetic attitude toward the Communists,
at home and abroad, and toward certain aspects of Communist theory. Carsun Chang, a proponent of a "third force"
in China and a great admirer of Sun, believes that "the
political status thus granted the Communist Party by Dr. Sun
provided the foundation for their present success." [8] Is this
really true, or can the success of the Communists in China be
attributed to other factors and developments? Many non-
Communist observers, in China and elsewhere, have professed
to be struck with certain basic similarities between the ideas
of Dr. Sun and the doctrines of Communism. In particular,
they are impressed by Dr. Sun's exposition of the Third
Principle. This is undoubtedly the most difficult principle of
the famous "Three Principles of the People" to interpret
correctly. Sun himself described it in many ways, and always
with a high degree of vagueness and lack of clarity. It is
particularly difficult to find a precise English equivalent for
the Chinese terms for this Third Principle—*Min-sheng*. It has
been variously referred to as the idea of the service state, as
socialism, and, most commonly, as the People's Livelihood.
The latter term, despite its popularity, is an awkward English
expression, and, indeed, a rather vague and meaningless one.
In his lectures on this Principle in 1924, Sun referred to
Communism in a very different sense from the meaning of the
term in the dictionary of Marxism-Leninism, and he went out
of his way to criticize the doctrine of the class struggle and
other ideas central to Communist doctrines. His "communism" was based on harmony and not on conflict; it was rooted
in Chinese history and traditions; it was a kind of vague
service concept. In short, it was not Communism at all in any
post-Marxist sense. Nevertheless, many later observers have
been led by the vagueness of his exposition, his associations
with the Communists, and his frequent references to Communism—plus their own lack of understanding of the situation
in China at the time, and of Chinese ways of looking at such
things, and plus their rather naïve and trusting approach to

Communism generally—to comment on the close relationship between the *Min-sheng* Principle and Communism. From this line of reasoning, it naturally follows that perhaps the Chinese Communists are the real heirs of Sun Yat-sen and that Communism in China is a logical sequel to Sun's teachings.

In the introduction to his essays on *India and China,* published in 1944, Dr. S. Radhakrishnan, now Vice-President of the Republic of India, wrote: "Something like Communism is a natural development of the third principle of Dr. Sun Yat-sen. It relates to the necessity for social justice and economic democracy." This statement should be considered in the light of Dr. Radhakrishnan's general approach to Communism. In the same introductory essay, he voiced a belief that "The broad principles of Communism—that there shall be no exploitation of one man by another, and that there shall be no private ownership of the means of production, are likely to be accepted to an increasing degree by democratic nations. By democratic methods it will be possible to achieve the third of Sun Yat-sen's principle [*sic*], livelihood for all." [9] This well-meant interpretation of the way in which the Third Principle might at one and the same time lead to "something like Communism" and yet be achieved by "democratic methods" hardly clarifies the nature of the Third Principle. Nevertheless, the views of the great Indian philosopher-statesman are held by many sincere non-Communists, who are more impressed by the similarities than by the differences between the Third Principle and basic Communist principles. Even so astute a student of international politics as Professor W. Friedmann wrote a few years ago: "It is the Communists who claim to be and, in the opinion of most unprejudiced foreign observers, are now regarded by the vast majority of the people as the more genuine executors of Sun Yat-sen's program. The principle of 'the people's livelihood' can comprise any program from moderate land reform and elementary social services to full-fledged Communism." [10]

For a very different interpretation we may turn to the views of a prominent Indian Communist and Comintern representative in China and elsewhere, who regarded Dr. Sun as not a true revolutionary at all. In his account of *Revolution and Counterrevolution in China,* written after his break with Communism, M. N. Roy offered the following interpretation of Sun's real attitudes toward Communism:

> The greatest service of Sun Yat-sen to the Chinese Revolution was that he understood the potential importance of the Communist Party, and resolutely maintained that the Kuo Min Tang must establish a close relation with it. He had no inclination whatsoever towards Communism. He made it quite clear, when he advocated cooperation with the Communist Party and friendly relations with the Soviet Republic. Far from being under any Socialist influence, he formulated his principle of People's Livelihood on the basis of a criticism of the doctrines of Karl Marx. His social outlook remained colored by an incompatible mixture of Confucian patriarchalism and capitalist liberalism. His policy of cooperation with the Communist Party was not the result of any agreement with, or sympathy for, either its philosophy or its program. In his last days, Sun Yat-sen showed a belated tendency towards Jacobinism, and even that was very defective.[11]

Conflicting opinions of this sort would have scarcely more than academic interest if they did not have a current applicability and significance. But they concern the greatest figure of modern China, whose influence is still omnipresent even though he died a generation ago; and they raise questions of his relations with the Chinese Communists, today the masters of the mainland of China, and with Communism, in whose name a ruthless group of men control the destinies of one-third of the population of the world, extending their tentacles into almost every country. Are the Chinese Communists carrying on the revolution, which Dr. Sun did so much to get started, as he wished it to go, or have they taken it in a radically different direction? Was Sun, a veteran revolutionary even before the Russian revolution, so profoundly affected by this revolution, by his studies of Communism, and by his associa-

tions with Chinese, Russian, and other Communists, that they
altered his ideas as well as his tactics? What precisely was the
relationship between Dr. Sun and the Communists and Communism, and what is the significance of this relationship at the
present time and for the future?

These questions relate to some of the most deep-seated
trends in modern China and to some of the most powerful
ideological currents of the present century. They center around
the greatest figure in modern Chinese history and around the
present leaders of the world's most populous nation. They involve an analysis of the two most powerful ideologies of
twentieth-century China, namely Sun Yat-senism and Communism. In the one case, we are dealing with a not-too-
coherent ideology, and in the other, we are encountering an
all-too-familiar type of ideological universalism, but in a form
which seems to have many peculiar characteristics. Thus, the
questions with which we shall deal have a deep significance, as
well as a current importance, for China and for the world.

For the course of events in China during the last half century, and even during the last two decades, Sun Yat-sen must
receive a fair share of credit and of blame. As Nathaniel Peffer
noted in 1924, "Without understanding Sun Yat-sen, we cannot understand latter-day China." Does it follow, therefore,
that Dr. Sun, even though unconsciously, launched China on
a path that could only end in Communist control? Was Communism the logical or even "inevitable" outcome of Sun Yat-
senism? In 1924 Peffer delivered the following verdict: "If
there is a republic in China today, the credit belongs to Dr.
Sun. If, also, the republic is a failure, the blame attaches to
Dr. Sun more than to any one individual. These two sentences
are, I believe, Dr. Sun's biography epitomized." [12] Even today,
a generation after Peffer wrote these words and after Sun
Yat-sen's death, it is still premature to judge whether the revolution which Dr. Sun envisaged has been a success or failure.
Almost certainly, he would argue that it is still incomplete,
and, in all probability, he would regard the Communist
victory as no more than a passing phase, perhaps even as a

perversion, of the revolutionary struggle. But it is time to present the record, and to let that record speak for itself. In so doing we shall be probing deeply into the mainsprings of thought and action of those who have done so much, for good or for ill, to shape the China of the twentieth century.

Chapter 2

Sun Yat-sen and the West

Before we can discuss in detail the complex question of Sun Yat-sen and Communism, it is relevant to consider first Sun's relationships with, and attitude toward, the West. While the subject of "Sun Yat-sen and the West" is itself a matter for another independent study, the present chapter confines itself to the discussion of a few chosen questions, in the hope of constructing a clear picture of Sun's early ideological orientation with which we can later evaluate the meaning and effects of his Russian alliance in the 1920's. The questions this chapter is chiefly concerned with are: To what extent was Sun exposed to the cultural impact of the West? In what manner did he interpret, accept, or reject Western ideas and institutions? How willing was he to accept aid from the West to carry out his revolutionary work? Was Japan regarded by him as a useful model for other Asian nations which wanted to undertake the same task of Westernization and modernization?

The impact of Western culture

The development of Sun's ideology can be divided into three
stages: (1) the formative stage, between the early years of his
life and the overthrow of the Manchus in 1911; (2) the stage
of experimentation and frustration, between the establishment
of the Chinese Republic in 1912 and Dr. Sun's negotiations
with the Communists in Shanghai in 1922; (3) the stage of
Russian orientation, between the Sun-Joffe joint statement
in 1923 and the death of Dr. Sun in 1925. Throughout these
stages Sun's revolutionary ideas and policies were in a continuous process of evolution. They changed according to "the
conditions in China and the general tendency of the world."
It was, however, in the first stage that Sun formulated the
general outline of his basic principles and programs: the Three
People's Principles, the Five-Power Constitution, and the concept of the three-stage revolution.

Professor Arthur N. Holcombe rightly describes Sun's
system of political thought as "a blend of Far Eastern political
philosophy and Western political science." [1] This blending can
be best appreciated if one looks into the tremendous impact
of foreign and indigenous cultural influences upon Sun Yat-sen,
and into his educational training and personal experience. In
describing his own cultural preferences, Sun wrote:

> In Chinese work I like the writings of the Three Dynasties
> and of the Two Hans. In Western work I am specially fond
> of Darwinism. Logic and politics are also among things
> I have often read. In religion I worship Jesus Christ. As
> for individuals, I admire China's Tang and Wu and Amer-
> ica's George Washington.[2]

That Sun was profoundly affected by the ancient Chinese
culture goes without saying.[3] Brought up in the Confucian
tradition, he was well acquainted with the Chinese classics
before he went to Honolulu. After his return from Hawaii, he
continued his Chinese studies with scholars like Chu Fêng-ch'ih
and Chen Chung-yao, a work which he carried on even in
medical school.[4] With such a background, Sun always took

pride in China's intellectual heritage and wanted to use it as a basis to develop a doctrine and a program to meet the demands of modern times. It is, therefore, no surprise that the doctrine and program he developed for China reflect the strong influence of Confucianism. The speeches and writings he made often had passages from the old classics. As a dedicated patriot, never in his life did Dr. Sun stop urging his countrymen to strive for the preservation of Chinese culture and the perpetuation of the Chinese nation.

Another aspect of Sun's ideological background is the cultural impact of the West. A genuine nationalist, who in later years developed a strong anti-imperialist attitude, Dr. Sun, nevertheless, was probably one of the most Westernized Chinese of his time in terms of studies, contacts, and foreign experience. It should be noted that a large part of Sun's lifetime was actually spent on foreign soil. In his teens he studied at Iolani School in Honolulu, and later he studied at Queen's College and at the Medical School of the Alice Memorial Hospital in Hong Kong. He made several trips to Europe, Japan, and the United States, and he had close and frequent contacts with many foreign friends, notably Dr. James Cantlie, Sir Patrick Manson, and Judge Paul Linebarger. In particular, Dr. Cantlie, an English medical missionary, had a powerful influence upon Sun in his formative years. It is, however, to the credit of Sun's own industrious study and keen observation that he acquired a knowledge of the West such as few non-Westerners have ever possessed. Dr. Cantlie has testified to the breadth of Sun's knowledge as well as to his diligence:

> Sun studied medicine as he has studied everything else, ardently. The liberal education medicine gives has stood him in good stead; since his energies have been directed to other spheres of activity he has had to study international law, military tactics, naval construction, finance in all its departments, statecraft, and politics in all its bearings. He has visited many countries, and studied their institutions and modes of government. When residing with us in London, Sun wasted no moments in gaieties; he was forever at work, reading books on all subjects which appertained to political, diplo-

matic, legal, military, and naval matters; mines and mining, agriculture, cattle-rearing, engineering, political economy, etc., occupied his attention and were studied closely and persistently. The range of his opportunities for acquiring knowledge has been such as few men have ever had, and the result is known to us.[5]

The Western influence was quite evident in the program Sun advocated during the early years of his political activities. In a letter to Viceroy Li Hung-chang in 1894, Sun outlined a plan for the economic and technological development of China through the adoption of the methods of the West.[6] Among the things he proposed were the expansion of schools, the improvement of agriculture, the exploitation of natural resources, the development of industries, the elimination of trade barriers, and the modernization of the transport system. In order to introduce scientific agricultural methods to China, he offered to make a personal study of agriculture and sericulture abroad. Later in 1894, when the Hsing Chung Hui (Revive China Society) was organized, Sun included republicanism as one of the goals of the revolution. The oath used by the Hsing Chung Hui listed three slogans: "Drive out the Manchus, restore the Chinese nation, and establish a republic." [7]

It was during the late 1890's and the early 1900's that Dr. Sun came to grips with ideas of democracy and of socialism. In London, he was introduced to the works of Henry George and Karl Marx, and probably he also met Lenin and the Russian revolutionary exiles.[8] In the United States, he came under the influence of the teachings of Abraham Lincoln and other liberal Americans. The frequent references to Rousseau, Montesquieu, Lincoln, Marx, Henry George, and others in his later writings and speeches showed how well-read Sun was, and how great an impact these Western thinkers had on his own thinking. Furthermore, it was during his stay in Europe and America that Sun came to the realization of the existing inequalities and tensions in Western societies and, consequently, decided to work out a program for China to solve political and social problems at the same time. In his autobiography he recorded:

After I escaped from the trouble in London, I stayed temporarily in the European countries to study their political
and social conditions and to get acquainted with their statesmen and other leaders. I learned a great deal during the two
years [1896-1898]. I found out that although the European
countries were powerful and wealthy and had well-developed democratic governments, they could not accord
complete happiness to their people. Therefore, many progressive Europeans were still engaged in a social revolution.
In an effort to seek a more permanent solution of China's
political and social problems, I adopted the Principle of
Min-sheng (People's Livelihood) along with the Principle
of *Min-tsu* (Nationalism) and the Principle of *Min-ch'üan*
(Democracy or People's Power) to form the Three Principles of the People.[9]

Between 1905 and 1906, following his second trip to Europe and America, Dr. Sun's revolutionary ideas began to take
a more definite form. When the T'ung Meng Hui was organized
in Tokyo in August 1905, the objectives stated in its Manifesto—the expulsion of the Manchus, the recovery of China,
the establishment of a republic, and the equalization of land
ownership—constituted the forerunner of the famous Three
People's Principles. The same Manifesto also embodied Sun's
concept of the three-stage revolution as a practical procedure
for the gradual accomplishment of his program. It declared
that the Chinese revolution would be carried out in the following three stages: (1) the rule of martial law, (2) the rule of a
provisional constitution, and (3) the rule of a permanent constitution.[10] Three months later, in a message to the *Min Pao* of
Tokyo, Dr. Sun, for the first time, officially used the term of
San Min Chu I (the Three People's Principles). He urged the
adoption of the Principles of Nationalism and Democracy to
liberate the Chinese from oppression, and the adoption of the
Principle of People's Livelihood to prevent in China those social and economic ills that were troubling the West. "If we can
nip economic evils in the bud, we may, by one stroke, reap the
fruits of both a political and a social revolution. Thus we may
outdistance the Western Powers." [11]

In a speech in October 1906, Sun further elaborated his concepts of the Three People's Principles. According to him, the objectives of the Chinese revolution were threefold: to achieve national, political, and social revolutions side by side. The *Min-sheng* Principle, he explained, did not require the killing of people or the confiscation of land; its "equalization of land ownership" policy only meant public appropriations of all future increases in land value, subsequent to the modernization of society.[12] In the same speech Sun also proposed the Five-Power Constitution for China. A synthesis of Chinese and Western systems, the proposed constitution would divide the power of government into five independent powers—namely, executive, legislative, judicial, examination, and control.[13]

Thus, drawing upon Chinese traditions and Western experiences, Dr. Sun by 1906 had worked out a long-range revolutionary program, designed to free China from the Manchu rule and to rebuild the country anew. He showed a great deal of farsightedness in his efforts to seek socio-economic solutions simultaneously with a political revolution. His deep interest in the problems of land and people's livelihood can be attributed to his peasant background.[14] It was also, obviously, the result of his study of Western conditions and doctrines. Sun's early land policy, in fact, was essentially urban rather than agrarian, and reflected the strong influence of the Henry George variety of social reform.[15]

Finally, a word should be said about the impact of the Christian religion on the life of Sun Yat-sen. He became converted to Christianity in his teens, as a result of his schooling in Honolulu. From the very beginning, he showed a strong faith in the Christian religion, and he resisted the pressure of his brother to force him to give it up.[16] His faith in Christianity was further illustrated by an incident in 1896, when he was detained in the Chinese legation in London. During this crisis, not only did he make a religious appeal to an English servant named Cole, but he also found courage and hope in his constant prayers to God. Later on, he recounted this experience with strong religious overtones:

My despair was complete, and only by prayer to God could
I gain any comfort. Still the dreary days and still more
dreary nights wore on, and but for the comfort afforded me
by prayer I believe I should have gone mad. After my release I related to Mr. Cantlie how prayer was my one hope,
and told him how I should never forget the feeling that
seemed to take possession of me as I rose from my knees on
the morning of Friday, October 16th—a feeling of calm-
ness, hopefulness and confidence, that assured me my prayer
was heard, and filled me with hope that all would be well.[17]

It is true that Sun often gave his own interpretation to
Christian doctrine. He once said: "I do not belong to the
Christianity of churches, but to the Christianity of Jesus, who
was a revolutionary." [18] It is also true that, in his later years,
he talked much less about religion and sometimes even became
suspicious of the motives of missionaries. On the other hand, at
no time did he repudiate his Christian faith. Nor did he express doubts about the existence of God. In fact, Christianity
gave him a sense of historical mission and destiny; it provided
him with religious and moral sanctions for his revolutionary
activities. Dr. Sun himself, in 1912, admitted the influence of
Christian teaching upon his life as a revolutionary: "Men say
that the revolution originated with me. I do not deny the
charge. But where did the idea of revolution come from? It
came because from my youth I have had intercourse with foreign missionaries. Those from America and Europe with whom
I associated put the ideals of freedom and liberty within my
head and heart. . . . The Republic cannot endure unless there
is that virtue—the righteousness for which the Christian religion stands—at the center of a nation's life." [19] Even on his
deathbed in 1925, Sun said to a Christian brother-in-law:
"You are a Christian; I too am a Christian," and "I am a messenger of God to help men to obtain equality and freedom." [20]

Sun's discussion of Western ideas and systems

After this review of the way Sun was exposed to Western influences, we can now consider briefly how he treated, in his
later lectures and writings, some of the political and economic

ideologies and systems of the West that had come to his attention. To begin with, it should be stressed that Sun was deeply
rooted in Chinese culture and never advocated wholesale Westernization. He was impressed by a number of Western thinkers, to be sure, but he always studied their works with a critical
mind. In the end, not only did he urge the adoption of Western
science and technology, but he also accepted democracy as an
ideology and as a system. What he really sought to do was to
select the best for China, and to work out an organic synthesis
between Confucian teachings and Western democracy to suit
the conditions and realities of the Chinese scene.

It is, therefore, relevant here to cite Sun's comments on
some Western thinkers and statesmen, as a clue to the breadth
of his information and the extent of Western influences upon
his doctrine. He praised Rousseau's contribution to the development of democracy and, at the same time, suggested that the
theory of "natural rights" was false:

> The theory in Rousseau's *Social Contract* that the rights
> and the powers of the people are bestowed by Nature is
> fundamentally in conflict with the principle of historical
> evolution, and so the enemies of democracy have used
> Rousseau's unsound argument to stop the mouths of the
> supporters of democracy. Rousseau's idea that democracy
> is naturally endowed was unreasonable, but for opponents
> to use one false conclusion of his as an argument against
> all democracy is just as unreasonable. . . . Why, if Rous-
> seau's philosophy was not based upon fact, did all the
> peoples welcome it? And how was Rousseau able to produce
> such a treatise? He saw the power of the people rising into
> a flood and espoused the people's sovereignty; his demo-
> cratic proposals suited the psychology of the time and made
> the masses welcome him. So, although his theory of democ-
> racy conflicted with the principles of historical progress,
> the spirit of democracy which was already coming to be
> a reality in the life of his day caused him to be warmly
> received in spite of his faulty arguments. And it may be
> added that Rousseau's advocacy of the original idea of de-
> mocracy was one of the greatest contributions to govern-
> ment in all history.[21]

Sun regarded Darwin's theory of evolution and Newton's law of gravity as the two greatest discoveries of men. But he pointed out that Darwin's theory had its limitations because it could not apply to human beings.[22] According to Sun, men were guided by the principle of mutual aid, whereas other creatures were governed by the law of the struggle for existence. He deplored the fact that, from the time of Darwin's discovery of the principles of evolution, scientists began to treat morality, love, justice, and friendship as a mirage, and to regard the law of struggle as the reality. "They even want to apply these laws of the animal world to mankind, but they do not understand that that only applied to a transitional period in the history of mankind—that the evolution of man has outgrown this principle which governs the world of animals."

With respect to Marx, Sun's views were quite critical. He rejected explicitly the Marxian theories of historical materialism, class war, and surplus value, and called Marx a mere social pathologist. He criticized the inconsistencies of Marxism and pointed out the contradictions between Marx's predictions and the actualities of the modern economic world.[23] In support of his argument, he referred to the theory of social revolution of Maurice William, whose book *The Social Interpretation of History* apparently had impressed him deeply and had helped fortify his own ideas. Sun said of William's theory:

> He set forth the view that the materialistic conception of history is wrong; that the social problem, not material forces, is the center which determines the course of history, and that subsistence is the heart of the social problem. This social interpretation of history, he believes, is the only reasonable one. The problem of livelihood is the problem of subsistence. This new theory of this American scholar tallies exactly with the third principle of our party. William's theory means that livelihood is the central force in social progress, and that social progress is the central force in history; hence the struggle for a living and not material forces determines history.[24]

The economic philosophy of Henry George, another American, was frequently mentioned in Sun's writings and speeches.

On one occasion, Sun called attention to the eloquent portrayal of social injustice in modern society by Henry George in *Progress and Poverty*.[25] On another occasion, Sun paid a high tribute to George's advocacy of public ownership of land, particularly to his theory of the single tax.[26] In an interview with American journalists in 1912, Sun declared: "The teachings of your single-taxer, Henry George, will be the basis of our program of reform. The land tax as the only means of supporting the government is an infinitely just, reasonable, and equitably distributed tax, and on it we will found our new system." [27] To be sure, Sun did not actually adopt the method of making the land tax the sole revenue of the state; however, it is generally agreed that his land policy of redistribution and confiscation of unearned increment was derived mainly from the theory of Henry George.[28]

In connection with economic policies, Sun also had great admiration for Bismarck and his State Socialism. In a speech on "The *Min-sheng* Principle and State Socialism," Sun called attention to the world-wide influence which Bismarck had had through the advocacy of State Socialism as opposed to socialism. Then he went on to say that China should adopt State Socialism to prevent the monopoly of big capitalists, and that his idea of nationalization of railroads was State Socialism.[29] In one of his lectures on the Three People's Principles, he further gave Bismarck his enthusiastic appraisal. First, the German statesman's political skills were highly acclaimed. "Germany was raised to her eminent position entirely by the creative arm of Bismarck. Within twenty years after he had taken charge of the government, Bismarck transformed a weak Germany into a powerful state." [30] Second, Bismarck's State Socialism was again praised:

> The Socialist Party advocated social reforms and economic revolution. Bismarck knew that they could not be suppressed by political power, so he put into effect a kind of state socialism as an antidote against the Marxian socialists' program. . . . He brought all the railways of the country under state ownership and control and put all the essential industries under state management. He determined upon

hours of labor and arranged for old-age pensions and ac-
cident insurance for the workers. . . . Moreover, he used
the profits from the state-managed railways, banks, and
other businesses for the protection of workers, which of
course made the workers very contented. . . . Bismarck met
socialism by anticipating it and by taking precautions against
it, rather than by a head-on attack upon it; by invisible
means he caused the very issues for which the people were
struggling to dissolve.[31]

These are only a few examples of Sun's comments on individual Westerners, designed to throw light on his ideological
basis and orientation. More will be gained by turning our attention now to his discussion of Western systems and institutions.

Through his studies and residence abroad, Sun had carefully observed democratic governments at work in Europe and
America. While recognizing their imperfections and limitations, Sun came to the conclusion that democracy was the best
political system men had designed. Nevertheless, he maintained
that China should not imitate the West blindly; rather, she
should work out a democratic machinery best suited to her own
traditions and requirements.

1. ADVOCACY OF DEMOCRACY

According to Sun, China's tide of revolutionary ideas came
from Europe and America,[32] and the Chinese revolution chose
democracy for two reasons: first, to follow the world current;
and second, to reduce the period of civil war.[33] Not infre-
quently, he liked to equate his revolutionary watchwords with
those of the West. Once he compared the Three People's Principles of Nationalism, Democracy, and Livelihood with President Lincoln's government of the people, by the people, and
for the people, which he translated into Chinese as *min yu*
(people possess), *min chih* (people govern), and *min hsiang*
(people enjoy).[34] At another time, he compared his Three
Principles with the watchword of the French Revolution—
"Liberty, Equality, Fraternity":

"Liberty" in the French revolutionary watchword and "People's Nationalism" in our watchword are similar. The People's Nationalism calls for the freedom of our nation. "Equality" is similar to our "Principle of the People's Sovereignty," which aims to destroy autocracy and makes all men equal. . . . The idea in "Fraternity" is similar to our "Principle of the People's Livelihood," which plans for the happiness of our four hundred millions.[35]

Furthermore, Sun often suggested that China learn from the experiences of Western democracies. "Although we cannot wholly copy Europe and America," he said, "yet we can observe them and study their experience in democracy very carefully. . . . Western nations . . . have gained not a little experience in the past century, and this experience, along with their various new theories, should be used as data in our study." [36] For instance, the ability of the United States to establish a stable, democratic republic was attributed to the existence of a highly developed local self-government, which, Sun felt, China should strive to achieve.[37] Likewise, the American policy of training the Filipinos for self-government was cited as a case to support his idea of political tutelage.[38] In a speech before the Chinese Republican Party in 1911, Sun pointed out that England and America had the most well-developed party politics in the world. In each country the two contending parties fought over important issues rather than partisan interests. Political parties in China, he advised, would do well to follow the model of such advanced countries as England and the United States.[39]

2. CRITICISM OF THE SHORTCOMINGS OF WESTERN SYSTEMS

Much as Sun stood for democracy, he never hesitated to point out the limitations and imperfections of Western systems. For one thing, he maintained that economic and social problems in the West were acute and remained to be solved. In a message to the *Min Pao* of Tokyo in 1905, Sun stated that "though the Western countries are powerful, their people are really in distress. Judging from the frequency of general strikes and the

growth of anarchism and socialism, a social revolution is not
far off." [40] In 1912, in an article for *The Independent,* he
wrote: "Today there are no wealthier countries than Britain
and America; there is no more enlightened country than
France . . . but the gap betwixt the poor and the wealthy in
these countries is too great. And so it comes to pass that
thoughts of revolution still rankle in the minds of many." [41]

Even in the machinery of democratic government, Sun
found much to be desired. In the West, he reasoned, the people
were given only the power of voting and had no other way of
controlling the men who were elected to office, whether they
turned out to be worthy or incompetent. This system could
neither satisfy the desires of the people, nor give them a complete measure of happiness.[42] Moreover, in his lectures on the
"Five-Power Constitution," he singled out the deficiencies and
defects of the "three-power constitution," as represented by the
American constitution. With the power of impeachment vested
in Congress, according to him, crafty congressmen could frequently employ it as a weapon to exert pressure on the government, so as to give the government no free hand in its actions.
In the absence of an examination system, the selection of civil
servants would be dominated by political parties, and, more
often than not, capable persons and real talents would consequently be buried in obscurity.[43] All in all, what Sun proposed
to do was to use Western experiences as material for study, and
to work out a program to make "China into a nation under
complete popular rule, ahead of Europe and America." [44]

The search for Western assistance

With his personal experiences and contacts, as well as his faith
in democracy, Sun had the natural inclination to turn first to
the West for assistance. To him, diplomacy was very vital to
the success of the revolution. For one thing, the least he could
hope to accomplish was to prevent foreign powers from inter-
vening in behalf of his enemies. Once he instructed his followers to "protect the lives and properties of the Europeans; respect their churches and ports open to international commerce,
in order that the foreign Powers may have no cause for inter-

vention." [45] More important, he expected outside help to make positive contributions to his revolutionary work. In one of his speeches, he pointed out that the victory of the American colonists in their War of Independence was due partly to French assistance, while the defeat of the T'ai-p'ing rebellion was largely because of the failure of its diplomacy.[46] On several occasions, he advocated that China should adopt an "open door policy" to attract both foreign capital and experts, on a large scale, to develop her industry and railroads. He supported this point by arguing that Russia, Japan, and, particularly, the United States sought outside assistance in developing their industries, too.[47]

In the early years of Sun's revolutionary career, progressive elements in the West took a sympathetic attitude toward his cause. Not only did he receive encouragement from private individuals, at times he even received the blessings of some Western governments. According to his own account, between 1902 and 1903, the French Minister in Tokyo extended him an invitation from the Governor of Annam. Later, when Sun visited Hanoi, the Governor had already left, but the latter's chief secretary was instructed to entertain him.[48] In 1906 a French officer, Bugarbé, representing the French Minister of War, approached Sun. He asked about the strength of the Chinese revolutionists and stated that "the French government would be happy to render any assistance to the Chinese revolutionary movement." As a result, he and several French officers assisted Dr. Sun in making military plans, and they were recalled later only after a change of the French government.[49] In a letter to Teng Tse-ju, dated July 17, 1911, Sun wrote that through some feelers he had found the American government quite sympathetic to his cause, and that he was now sending people to approach the English authorities with the expectation of an equal success. Since the French government was already on its side, he continued, the Party could be assured that in the future revolution England, France, and the United States would not only refrain from intervention but would also prevent others from interfering in Chinese internal affairs.[50] When the revolution broke out in Wuhan in October 1911, foreign consuls there called a meeting to decide their stand. At the meeting, the French consul, an old acquaintance of Dr. Sun's, declared that the followers of Sun Yat-sen were not a mob like the Boxers but were dedicated, genuine revolutionaries, and that, as such, they should not be interfered with. The majority of the consuls went along with the French consul and passed a resolution of nonintervention and strict neutrality.[51]

On several occasions before 1911, Sun also made attempts to secure loans from Britain, France, and the United States.[52] Upon hearing the news of the 1911 Wuhan outbreak while he was abroad, Sun immediately went to England and put three demands before the British government: first, to stop all loan negotiations with the Manchu government; second, to prevent Japan from giving assistance to the Manchus; and third, to revoke all orders excluding him from British territory. To all these requests, he received satisfactory answers from the English. Having achieved this, Sun left for Paris, where French politicians, especially Clemenceau, gave him an equally favorable reception.[53] After the founding of the Chinese Republic, Sun continued his efforts to win the sympathies of the West, in the hope of establishing better relations with the foreign powers and of receiving their help in building up a democratic and prosperous new China.

Of all the Western powers to which Sun turned for assistance, the United States stood in his eyes as probably the best hope. In a pamphlet entitled "The True Solution of the Chinese Question," written in 1904, Sun made a direct appeal to the people of the United States by saying that the Chinese expected sympathy and support from them more than from any other people in the world. Because the Americans were a Christian people, the leaders of Western civilization, and inspiring examples for a new China, he reasoned, there must be many Lafayettes among them willing to give a helping hand.[54] In his letters to the Chinese National Assembly and to Ts'ai Yüanp'ai, in 1918, Dr. Sun said that he had cabled the American President to explain the reasons why the Kuomintang-led southern regime was fighting against the Peking government which was dominated by the warlords. It was his hope that, in the future, President Wilson would be persuaded to uphold justice and to help the Kuomintang to realize the objective of its "protecting the Constitution" campaign.[55] In 1919, writing separate but almost identical letters to T'ang Chi-yao in Yunnan and Lin Shen in Kwangtung, he introduced to them an American military attaché, who was paying a visit to southern China. According to Sun's words, the United States had a sincere intention to help China, but being unfamiliar with the Far East, she did not know how to start. Now that the American officer had a mission to investigate and to report on the Chinese situation, he should be told in detail about all the political, economic, and social problems in the South, thereby providing the necessary information for the United States to work out a program to assist China.[56] In 1920, when he was interviewed by a reporter on the Shantung question, Sun maintained that China should cooperate with the United States in seeking a solution of this problem.[57] Speaking before a group of visiting American congressmen in Shanghai, in the same year, he urged the Americans to follow the direction of John Hay's Open Door Policy. "As you are going to Japan as guests," he concluded, "I believe that you will be able to use your influence to promote the abolition of the Twenty-One Demands—the only way to solve China's problems." [58] In a letter to President Harding in 1921, Dr. Sun further appealed to the United States to help China by extending recognition to his Southern regime. He said he made this special appeal for the reason that "we regard America as the Mother of Democracy, and the champion of liberalism and righteousness, whose disinterested friendship and support of China in her hour of distress has been demonstrated to us more than once." [59]

All these are just a few examples of Sun's persistent efforts to seek assistance from the West in general, and the United States in particular, before he turned to Russia in later years. There were many other similar instances, some of which will be discussed in the next chapter.

Sun and Japan

Inasmuch as Japan was the only Westernized country in Asia in Sun's time, some comments should be made about his attitude toward this neighboring Asian country.[60]

During his early years of revolution against the Manchus, Dr. Sun received assistance and support from a number of Japanese friends, and he used Japanese soil as the base of his operations. At the turn of the century, Sun came to know Inukai Ki, Miyazaki Torazo, Toyama Mitsuru, and other influential Japanese leaders, who helped his revolutionary movement from time to time by supplying him with advice, money, and arms. In 1900, Sun used Formosa as his sanctuary to direct the Waichow revolt, and a Japanese, Yomada Yoshimasa, became "the first foreigner who sacrificed his life for the Republican cause of China." [61]

In 1905, the T'ung Meng Hui was formed in Tokyo and became a training ground for thousands of young Chinese revolutionary recruits. The change in Japanese politics and Sun's expulsion from Japan in 1907 did hamper Chinese revolutionary activities in that country, but it did not dampen Sun's faith in the friendship of the Japanese people, as distinguished from their government. Writing his autobiography later, he not only listed a few names of those Japanese who helped him directly in promoting the Chinese revolution, but said: "There were many others who helped indirectly. We must wait for the official history of our Party to record in greater detail the invaluable work of our Japanese friends." [62]

Sun's friendly attitude toward Japan can be attributed to several factors. First, Japan being China's close neighbor, Sun felt that it was both important to have her assistance and convenient to use her as a base to direct the anti-Manchu movement.[63] Second, from his point of view, Chinese and Japanese were bound together by a common cultural and racial heritage. Japan's victory over Russia, therefore, gave him a great satisfaction, as it symbolized the resurgence of Asia against European imperialism. This type of feeling accounted for the expounding of Pan-Asianism by Sun in later years. Third, probably more important was the Chinese leader's admiration for Japan's progress and modernization. For Sun, the secret of Japan's rise to power lay in her adoption of Western institutions and science; her success gave China and other Asian nations both a new confidence and an inspiring model to encourage them to undertake the experiment of Westernization. The following words of Dr. Sun, stated in 1919 and 1924, respectively, represent this point of view most tellingly:

> When Japan began her reforms, she was a very weak country, with a population not more than one-tenth the size of ours, and with a territory equivalent to one of our provinces. . . . And yet now Japan is one of the strongest Powers in the world. Her people have given up their old prejudices, they have learned the lessons of the West, reformed their administration, created an army and fleet, organized their finances, and have done all this in the space of fifty years. . . . Consequently, if we base ourselves on these standards and relationships, China can become a very powerful State if she concentrates on the work of her transformation for the space of, say, ten years.[64]

> In recent years . . . a new Japan, transformed into a first-class power, has risen, and Japan's success has given the other nations of Asia unlimited hope. . . . Japan has been able to learn from Europe and, since her modernization, to catch up with Europe. . . . We may infer, therefore, that what the white races can do, Japan can evidently also do . . . Japan's rise has brought prestige not only to the Yamato race, but it has raised the standing of all Asiatic peoples. We once thought we could not do what the Europeans could do; we see now that Japan has learned from Europe and that, if we follow Japan, we, too, will be learning from the West as Japan did.[65]

Conclusion

This chapter has shown that Dr. Sun throughout his life, and particularly during the formative stage of his ideology, had been subject to the influences of the West in one aspect or another. With all his reservations, he admired Western democracy and wanted to work out a modified version to suit the

needs of China. In fact, his early pro-Japanese attitude was
based largely on the hope that Japan could serve as a model, as
well as a friend, for other Asian nations that sought to travel
the same road of Westernization as she did. Consequently, it is
no surprise to find that Sun, for many years, had looked toward the Western powers, especially the United States, for
assistance in carrying out his revolutionary work. Indeed, the
West had a golden opportunity to be a good friend of Dr. Sun
and could have influenced the direction of the Chinese revolution through cooperation with him. The truth of the matter,
however, is that it missed this opportunity. The following chapters will show how the founder of the Kuomintang turned
away from the West to seek the assistance of the Russians.

Chapter 3

The Background
of Sun Yat-sen's Soviet Alliance

Sun Yat-sen's alliance with Soviet Russia in the 1920's unquestionably stands as one of the most important and complex
events in China's modern history. Interpretations of the motives, nature, and significance of this alliance are divergent and
often confusing, with the Kuomintang and Communist spokesmen holding the two extreme views.[1] A careful re-examination
may cast new light on the Chinese revolution and on Sino-
Soviet relations.

In this chapter we shall study the background and the reasons for Sun's policy of allying his Party with the Bolsheviks.
The years to be covered are those between early 1912 and late
1922—the second period of Sun's ideological development.
This period witnessed the tragic failure of the experiment of
republicanism in China and the gradual disillusionment of Dr.
Sun with the West. It also saw the continuous growth and

development of Sun's revolutionary theory and program in response to the problems of China.

To begin with, a quick review of the evolution of Sun's ideology is in order. With the inauguration of the Chinese Republic in 1912, his views on the Principle of Nationalism changed from the previous anti-Manchu stand to the advocacy of "equality and unity of all the five races in China." [2] In the constitution of the Chung-hua ko-ming-tang (the Chinese Revolutionary Party) in 1914, the strategy of the three-stage revolution (military rule, political tutelage, and constitutional government) received a renewed emphasis, and the idea of one-party government found its first expression.[3] In a speech in 1916, Sun introduced into his Principle of Democracy the concept of direct democracy in the form of the four "people's rights" of suffrage, recall, initiative, and referendum.[4] As early as 1912, he began to talk about "regulation of capital," in addition to the policy of "equalization of land ownership," which was originally embodied in the Principle of People's Livelihood.[5] In 1919, he formally put the program of "regulation of capital" in his plan for the industrial development of China.[6] Between 1917 and 1919, to provide concrete measures to implement his revolutionary theory, Dr. Sun completed the *Plans for National Reconstruction* in three parts: *Psychological Reconstruction* (Sun Wen's Doctrine), *Social Reconstruction* (the Preliminary Step of Democracy), and *Material Reconstruction* (the International Development of China). All in all, during the period under discussion, the process of Sun's ideological development continued, but in his efforts to put his ideas into practice, he experienced more failures than successes. The following pages will discuss the factors that combined to influence Sun's decision to move in a new direction, culminating in an alliance with the Russians.

Frustration of the Chinese revolution

Among the factors leading to Dr. Sun's Soviet alliance was his frustrated experience with the Chinese revolution after 1911. He had high hopes for his country when the new Chinese Republic was first established to replace the Manchu dynasty. In a speech in 1912, Sun told his Party members that, since the Principles of Nationalism and Democracy had been realized, from now on what they should urgently promote was the Principle of People's Livelihood.[7] Writing in an American magazine in the same year, Sun again stated: "Having finished the task of bringing about a political revolution, I am now devoting my thought and energies to the reconstruction of the country in its social, industrial, and commercial conditions." [8] Nevertheless, his early optimism about the Republic was soon shattered; to his dismay he later saw the futility of parliamentarianism in China, the disintegration of the country under warlords, and the intense suffering of the people. Between 1912 and the 1920's, first Yüan Shih-k'ai and then a succession of Pei-yang generals controlled Peking and formed a military rule designed merely to promote their personal interests and ambitions. The Kuomintang opposition in the parliament was rendered ineffectual in restraining the government, and the rival regime Sun and his followers established in the South in 1917 found itself maintaining only a precarious existence under the protection of Southern militarists. The country, as a whole, was plunged into long years of civil war, political anarchy, and economic impoverishment. As one author puts it, democratic institutions and representative forms of government in China "became disastrously associated with militarism, disorder, insecurity, and poverty." [9] In explaining all this, Sun wrote in 1923:

> The fault was the failure to enforce the revolutionary fundamentals. The revolutionary fundamentals . . . divide the course of revolution into three stages: first, military rule; second, political tutelage; third, constitutional government. These are the inevitable stages leading from malgovernment to good government, and none of them should be overlooked. China cannot be a true republic unless she undergoes such a transition. It was a matter of deep regret that the revolution of 1911 neglected the revolutionary fundamentals: they were shelved and obstructed. As a basic error engenders many side issues, the ship of state was left to steer in an uncharted sea.[10]

The failure to carry out Sun's revolutionary program, in turn, was attributed to the defects of his Party. The T'ung Meng Hui, which Sun formed in 1905 and which was instrumental in the 1911 revolution, was a heterogeneous group. It consisted of different social elements and interests, ranging from radical intellectuals to conservative landed gentry. The Party had no central organization and no Party discipline. Beyond the overthrow of the Manchus, there was no common objective among the various constituent elements. Consequently, as soon as the Manchus were forced to abdicate, the unifying sentiment of the Party began to vanish. The majority of Sun's Party members started to entertain differences of opinion, and they refused to follow what they called his "impractical ideas." [11] Most illustrative of the Party conditions in 1921-1924 was a letter from Ch'en Chih-mei to Huang Hsing, both influential Party leaders:

> But there also exists the opinion that Sun Yat-sen is a great idealist, and this prejudice greatly hindered the application of his ideas; this is used as reproach against Sun Yat-sen, this is made use of by his enemies to attack him. But all the facts of the past indicate that the biggest defeats suffered by our Party arose from the fact that we failed to appreciate Sun Yat-sen's ideas, considered them unattainable, and rose up against them. Thereby we brought our own defeat.[12]

In recollection Sun felt bitter about this and put the blame on his Party comrades for the failure of the Republic:

> Unfortunately the revolution was scarcely completed when the members of our Party turned out to be of a different opinion from myself, considering my ideals too elevated and unobtainable for the reconstruction of modern China. Some of my comrades even began to entertain doubts concerning the realization of our program. So it came about that my program had less chance of being realized when I held the position of President than when I was the leader of the Party preparing the revolution. On the other hand my Party comrades cannot escape the reproach of insufficient conviction and effort in the realization of our revolutionary ideals and the carrying out of our revolutionary program.[13]

Although between 1912 and 1922 Dr. Sun made several attempts to reorganize and strengthen his Party, the revolutionary spirit was never revived. The secret revolutionary organization, the T'ung Meng Hui, was transformed, in 1912, into the Kuomintang (a nonsecret party), which soon suffered from disunity and bureaucracy. In 1914, Sun inaugurated the Chung-hua ko-ming-tang with "the object of removing all social and political evils and restoring the supremacy of law." Though reconstituted as a secret society, this new Party held its members together merely by the personality of Dr. Sun. In 1920, the Party again was reorganized into the Chung-kuo Kuomintang. This reorganization enlarged the membership but failed to energize the Party, since there was no effective Party constitution.[14] The Party continued to be based on personal relationships. No solidarity existed and no concerted action was possible, as many Party members neither understood nor believed in what the Party stood for. Careerists and counterrevolutionaries had infiltrated the Kuomintang in large numbers.[15] There was no effective contact between the Party and the masses. Nor was there any definite connection between the Party and the military and political power.

The best summary of the Kuomintang's difficulties is given by Dr. Leonard S. Hsü, who lists four factors that prevented Sun's Party from making the Chinese revolution a success:

> In the first place, the Kuomintang consisted largely of intellectuals and of old politicians, who bargained and negotiated with feudal lords and militarists and sought to get the place of power by virtue of the reputation of Dr. Sun Yat-sen, whom they often betrayed. The spirit and principle of the Party had scarcely reached the common people. . . . In the second place, there was no definite program besides the expulsion of the Manchus and the establishment of a republic. The idea of representative government was not understood by the average Chinese, and the Kuomintang made no effort in the way of training the Chinese for self-government beyond introducing a few courses of political science in colleges and high schools. . . . In the third place, Dr. Sun and other Kuomintang leaders had always expected

foreign assistance: moral, financial, and even military, especially from the United States and Japan. . . . In the fourth place, the Kuomintang itself paid little attention to the cultivation of military strength. . . . The Party lacked organization, discipline, and propaganda. Its influence scarcely reached the labor, peasant, and merchant classes. . . . Indeed, the only force that had kept the Kuomintang from dying a natural death during these years of difficulties was Dr. Sun's enthusiasm and perseverance.[16]

In their efforts to unify China through military means, Sun and his followers had to rely upon armies that were not their own.[17] Oftentimes Sun found himself allied with provincial militarists against warlords in Peking. These alliances were naturally unreliable and could result only in a series of disappointments and defeats for Sun. The last defeat he received was from Ch'en Ch'iung-ming, whose revolt in June 1922 climaxed Sun's frustration and forced him to flee from Canton to Shanghai. All his old-style efforts of organizing the Party and of using warlords had ended in failure. Although new attempts were being made to form an alliance with Generals Wu P'ei-fu and Chang Tso-lin,[18] it became quite apparent that if the Chinese revolution were to be accomplished, he must seek a new basis of power by attempting a thorough reorganization of the Kuomintang along radically different lines. In this new attempt, he was in a mood to welcome whatever assistance he could possibly get.

Sun's disillusion with the West

The Western powers' blunders since the revolution of 1911 also did much to drive Sun Yat-sen into Russian arms. Sun's attitude toward the Western powers had been a complex one. Educated, and often exiled, abroad, Sun came to know and admire some Western ideas and institutions. Being a patriotic nationalist, he resented, at the same time, the humiliations China suffered at the hands of the West, and he wanted to see his country independent and free of foreign control. Nevertheless, before 1911, Sun directed the Chinese revolution only against the Manchus and not against the foreign powers, for he attrib-

uted China's internationl troubles not so much to foreign imperialism as to the stupidity of the Manchu regime.[19] He
believed that relations between China and the foreign powers
would be improved if the Manchus were overthrown, and that
the cause of the Chinese revolution would be furthered if foreign aid were forthcoming.

When the revolution broke out in Wuhan in October 1911,
Sun was in the United States. Informed of the news, Sun delayed his return home to concentrate his efforts on winning the
sympathies of the United States and Europe. To him, the diplomatic front was even more important than the military front,
insofar as the fate of the Chinese revolution went. In his recollection, he analyzed the international situation as follows:

> There were six Powers who at that time took a very intimate
> part in the affairs of China. Of these, France and America
> took the side of the revolution, Germany and Russia were
> opposed to the revolution. England had not yet defined her
> policy, though her people also expressed its sympathy with
> the revolution, and, while the Japanese Government was
> against the revolution, the Japanese people sympathized
> with it.
>
> Thus, the international situation was a question of life or
> death for the Chinese revolution. The most important of all
> for us, at the moment, was the attitude of England, for we
> considered that, if England took our side, Japan would not
> delay in following her example. . . .[20]

Upon the assumption of the provisional presidency in January
1912, Sun issued a proclamation to pledge the Republic of
China to carry out the duties of a civilized nation, to wipe out
all the past humiliation and anti-foreign feeling, and to win for
China a respectable place in international society.[21] Again in
February, he issued a manifesto to the foreign powers assuring
them that his government would respect legitimate foreign interests in China and the existing treaties that had been
concluded before the revolution.[22] The intention of the Kuomintang to protect foreign rights was reiterated even as late as
May 1921, when Sun became the President of the Canton
regime.[23] All this indicated Sun's desire to open a new rela-

tionship with the foreign powers, as well as his hope of securing the support of progressive elements in the West.

Nevertheless, it was not long before Sun gradually became disillusioned. For one thing, the experiment of Western parliamentarianism in the Chinese Republic was a complete failure, because there was little foundation in China for such a system.[24] For another, the foreign powers had not changed their aggressive designs on China even after the establishment of the Republic, as is evidenced by the British invasions of Tibet and the Russian occupation of Mongolia. What is more, the powers adopted a policy of supporting Yüan Shih-k'ai, and other warlords in Peking, against Sun and his Party. They generally underestimated the strength of the Kuomintang and favored some other group to run the Chinese government.[25] This attitude can be best illustrated by the China policy of the United States during the 1910's and the 1920's. Even under the administration of President Woodrow Wilson, for whom Dr. Sun had great respect, the American policy was one of supporting the Peking government in general, and Yüan Shih-k'ai in particular.[26] In the minds of President Wilson and his successors, the Peking regime was the only "legitimate" Chinese government the United States had recognized; Yüan Shih-k'ai and other Northern militarists were the only strong men who could bring peace, order, and stability to China. Any movement or revolution aiming at the overthrow of the regime at Peking was viewed by the American government as injurious to the Chinese nation. Small wonder that Sun's appeal to the United States for aid never got any response. In 1914, informed of the impending visit of Huang Hsing, one of Sun's trusted aides, to Washington, Secretary of State William Jennings Bryan assured Peking that there would be no encouragement to persons intriguing against a friendly government and that President Wilson would not receive Huang Hsing in any audience.[27] In 1921, upon receiving a personal letter from Dr. Sun to President Harding, the State Department refused to transmit this letter and instructed the American Consulate General at Canton against making "itself a vehicle of official communication for an organization in revolt against a Government with which the United States is in friendly relations." [28]

The Chinese policy adopted in Washington, in fact, does not seem so strange if we take a look at the unfavorable reports on Dr. Sun and his group that were frequently sent back by American Foreign Service officers in China. For instance, in a report to the State Department in 1913, E. T. Williams, American Chargé d'Affaires at Peking, described Yüan Shih-k'ai as the "real founder of the Republic" and pictured Sun and his followers either as "impractical" men or as "disreputable" characters.[29] In 1921, Charles R. Crane, American Minister in China, informed the Secretary of State that "the associates of Sun Yat-sen ever since the Revolution of 1911 have been greatly embarrassed by his impracticable and grandiose schemes. He is reported to be a man of great personal vanity, although sincere in his motives, and much given to initiating projects of national magnitude that he has not as yet in any case brought to fruition." [30] Reporting to Washington on the revolt of Ch'en Ch'iung-ming in 1922, Crane's successor, Jacob G. Schurman, expressed the opinion that Sun Yat-sen was the "one outstanding obstacle" to the reunification of China, and that it would be better to let Ch'en Ch'iung-ming or the Peking government bring about Sun's "retirement." [31] There were, of course, some Americans who had a different estimation of Dr. Sun and his revolutionary work. According to Ernest B. Price, United States Vice Consul at Canton, the leaders of the Southern regime "are enlightened men, acquainted with foreign ideas and methods and . . . are making a praiseworthy attempt to demonstrate their ability to work together and to govern the people over whom they are exercising power to the satisfaction of the people themselves." [32] Nevertheless, Mr. Price was absolutely in the minority. By and large, American officials had misgivings about Dr. Sun and preferred to deal with the "legal" government of China in Peking. The same can be said about the official attitudes of the European countries.

To the Western powers' policy of supporting his enemies in the North, Sun's reaction was a mixture of anxiety and bitterness. When Yüan Shih-k'ai was negotiating a loan with the Consortium bankers in 1913, Sun warned that the money "would be used in waging war against people" and appealed to the West to assist "in averting unnecessary bloodshed" by not making the loan.[33] This protest went unheeded, and Yüan secured a loan of two hundred and fifty million dollars. Sun was bitterly disappointed at this action. In a letter to a friend in 1916, he attacked the support of Yüan by the leading Western power, Britain:

> The English officials in Hong Kong, Shanghai, and Singapore zealously cooperate with Yüan in persecuting our patriots, and act as if they receive orders from Yüan Shih-k'ai and not from their own Government; as [though] Yüan was their master and superior. . . . The English Government should not keep her eyes glued to the present and the temporary, but look further into the future if she desires friendship and not enmity from the younger generation of China.[34]

During 1916-1917, when the problem arose of China's entering World War I on the side of the Allied Powers, Sun was strongly opposed to participation. He even cabled British Premier Lloyd George in 1916, to the effect that China's participation might create anarchy in the country and would only weaken the cause of the Allies.[35] His main argument for China to maintain her neutrality was expressed by a book written in 1917—_Chung-kuo ts'un-wang wen-t'i_ [_The Question of China's Survival_]. In the first place, he saw no difference between Germany, on the one hand, and England and France, on the other, so far as their colonial policies were concerned. Second, he doubted that China could possibly benefit from helping the Allies, regardless of how the war was concluded. If Germany was victorious, China's position would become worse. If the Allies won the war, China would be left in the same position as she was before. Consequently, he maintained that China should stay out of the war and concentrate on her own problems. In order to develop her resources, China must, in Sun's opinion, seek help from the United States and Japan, "whether it be in the form of personnel, capital, or material." To him, these two countries were China's logical friends because they were politically or racially bound to her.[36] Notwithstanding the opposition of Sun and the Kuomintang, the Peking government under Premier Tuan Ch'i-jui went ahead to declare war against Germany in August 1917. Tuan and his military backers apparently saw in the war an opportunity to secure Allied loans to entrench themselves in power. Disgruntled and irate, Dr. Sun and his followers set up a rival regime at Canton.

While opposed to foreign powers' support of Northern militarists, Sun continued his efforts to seek genuine foreign assistance to help China and the revolution. These efforts culminated in a project called "The International Development of China," which was completed about the end of World War I. The basic idea of this ambitious project was to promote rapid industrialization of China with the aid of international capital. In outlining the project, Sun counted on foreign capital and experts to come to China to develop railroads and highways, river conservation and irrigation, new ports and modern cities, basic industries and public utilities. He wanted to "make all the national industries of China into a Great Trust owned by the Chinese people, and financed with international capital for mutual benefit." [37] "In a nutshell," he wrote, "it is my idea to make capitalism create socialism in China so that these two economic forces of human evolution will work side by side in future civilization." [38] The project was submitted to various Western nations immediately after the war, but it came to nothing for lack of any favorable response. Although Sun did receive some polite replies, most of them expressed doubts about the practicability of his colossal plan.[39] Whatever its shortcomings, the project actually proposed what may be regarded as the post-1945 variety of international investment and cooperative economic endeavor—the Marshall Plan, the Point Four Program, the Technical Assistance Program of the United Nations, etc. Like some other ideas of Dr. Sun, however, it was just too far ahead of his time and too "impractical" to be appreciated by his contemporaries.[40]

The result of the Versailles Peace Conference, which "betrayed" China by awarding the former German rights in

Shantung to Japan, shocked Sun Yat-sen and his fellow countrymen into reconsidering their judgment of the West. The
resentment at the decision of the Conference turned into a
new, nation-wide anti-imperialist campaign in China, better
known as the May Fourth movement of 1919.[41] In a manifesto
issued in May 1921, Sun still urged the foreign powers to
change their policy and to assist China's economic development: "The vast resources of the country, natural and industrial, shall be developed so that the whole world, suffering
from the disastrous effects of long years of war, will be benefited. For this purpose foreign capital and expert knowledge
will, in pursuance of an open door policy, be welcomed." [42]
Again, this appeal was unheeded. The Washington Conference
of 1921-1922 further disappointed Dr. Sun, as the Western
powers refused to deal with his Canton government and continued to recognize the Peking militarists as the "legitimate"
Chinese authority. The bitterness at Canton was expressed
by Wang Ching-wei, who pictured the Conference as freeing
"China from the Japanese policy of independent violent encroachment," only to leave it victim "to the cooperative slow
encroachment" of all the powers.[43]

By the time Sun went to Shanghai in August 1922, as a
result of Ch'en Ch'iung-ming's revolt, the revolution was at
the lowest ebb and his disillusion with the West became complete. All his efforts since 1911 to secure cooperation from the
Western nations had been frustrated. Instead, the latter had
rendered every assistance to the warlords in Peking to obstruct the emancipation of the Chinese people. Sun came to
realize that foreign imperialism, as well as internal reactionaries, was responsible for his failures. He charged that the
foreign powers "have intervened in China's internal affairs by
practically imposing upon the country a government repudiated by it. They have, by supporting a government which
cannot exist for a single day without such support, hindered
China from establishing an effective and stable government." [44]

Besides his disillusion with the West, Sun also became
highly disappointed with Japan by 1922. In his early years of
revolutionary work, he had frequently been helped by some

Japanese friends, and he had a personal belief that Japan was China's natural friend because of their common racial and cultural heritage. Nevertheless, after the revolution of 1911 succeeded in overthrowing the Manchus, the expectation of genuine assistance from Japan never materialized. Instead, the Japanese government capitalized on every opportunity to advance its interest at the expense of China. During his exile in Japan from 1913 to 1916, Sun's fortunes hit a new low, and he needed Japan's support for another revolution to overthrow Yüan Shih-k'ai and to put the Kuomintang back in power. With little bargaining power, and in a desperate mood, he made some extremely ill-advised bids for full Japanese support during the negotiations for the notorious Twenty-One Demands. The Japanese authorities not only gave no help to Sun, but used his pleas as threats in extorting sweeping concessions from Yüan Shih-k'ai.[45] After the death of Yüan Shih-k'ai in 1916, Japan continued a policy detrimental to the interest of China and the Chinese revolution. Tokyo's support of the pro-Japanese warlords in Peking and its acquisition of the Shantung properties from the Versailles Conference must have been a severe blow to Sun's dream of a friendly Japan. Between 1917 and 1918, several letters were written by Sun to his Japanese friends, urging that Japan stop aid to General Tuan Ch'i-jui and other Pei-yang generals.[46] In both his reply to a Japanese reporter in 1919, and his letter to Miyazaki Torazo, Sun charged that the militarists in Japan treated China even worse than did the Europeans and Americans. Unless this policy was changed, he warned, China would be forced to ally with the whites to resist Japan.[47] When all these efforts proved to be of no avail, and when all his pleas for Western aid fell on deaf ears, Sun had no other resort but to turn to Soviet Russia for aid.

The appeal of the Russian revolution

In addition to the internal and external factors that created a favorable atmosphere for a Russian orientation of the Kuomintang, the appeal of the Russian revolution itself played a potent part in influencing the decision of Sun Yat-sen. According to

Sun's own account, he came in contact with Russian revolutionaries in Europe, before the success of the Chinese and Russian revolutions. He was tremendously impressed by their spirit and program.[48] Subsequently, when the revolution broke out in Russia in 1917, Sun viewed its progress with keen interest and sympathy. In 1918, Sun was in Shanghai and managed to send, through many intermediaries, a message to Lenin, congratulating him on his success and encouraging him to continue his hard struggle. This message was sent at a time when all the powers were against Soviet Russia. Upon receiving it, Lenin is said to have been highly moved and to have regarded the message as "the light of the East." [49] Between 1919 and 1920, Dr. Sun, while still in Shanghai, began to have contacts with the Russians and was even contemplating the sending of Liao Chung-k'ai and others to Russia for study.[50]

Sun's sympathy with the Russian revolution stemmed from the fact that there existed something in common between China and Russia. Both were noncapitalist and "backward" countries. Both were undergoing a struggle against internal as well as external enemies. Their revolutions, in the words of Sun's 1918 message to Lenin, had common aims and were "leading to the liberation of the peoples and to the establishment of enduring peace" based on the recognition of the community of interests of the Chinese and Russians.[51] The renunciation by Russia of all the unequal treaties she had concluded with China in the Tsarist days had a special appeal to Chinese patriots. The success of the Soviet regime, in resisting foreign and White Russian armies and in extending its control throughout the country, was undoubtedly inspiring to Sun and his followers, who had suffered one defeat after another since 1911. To them, Russia's ability to withstand foreign intervention and her anti-imperialist slogans gave a great lift to the cause of the oppressed everywhere. Once Sun remarked: "Because of the Russian revolution, mankind of the world has found a great hope." [52]

Furthermore, to his satisfaction, Sun Yat-sen also found some striking resemblances between his ideas and those of the Bolsheviks. This strengthened Sun's confidence in the feasibility of his program, as well as provided him with a Russian model from which he could adopt specific tactics and methods. Among the ideas held in common was that of one-party government, which Sun had developed in his theory of the three stages of revolution.[53] It should be noted that as early as 1905 the three stages of revolution were mentioned in the Manifesto of the T'ung Meng Hui. However, the ruling power referred to in this document was a military rather than a party government.[54] The unsuccessful experiment of republicanism in China, immediately following 1911, convinced Sun of the necessity of pursuing his revolutionary program. Consequently, in drafting the constitution of the Chung-hua ko-ming-tang in 1914, he reiterated the three stages of revolution with special emphasis on political tutelage. The idea of one-party government was then explicitly put forth by Sun, as he stated that "all the military and civil affairs of the country will be the responsibility of the members of our Party," during the revolutionary period "between the first action of the revolutionary army and the promulgation of the constitution." [55]

The political tutelage of the Kuomintang, in Sun's opinion, was the necessary measure to prepare China for democracy. "Our Chinese people," he reasoned, "have long been under the domination of monarchy. The slave psychology has left in its soul a deep impression, which cannot be destroyed without first passing through a period of preparatory training." [56] During this period of tutelage, the people must be under the care of the elite (Kuomintang), their relationship being one of child to parent.

> The Kuomintang bore this infant, and is obliged to nurse it like a mother and train it, and only by training the people can it carry out its parental duty. And for this the period of preparatory training is necessary, so that the child can be given experience and trained up to years of discretion, up to the moment when it can take over power itself.[57]

Although this theory of one-party rule was formed by Sun before the Russian revolution, he had never been able to put

it into practice in China. Therefore, when he later learned of
the dictatorship of the proletariat of the Bolsheviks, he was
delighted to see the parallelism to his idea.[58] Not only did the
success of the Soviet experiment confirm his belief in the
correctness of the principle, but he also could learn from
the Russians the techniques of party organization and their
methods of securing mass support.

The New Economic Policy of Soviet Russia also appealed
to Sun Yat-sen. For many years, he had been interested in
social and economic problems of the masses. His answer to
those problems was the Principle of Livelihood, which included the two essential policies of "equalization of land"
and "regulation of capital." This Principle of Livelihood had
not been popular with many of his followers and was included
in the revolutionary program only through Sun's insistence.
For instance, during the period of Sun's presidency at Nanking, Sung Ch'iao-jen, a prominent Party member, advised
him "to talk no longer about the Principle of Livelihood." This
invited an angry reply from Sun: "The revolution aims at the
welfare of the people and the solution of the problem of livelihood. If we discard the Principle of Livelihood, we may as well
give up the whole revolution." [59] In 1921 he met Maring, the
Comintern's representative, in Kweilin. After their talk, he
came to believe that the New Economic Policy of Soviet
Russia was not Communism but actually his Principle of Livelihood. In a telegram to Liao Chung-k'ai, one of his most
trusted aides, Sun said that he was at first surprised at the
adoption of Communism by Soviet Russia because her economic conditions were not ready for it. However, after Maring's
visit, he continued, he realized that Russia's New Economic
Policy was little different from his plan for the industrial
development of China, and he was therefore highly pleased.[60]
Sun's pleasure, indeed, was quite understandable, as the Russian example seemed to vindicate the economic programs he
had been championing in China for years.

Even before Ch'en Ch'iung-ming's revolt in June 1922,
Sun had gradually oriented himself toward Russia in the way

of seeking advice and alliance. In a letter to Chicherin on August 28, 1921, he said:

> . . . I am extraordinarily interested in your work and in particular in the organization of your Soviets, your army, and education. I would like to know all that you and others can tell me of these matters, particularly about education. Like Moscow, I would like to lay the foundation of the Chinese revolution deeply in the minds of the younger generation—the workers of tomorrow.[61]

On board a warship on August 9, 1922, after Ch'en's rebellion, Sun discussed foreign policy with his followers and stressed the necessity for China to pay special attention to Russia and Germany. In the case of Russia, he said that no foreign power was more important than she in terms of "geographical proximity and close relations" with China. Calling the fear of Russian Bolshevism groundless, he pointed out that the New Economic Policy of Russia had long changed Communism to "state capitalism" and had relaxed the ban on private ownership.[62] In September 1922, the *Hong Kong Telegraph* published a series of Sun's private papers, which had been stolen from his residence by Ch'en Ch'iung-ming. These papers showed that Sun had been in secret correspondence with Russia and Germany, contemplating an alliance. This disclosure surprised some of his followers, but he publicly acknowledged the authenticity of these papers.[63]

In short, the Russian revolution attracted Sun Yat-sen both by its programs and its spectacular success. On the one hand, the existence of some similarities between his ideas and those of the Bolsheviks was indeed inspiring and reassuring to a man like Sun, who had been frustrated in his revolutionary efforts. On the other hand, he could not but admire the Soviet regime for its ability to achieve what he failed to do in China. This convinced him of the desirability of learning from the Bolsheviks about party organization and political techniques. Therefore, once the opportune time came, Sun was quick to accept the offer of Soviet assistance and to use the Russian methods as a model for the Chinese revolution.

Soviet policy toward China

If Sun had good reasons for a Russian orientation, the Soviet regime was also anxious to cooperate. In their early years in power, the Bolsheviks met with bitter opposition from the Western powers and were completely isolated from the outside world. To search for allies, they quickly turned their attention to the Far East, especially China, where the oppressed masses offered great potentialities in the struggle against imperialism. As a gesture of friendship to the Chinese people, the Soviet government, in two declarations in 1919 and 1920, renounced all the indemnities, special privileges, and territories wrested from China by the Tsarist government.[64] It is true that these declarations to some extent made a virtue of necessity, since Soviet Russia was at this time powerless to regain what she renounced. It also should be noted that the Soviet position was equivocal in regard to the Chinese Eastern Railway and to Outer Mongolia. But the fact that Soviet Russia was the first foreign power to offer China a new relationship on the basis of equality attracted all the patriotic Chinese, and won many friends for the Bolsheviks in China.[65]

The immediate objective of Soviet policy in China was to seek official recognition and to establish friendly relations. For this, Moscow had to deal with the nominal Chinese government at Peking, notoriously reactionary and pro-imperialist as the latter was. The long-range China policy of the Bolsheviks, however, was based on Lenin's theory of revolution in colonial and semicolonial areas.[66] According to Lenin, in oppressed countries like China, where a modern industrial proletariat scarcely existed, the first task of revolution was to overthrow foreign imperialism. The liberation of these areas would deprive the capitalist world of its main resources and incomes, and would contribute to its final downfall. It was necessary, therefore, for the Communists to arouse the revolutionary spirit of the oppressed people, and to cooperate with whatever forces were fighting for the expulsion of foreign imperialism. In outlining Communist strategy, Lenin said: "The Communist International must enter into a temporary alliance with bourgeois democracy in colonial and backward countries, but must not merge with it, and must unconditionally preserve the independence of the proletarian movement even in its most rudimentary form." [67] He also listed the conditions for such an alliance: "We Communists should, and will, support bourgeois liberation movements in the colonial countries only when these movements are really revolutionary, when the representatives of these movements do not hinder us in training and organizing the peasants and the broad masses of the exploited in a revolutionary spirit." [68] In other words, while the national revolution was being carried on during the temporary alliance, ways also must be paved for the future realization of Communism in the colonial and semicolonial areas.

In view of the diversity of her objectives in China, it was not surprising to find that in the early 1920's Soviet Russia pursued a course of conducting negotiations with Peking, on the one hand, and of helping to organize a Chinese Communist Party and making contacts elsewhere, on the other. With the aid of such Comintern agents as Voitinsky and Maring, the Chinese Communist Party was formed in 1921.[69] Of course, it was yet too weak and immature to be effective in China. In the search for allies, the Russians at times were even attracted by the military strength of General Wu P'ei-fu—they called him a bourgeois nationalist.[70] Nevertheless, it was to Sun Yat-sen that they finally turned their attention.

As early as 1912, Lenin showed considerable interest in Sun's ideas and activities. In an article titled "Democracy and Narodism in China," written in July 1912, Lenin described the Chinese leader as a "petty-bourgeois democrat" standing close to the Russian Narodnik.[71] While criticizing some of his ideas, such as the possibility of "preventing capitalism in China," as reactionary and naïve, Lenin nonetheless praised Sun's platform as "a really great ideology," with a "sincere spirit of democracy" and a "warm sympathy for the masses." In another article, written in November of the same year, Lenin had this to say about the Kuomintang: "The 'National Party' . . . is mainly the party of the more industrial, more progressive, and more developed in Southern China. The 'National Party' ob-

tains its main support from the wide masses of the peasants.
Its leaders are the intelligentsia who have been educated
abroad." [72] As has been stated, Sun Yat-sen was the first
prominent foreign figure to congratulate Lenin after the success of the Bolshevik revolution. In a reply to Dr. Sun on
August 1, 1918, Commissar of Foreign Affairs Chicherin took
the opportunity to stress the Sino-Soviet solidarity: "For our
victory is your victory. Our defeat is your defeat. Let us close
the ranks in the great fight for the common interests of the
world proletariat." [73] However, this letter did not reach Sun,
apparently because of communication difficulties. In fact, no
Soviet message ever reached him until the summer of 1921,
when Chicherin's letter of October 31, 1921, proposing the
re-establishment of trade relations between Russia and China,
was received in Canton. In his fervent reply Sun informed
Chicherin that:

> This is the first and only letter received by me from you or
> from anyone in Soviet Russia. In the course of the past two
> years, there have been several reports in the capitalist press
> concerning formal proposals allegedly made to me from
> Moscow. No such proposals have been communicated to
> me by letter or by any other means.[74]

Nevertheless, other evidence indicates that there had been
some informal contact between the Kuomintang and the
Comintern during 1920-1921. For instance, when the Congress of Toilers of the Far East was held in January and February 1922, in Moscow and Petrograd, a Kuomintang delegate
came to take part and to explain the policies of the Canton
regime.[75] At the Congress Grigori Zinoviev, the spokesman of
the Third International, ridiculed the Open Door Policy of the
United States, attacked the Washington Conference, and called
the Four-Power Treaty the "Alliance of the Four Blood-
suckers." He chided those adherents of Sun Yat-sen who
looked to America for help, and he hoped that the Washington
Conference would convince the more farsighted leaders in
Southern China of American hypocrisy. In the end, he offered
the full support of the Comintern to the Chinese people to

"achieve elementary freedom and independence" and to "bring about the day when the Japanese, American, and English bourgeoisie and officers will no more be able to mock the masses of China, to behave there as if they were in a stable, will not be able to commit the atrocities which they committed with impunity during the suppression of the Boxer Rising, the rising for which you paid not only with your blood and tears, but also with your gold." [76] Throughout the Congress the Kuomintang received considerable criticism for its bourgeois outlook and was urged to adopt a more radical policy. The Chinese Nationalist delegate took pains to explain the position of his Party and to point out the resemblance between the Kuomintang program and that proposed by the Comintern. [77]

More important were personal meetings between Sun Yatsen and some Comintern agents. In the autumn of 1920, Gregory Voitinsky, head of the Eastern Department of the Communist International, had an interview with Dr. Sun in Shanghai. The Chinese leader asked the Comintern representative about Russia and the Bolshevik revolution, and he expressed the hope that the Russians might place a very powerful radio station in Vladivostok or Manchuria in order to communicate with Canton. [78] In the spring of 1921, Alexieff, another Soviet agent, came to Canton to exchange views with Dr. Sun and to establish the Rosta News Agency to help Chinese propaganda work. [79] In the summer of the same year, Maring also met Sun in Kweilin. It was through the meeting of this Comintern representative and Dr. Sun that the first definite step toward a Kuomintang-Bolshevik entente was taken.

Maring, whose real name was Sneevliet, was sent to China by Lenin, in the spring of 1921, as the Comintern's representative to observe revolutionary possibilities there. He first met General Wu P'ei-fu in the North and then went south to confer with Dr. Sun Yat-sen at Kweilin and later at Canton. In their interviews, Maring informed Sun of the real conditions in Russia, especially the revolutionary methods of the Bolsheviks and the New Economic Policy. He was impressed with Sun's movement, but he quickly pointed out that the Kuomintang could not shoulder revolutionary responsibilities due to its weakness in organization and propaganda, and its dependence on General Ch'en Ch'iung-ming.[80] Consequently, he presented to Sun two concrete proposals. First, to carry out the Chinese revolution, there must be a good political party allied with all classes, especially the proletariat and peasantry. Second, to obtain armed forces for revolution, a military academy must be established.[81] Although these resulted in no definite commitment, Sun expressed his interest in Maring's proposals and a way for future cooperation was paved.

His interviews with Dr. Sun, together with his observation of the conditions in China, convinced Maring that the Kuomintang was the nucleus of the Chinese national-revolutionary movement, and that Soviet interests lay in cooperation with it. These views were expounded in an article on South China, published in *Kommunistichekii International* in 1922, in which, while critical of the Kuomintang in some respects, Maring focused his attention on improving Communist relations with Sun's Party—in opposition to the warlords in China.[82] His recommendations won the approval of the Kremlin and helped to start a new orientation of Soviet policy in China. Nevertheless, there was no unanimity in approach to Dr. Sun Yat-sen and the Chinese problem among the Soviet elite in the Comintern, the Narkomindel (the People's Commissariat for Foreign Affairs), and the Profintern (the Red International of Trade Unions). Within the Comintern, Lenin and Maring continually stressed the positive features of Sun's regime, favoring a policy of cooperation, but Zinoviev, G. Safarov, and M. N. Roy "featured the negative aspects of the Canton regime, constantly referring to the time when the Chinese bourgeoisie could be overthrown and smashed." [83] Roy, in particular, was always very critical of Sun Yat-sen. In fact, he dismissed Sun quite contemptuously as "impractical," "positively reactionary," and "a schemer." [84] In contrast, Narkomindel writers wrote encouragingly of the Chinese bourgeoisie and regarded both Sun Yat-sen and Wu P'ei-fu as representing the most promising force in China. Profintern publicists, however, took an entirely independent line. They were frankly skeptical of any positive program in China and highly critical of General Wu's anti-labor activities, as well as Dr. Sun's compromise tactics.[85] Although the policy of alliance with the Kuomintang finally prevailed, differences of opinion among Soviet leaders continued to exist, and they formed a basis for the future debate on China.

Before his return to Russia in September 1922, Maring personally laid the foundation for cooperation between the Chinese Communists and the Kuomintang. From the Soviet point of view, such a step was necessary not only for a possible Moscow-Canton alliance, but also for the growth of Chinese Communism. Making use of the Kuomintang, the young Chinese Communist Party could widen its contacts among the masses and prepare a basis for its future hegemony. The question was, however, how to bring the Kuomintang and the Chinese Communists together.

Apparently in line with Lenin's theory of revolution in semicolonial countries, the Chinese Communists in the summer of 1922 made friendly overtures to the Kuomintang and all other democratic forces in China. In the First Manifesto of the Current Situation of June 1922, the Central Committee of the Chinese Communist Party proposed a "united front" of democratic revolution to liberate the Chinese people from a dual yoke—imperialism and feudalism. It went on to invite "the revolutionary elements of the Kuomintang" to a conference to discuss the creating of such a front.[86] Again, in their Manifesto of the Second National Congress of July 1922, the Chinese Communists called for a "democratic united front of workers, poor peasants, and petty bourgeoisie" in the pursuit of certain common revolutionary objectives. Nevertheless, they made it clear that they were the party of the proletariat and would work for the proletarian revolution even during the democratic alliance:

> The Chinese Communist Party is the party of the proletariat. Its aims are to organize the proletariat and to struggle for [the establishment of] the dictatorship of the workers and peasants, the abolition of private property, and the gradual attainment of a Communist society. At present, the Chinese Communist Party must, in the interest of the workers and

poor peasants, lead the workers to support the democratic
revolution and forge a democratic united front of workers,
poor peasants, and petty bourgeoisie. . . . However, the
workers must not become the appendage of the petty bourgeoisie within this democratic united front, but must fight
for their own class interests. Therefore, it is imperative that
the workers be organized in the Party as well as in labor
unions. Ever mindful of their class independence, the workers must develop the strength of their fighting organization
[in order to] prepare for the establishment of soviets in con-
junction with the poor peasantry and in order to achieve
[the goal of] complete liberation.[87]

The response of the Kuomintang to this offer of a united
front was not favorable. What the Chinese Communists actually offered was a sort of two-party alliance, that is, cooperation with the Kuomintang on equal terms. This appeared to be
rather presumptuous in view of the fact that the Kuomintang
had some 150,000 members, while the Chinese Communist
had less than three hundred.[88] Despite their new defeat in the
revolt of Ch'en Ch'iung-ming, Sun Yat-sen and his followers
had no intention of relinquishing their dominant role in guiding the Chinese revolution. Instead of a two-party alliance,
Sun suggested that the Chinese Communists join the Kuomintang to work for the realization of its program.[89] It was at
this point that Maring came to intervene on behalf of Moscow.
In August 1922, the Comintern representative called a special
plenum of the Central Committee of the Chinese Communist
Party at Hangchow, and proposed that the Party members join
the Kuomintang. According to Ch'en Tu-hsiu's account, Maring contended that the Kuomintang was not a bourgeois party
but a coalition party of all classes, and that by joining it the
Communists could transform the Kuomintang into a driving
force of the revolution. At first Maring's suggestion was
strongly opposed by Ch'en Tu-hsiu and the others present, on
the ground that entry into the Kuomintang would confuse class
structure and curb the Communist Party's independence. However, when Maring invoked the authority of the Comintern, his
proposal was adopted by the special plenum.[90] Thus, in the

interest of political reality and long-range gains, the Chinese Communists were forced to fall in line with Moscow's strategy to win the friendship of Sun Yat-sen.

Sun's negotiations with Soviet representatives in Shanghai

By the latter part of 1922, conditions had become favorable for a Kuomintang-Soviet alliance. Frustrations in the revolution, disillusion with the West, and admiration for the Bolsheviks—all had influenced Sun's Russian orientation. As for the Kremlin, the necessity of finding a new ally in China and the plan to use the bourgeois revolution for the preparation of Communist victory also pointed in the direction of collaboration with the Kuomintang. It was under such circumstances that Dr. Sun entered into negotiations with Soviet representatives in Shanghai.

Sun went to Shanghai in August 1922, following his ousting from Canton by Ch'en Ch'iung-ming. After his arrival in Shanghai, Sun immediately came into contact with Soviet representatives. Among those who carried on discussions with him were Maring and V. Dalin, a delegate of the Young Communist International.[91] Adolf Joffe, the new Soviet envoy to Peking, was also having correspondence with the Kuomintang leader.[92] In a letter to Chiang Kai-shek on August 30, 1922, Sun stated: "Their representative has recently sent a special messenger with a letter to inquire about the Far Eastern problems and the means of solving them. I have answered all his questions in detail. Now that we have exchanged correspondence with each other, all matters will be easy to discuss. He [the representative] has brought along a military aide with him and I have asked him to send the aide to Shanghai first for detailed consultation on the military situation. I am expecting the arrival of this aide soon." [93]

In their negotiations, Dr. Sun and the Russians not only sought agreement on the nature and scope of their future cooperation, but also tried to iron out some differences over such issues as the Chinese Communist Party, the Chinese Eastern Railway, and Outer Mongolia. While not in a strong position to negotiate, Sun nevertheless did his best to strike a good bargain with the Russians. For instance, in a meeting with Dalin in August 1922, he flatly rejected the proposal for a two-party alliance between the Chinese Communists and the Kuomintang, but expressed a willingness to allow the Communists to enter his Party as individuals.[94] Shortly after the Hangchow plenum of the Chinese Communist Party, Li Ta-chao, a prominent Communist leader, conferred with Dr. Sun in Shanghai. They agreed on a formula whereby the Chinese Communists would enter the Kuomintang as individuals to work for the Three People's Principles and the national revolution, but, at the same time, the Communist Party would continue to maintain its separate existence.[95] With this compromise formula, Li Ta-chao and other Communists began to make arrangements to join the Kuomintang, and Sun's negotiations with the U.S.S.R. moved a step forward toward a fruitful conclusion.

On November 21, 1922, when the negotiations were about reaching the final stage, Sun again wrote Chiang Kai-shek about the situation in Shanghai. Among other things, he discussed the prospects of the negotiations, the difficulties he was encountering, and the necessity for the Kuomintang to have its own strength in order to win Russia's respect and assistance:

> You previously had the intention to contact the West [Russia]. Recently in Shanghai I have worked on that, and now I have found important connections. But the matter [dealing with the Russians] is very complicated and difficult, probably ten or a hundred times more so than the conditions in Foochow. No wonder all our countrymen who went to their capital [Moscow] in high spirits came back dejected. Fortunately, I have found the way and shall be able to develop closer relations with them [the Russians] from now on. But fundamentally we must have a base to rely on before we can do much. Without anything to rely on, even though the young Chinese Communists share their doctrine, what good can those youngsters do? That is why the leaders in Moscow have advised the Chinese Communists to join the Kuomintang. All this tells us that we must secure a base first. To get that we must recapture Kwangtung. If Kwangtung is recovered this time, then we shall be able to unify

the Southwest. With the Southwestern provinces as a base, we certainly can go places.[96]

Dr. Sun's negotiations with Soviet representatives climaxed in his meeting with Adolf Joffe. Succeeding Ignatius Yurin and Alexander Paikes, Joffe was sent to Peking by Moscow, in the autumn of 1922, to continue the negotiations with the Chinese government in the North regarding the possible establishment of formal Sino-Soviet relations and the settlement of the Mongolian and the Chinese Eastern Railway question.[97] After several months of futile negotiations in Peking, the Soviet envoy came to Shanghai in December 1922, to discuss an alliance with Dr. Sun directly.[98] Their meetings resulted in an agreement jointly announced in January 1923, which became the foundation of the Kuomintang-Soviet entente.

Chapter 4

Sun Yat-sen's Alliance with Soviet Russia

The period from 1923 to 1925 was a very eventful one in the history of the Chinese revolution. It was the period of Sun Yat-sen's Soviet alliance. It was also the last, but unfinished, stage of Sun's ideological development. In the preceding chapter, we discussed the reasons for Dr. Sun's new Russian orientation. This chapter will examine the nature and scope of the Kuomintang-Soviet alliance, the inherent differences between the two allies, and the extent to which Sun's doctrines and policies underwent changes under Soviet influence.

The joint Sun-Joffe declaration in 1923

In December 1922, Joffe arrived in Shanghai to negotiate with Dr. Sun on the question of collaboration between the Kuomintang and the Bolsheviks. After a series of discussions, they reached an agreement on the general conditions of cooperation. This agreement was announced in the form of a joint statement issued on January 26, 1923:

1. Dr. Sun Yat-sen holds that the Communistic order or even the Soviet system cannot actually be introduced into China, because there do not exist here the conditions for the successful establishment of either Communism or Sovietism. This view is entirely shared by Mr. Joffe, who is further of opinion that China's paramount and most pressing problem is to achieve national unification and attain full national independence, and regarding this great task he has assured Dr. Sun Yat-sen that China has the warmest sympathy of the Russian people and can count on the support of Russia.

2. In order to clarify the situation, Dr. Sun Yat-sen has requested Mr. Joffe for a reaffirmation of the principles defined in the Russian Note to the Chinese Government, dated September 27, 1920. Mr. Joffe has accordingly reaffirmed these principles and categorically declared to Dr. Sun Yat-sen that the Russian Government is ready and willing to enter into negotiation with China on the basis of the renunciation by Russia of all the treaties and exactions which the Tsardom imposed in China, including the treaty or treaties and agreement relating to the Chinese Eastern Railway. . . .

3. Recognizing that the Chinese Eastern Railway question in its entirety can be satisfactorily settled only at a competent Russo-Chinese Conference, Dr. Sun Yat-sen is of the opinion that the realities of the situation point to the desirability of a *modus vivendi* in the matter of the present management of the Railway. . . .

4. Mr. Joffe has categorically declared to Dr. Sun Yat-sen . . . that it is not and has never been the intention or purpose of the present Russian Government to pursue an imperialistic policy in Outer Mongolia or to cause it to secede from China. Dr. Sun Yat-sen, therefore, does not view an immediate evacuation of Russian troops from Outer Mongolia as imperative or in the real interest of China. . . .[1]

This joint statement received wide publicity in China, but its significance was generally overlooked abroad. Whatever

secret agreements there may have been between Dr. Sun and
Joffe, a careful examination of their statement itself reveals
some interesting points. First, the Sun-Joffe declaration officially marked the beginning of friendly cooperation between
the Kuomintang and Soviet Russia and constituted the basis for
their alliance. While no formal alliance against Chinese warlords and Western imperialism was announced in this document, Russia did pledge to support the Kuomintang in its
efforts to "achieve unification and attain full national independence" of China. Furthermore, it was the first time that a
European power treated a Chinese regime on equal terms.
Second, the declaration indicated that the alliance Sun sought
with Russia was a qualified arrangement. He accepted Soviet
aid, in his attempt to achieve the Chinese revolution, only
after the Russians pledged not to impose Communism on China
and agreed to surrender all their special positions in China.
So far as the Bolsheviks were concerned, they did not try to
convert Sun to Communism. For the fight against a common
enemy—foreign imperalism—and for their future success in
China, they were willing to make temporary concessions to
win the confidence of Dr. Sun and his followers. Third, the
joint statement was obviously the result of prolonged, give-and-
take negotiations, as the spirit of compromise was quite in
evidence. Taking the Chinese Eastern Railway question as an
example, while both sides agreed that the whole issue should
be settled at a future conference, Dr. Sun in the meantime had
to accept "a *modus vivendi* in the matter of the present management of the Railway." On the question of Outer Mongolia,
Russia recognized Chinese sovereignty and denied having any
imperialist designs, and, once again, Sun accepted the realities
of the situation by agreeing not to "view an immediate evacuation of Russian troops from Outer Mongolia as imperative or
in the real interest of China."

Immediately following the conclusion of the Sun-Joffe
agreement, Eugene Ch'en, personal secretary and right-hand
man to Dr. Sun, publicly lauded the collaboration between
the Kuomintang and Soviet Russia, and predicted defeat for
the encircling policy of the "Anglo-Latin conquerors." Ac-

cording to Ch'en, the conversations with Joffe necessarily altered the international rating of Sun Yat-sen, who emerged as a world force with the support of Russia. The ultimate outcome of the policy underlying the conversations, Ch'en emphasized, depended on the attitude of the great powers toward Russia and toward Sun Yat-sen. "That outcome might be the contemplation of Russia and China in making available their resources to the uses of humanity—or a continued hostility to Russia, and what appears like hostility to Sun Yat-sen on the part of certain great powers might forge an iron alliance between China and Russia directed to other ends." [2]

In spite of the new development in Sun's relations with Russia, the West still maintained a rather contemptuous attitude toward the Kuomintang leader. This attitude was reflected in an editorial of *The New York Times* on January 29, 1923, which commented on the Sun-Joffe meeting in Shanghai:

> . . . Mr. Joffe further assured Dr. Sun that Russia would do all it could to further the reunion and independence of China. That is Dr. Sun's ideal, though whenever there are signs that China is about to become reunited and independent under somebody other than Dr. Sun he starts a fight. He has been accused very plausibly of being a more or less innocent tool of those Japanese interests which want anything rather than the reunion or independence of China. He works with General Chang Tso-lin, according to the well-known liberal doctrine that a militarist reactionary who will help orthodox liberals is a better man than a well-intentioned, middle-of-the-road statesman who keeps a liberal out of office. There isn't much mystery about the relations between Chang Tso-lin and Japan. If Mr. Joffe is genuinely enthusiastic for the reunion and independence of China, he is in strange company.

The coming of Borodin

On January 15, 1923, a few days before Sun's joint declaration with Joffe, his supporters recovered Canton from the hands of Ch'en Ch'iung-ming. In February, Dr. Sun again returned to power in Canton. Meanwhile, one of his trusted aides, Liao Chung-k'ai, had accompanied Joffe to Japan to continue the negotiations.³ After a month of detailed discussions with Joffe on the real situation in Russia, the Bolsheviks' policies and techniques, and the question of Kuomintang reorganization, Liao reported to Sun and helped push forward the Canton-Moscow collaboration. According to one account, in their talks Liao asked Joffe about the time needed for Communism to be realized in Russia and received the answer that it would probably take a hundred years. This prompted Liao to remark to a friend: "What is the use of dreaming about a Utopia which might or might not be realized, when we are all dead? Let us all be revolutionaries today, and work for the accomplishment of the national revolution on the basis of the Three People's Principles. These we can realize within our lifetime. We must, however, unite with all the revolutionary forces available, and agree on an immediate common aim no matter what our ultimate ideals are." ⁴ There is little doubt that Liao also used the same argument to lessen the fear of many Kuomintang leaders and to convince them of the necessity of cooperating with the Communists.

In August 1923, Dr. Sun sent a delegation headed by General Chiang Kai-shek, his Chief-of-Staff, to Moscow to study Soviet conditions and to negotiate for Russia's aid. Chiang carried with him identical letters of introduction from Dr. Sun to Lenin, Trotsky, and Chicherin. The following month, in a reply to the greetings from Leo Karakhan, who had just arrived in Peking to replace Joffe as Soviet envoy, Dr. Sun stated that the purpose of Chiang's mission to Russia was "to discuss ways and means whereby our friends there can assist me in my work in this country. In particular, General Chiang is to take up with your government and military experts a proposal for military action by my forces in and about the regions lying to the northwest of Peking and beyond. General Chiang is fully empowered to act in my behalf." ⁵

During their three months in Russia, Chiang and his group studied the military and political organizations, examined the industrial and agricultural systems, and attended mass meetings and discussion groups. Chiang met many Soviet leaders and had various talks with them. He was impressed by men like Trotsky, Zinoviev, Radek, Kamenev, Chicherin, and Joffe, who expressed regard for Dr. Sun and a sincere desire to cooperate with China in her national revolution. On the other hand, Chiang also found that the Soviet attitude toward Outer Mongolia was very evasive, and he was offended by the "shocking" resolution on the Kuomintang passed by the Comintern. Therefore, he began to entertain some doubts about the sincerity of the Russians.[6]

In the meantime, important steps had been taken by Moscow to assist Dr. Sun and his regime. The disillusion with General Wu P'ei-fu, who in February 1923 massacred many workers taking part in the Communist-organized Peking-Hankow Railway Strike, further convinced the Russians that Sun was the only influential ally they could find in China.[7] In September, Moscow dispatched Michael Borodin to Canton as political adviser to the Kuomintang. Ostensibly, he was to serve only in a private capacity, but, in actuality, he was appointed as an official representative of the Soviet government in Canton. He was to "take his orders direct from Moscow" and to have an important role in shaping up Soviet decisions and measures "regarding questions of the general policy of the Kuomintang in China."[8] An experienced organizer who had served abroad as an agent of the Third International, Mr. Borodin was highly recommended to Dr. Sun by a personal letter from Leo Karakhan:

> The absence in Canton of a permanent and responsible representative of our government has long been keenly felt at Moscow. With the appointment of M. M. Borodin, an important step has been taken in this direction. Comrade B. [sic] is one of the oldest members of our Party, having worked for a great many years in the revolutionary movement of Russia. Please regard Comrade B. not only as a representative of the government but likewise my personal representative with whom you may talk as frankly as you would with me. Anything he says, you may rely upon as if I had said it to you personally. He is familiar with the whole situation and besides, before his leaving for the South, we

had a long talk. He will convey to you my thoughts, wishes, feelings.[9]

The main objectives of the Borodin mission were to use the Soviet example to help reorganize Sun's Party and Army, to formalize the relations between the Kuomintang and the Chinese Communists, and to turn the Chinese revolution into an antimilitarist, anti-imperialist mass movement. Concerned over the Kuomintang's failure to organize the masses, the Russians repeatedly told Sun of the importance of broadening the basis of his Party. In a letter to the Chinese leader on December 4, 1923, Chicherin declared: "We think that the fundamental aim of the Kuomintang Party is to build up a great, powerful movement of the Chinese people and that therefore propaganda and organization on the biggest scale are its first necessities." Citing Soviet experiences as a significant example, he explained that "our military activities were successful because a long series of years had elapsed during which we organized and instructed our followers, building up in this way a great, organized party throughout the whole land, a party capable of vanquishing all its adversaries." [10] Karakhan also wrote to Dr. Sun on January 7, 1924, to the same effect. He urged Sun to carry out land reform, to mobilize popular support, and, above all, to strengthen the Kuomintang.[11]

When Borodin arrived in Canton in October 1923, he found Sun's regime in a precarious position, constantly threatened by Ch'en Ch'iung-ming's forces. He first assured Dr. Sun that Communism was not suitable for present conditions in China, and that he would support the fight for the realization of the Three People's Principles. Then he was quick to point out certain serious shortcomings with the Kuomintang: "In the first place, the Kuomintang organization is very incomplete, and there is no discipline worth speaking of. Second, there are many impure elements in the Kuomintang, corrupt bureaucrats and adventurers. Then the Kuomintang lacks a popular basis in the form of the organization of the masses." [12] All these things had to be rectified, said the Soviet representative, before the Kuomintang could become an effective revolutionary weapon. To this suggestion, Dr. Sun agreed completely. Borodin also promised Sun to obtain arms and munitions on easy terms from Soviet Russia and to provide a corps of military and civilian experts to help Canton in the reorganization work.[13]

There is little doubt that Borodin quickly won Sun's confidence and soon became the "reorganizer" of the Kuomintang. In a speech given on November 25, 1923, Dr. Sun told his followers that the Russian Communist Party actually advocated the Three People's Principles of the Kuomintang. The reason for the success of the Russian revolution was that the Russians had good methods and organization, and that their Party members struggled for the realization of their principles. In order to learn their methods, Sun said, he had asked Mr. Borodin to undertake the task of training the Kuomintang members. "Since Mr. Borodin is extremely experienced in Party management," Sun continued, "all the comrades are expected to sacrifice their personal prejudices and to learn faithfully his methods." [14] Thus, with the backing of Sun and the help of other Russian advisers, Borodin started an unprecedented job of reorganizing the Kuomintang, and revolutionizing its army, all along Soviet lines.

The admittance of the Chinese Communists into the Kuomintang

The story of the Moscow-Canton entente will not be complete if the admission of the Chinese Communists into the Kuomintang is left unexamined. It should be recalled that, under the pressure of Maring, the Chinese Communist Party in 1922 made concessions to the Kuomintang, in the search for a formula for their cooperation. Nevertheless, there was apparent reluctance on the part of the Chinese Communist leadership to seek such an alliance, and this attitude was criticized as being impractical by Karl Radek at the Fourth Congress of the Comintern, in November 1922.[15] The Executive Committee of the Communist International, in a resolution of January 12, 1923, further laid down the proper course of action for the Chinese Party. Calling the Kuomintang the only important national-revolutionary group in China, the resolution stated: "Insofar as the independent working class

movement in the country is still weak, insofar as the central
task confronting China is to carry out the national revolution
against the imperialists and their feudal agents . . . the
E.C.C.I. considers that it is necessary to coordinate the activities of the Kuomintang and of the young Communist Party of
China." [16] The Party was, however, advised not to merge with
the Kuomintang but to preserve its complete political and
organizational independence, while working inside the latter.
It was against this background of the Kremlin's pressure, together with the demoralizing failure of the Hankow strike of
February 1923, that the Third National Congress of the
Chinese Communist Party in June 1923 officially approved
the formula of entering the Kuomintang. The Congress Manifesto described the Kuomintang as "the central force of the
national revolution" and called upon "all the revolutionary
elements in our society" to "rally to the Kuomintang, speeding
up the completion of the national-revolutionary movement."
At the same time, it made clear that "the Chinese Communist
Party never forgets for one moment to support the interests of
the workers and peasants. . . . Our mission is to liberate the
oppressed Chinese nation by a national revolution, and to
advance to the world revolution, liberating the oppressed
peoples and oppressed classes of the whole world." [17]

With the Chinese Communists' formal concession of the
leadership to the Kuomintang, the Moscow-Canton entente
passed its final hurdle. Although certain elements in the Kuomintang were, from the beginning, opposed to the idea of
admitting the Communists into the Party, Dr. Sun was able
to bring them into line. [18] In January 1924, Sun's policy of
alliance with Soviet Russia and of admitting the Communists
into the Kuomintang received official endorsement from the
First National Congress of the Kuomintang, held in Canton.
In presenting his new policy, Sun told the Congress of its
necessity for the Chinese revolution, and of the good intentions
of Soviet Russia in helping the Kuomintang. Concerning the
admittance of the Chinese Communists into the Party, he
pointed out: "The Communists are joining our Party in order
to work for the national revolution. We are, therefore, bound

to admit them. If our own members are only active in their propaganda of the principles of the Party, and build up a strong organization and submit unquestioningly to Party discipline, we need have nothing to fear from Communist machinations. In any case, if the Communists betray the Kuomintang, I will be the first to propose their expulsion." [19] In spite of Sun's explanation, some members were still not satisfied. They proposed a strict Party regulation that "a Kuomintang member should not join the other Party," as a means to restrict the Communists. Li Ta-chao, a Communist delegate, then assured the Congress with the following statement: "We join this Party as individuals, not as a body. We may be said to have dual Party membership. But it may not be said of Kuomintang that there is a Party within a Party. . . . Since we have joined the Party and so long as we remain its members, we shall carry out its political program and abide by its constitution and bylaws. We shall obey the disciplinary measures or punishment imposed by this Party in case we fail to do so." [20] This statement was accepted by the Congress, and admission of the Communists became an official Kuomintang policy. A few Communists even became members of the Central Executive Committee of the Kuomintang.[21]

Nevertheless, this did not mean that the Kuomintang and the Chinese Communists really saw eye to eye regarding their new relationship. For the Kuomintang, the policy of "Jung Kung," admission of the Chinese Communists, was based upon a subordinate-master relationship under which the Chinese Communists were *allowed* to join the Kuomintang and were expected to work for its revolutionary program, to submit to its discipline, and to undertake *no improper activities* within the Party. For the Chinese Communists, however, their joining the Kuomintang constituted no more than an opportunity for them to form a "bloc within," to reach the masses through the Kuomintang's organizational apparatus, and eventually to achieve "proletarian hegemony" in the Chinese revolution. A statement by Liu Jen-ching to the Fourth Congress of the Communists International in Moscow suggests the motives of the Chinese Communists in collaborating with the Kuomintang:

> There are two reasons for this [joining the Kuomintang].
> In the first place, we want to propagandize the many or-
> ganized workers in the national-revolutionary Party and
> win them over for us. In the second place, we can only
> fight imperialism if we can combine our forces, the forces
> of the petty bourgeoisie and the proletariat. . . . If we do
> not join this Party, we shall remain isolated and we shall
> preach a Communism which consists of a great and noble
> ideal, but one which the masses do not follow. The masses
> certainly would follow the bourgeois Party, and this Party
> would use the masses for its purpose. If we join the Party,
> we shall be able to show the masses that we too are for a
> revolutionary democracy, but that for us revolutionary
> democracy is only a means to an end. Furthermore, we shall
> be able to point out that although we are for this distant
> goal, we nevertheless do not forget the daily needs of the
> masses. We shall be able to gather the masses around us
> and split the Kuomintang Party.[22]

Consequently, the decision of the First National Congress notwithstanding, some leaders of the Right Wing of the Kuomintang, while recognizing the necessity of the Soviet alliance, remained unconvinced of the wisdom of admitting the Chinese Communists. Prominent among those dissenters were Tai Chi-t'ao, Chang Chi, Tsou Lu, Lin Shen, and Hsieh Ch'ih, who did not openly challenge Sun's policy, but who frequently expressed their distrust of the Chinese Communists.[23] General Chiang Kai-shek, who had just returned from Russia and was cooperating with Russian advisers to organize a military academy, also expressed his doubts about the sincerity of the Communists in a letter to Liao Chung-k'ai, on March 4, 1924: "According to my observation, the Russian Party does not have any sincerity. Even when I told you that only 30 per cent of the words of the Russians may be believed, it was said only because you were so enthusiastic in trusting the Russians that I did not want to upset you too much. Those who have deep respect for Dr. Sun are not Russian Communists but members of the Communist International. As for Chinese Communists in Russia, they have only slanders and suspicion for Dr. Sun. The Russian Party has only one objective in China, that is, to build up the Chinese Communist Party as its legitimate heir. It never believes that our Party can cooperate with it permanently for mutual benefits. As for its policy toward China, the Russian Party wants to have Manchus, Tibetans, Mongolians, and Moslems all under Soviet domination; it may even harbor sinister designs on China Proper." [24] On June 18, 1924 the Central Control Committee of the Kuomintang, led by Chang Chi and Hsieh Ch'ih, proposed an "impeachment of the Communist Party." Offering a Communist document, "Resolutions of the Socialist Youth Corps, August 1923," as evidence, the impeachment proposal charged that the Chinese Communists were not acting as individuals but as a Party within the Kuomintang and were taking orders from the Central Committee of the Chinese Communist Party, contrary to the best interest of the Kuomintang.[25] A few days later Chang Chi and Hsieh Ch'ih further questioned Borodin about the fact that the Communists were working as "a Party within a Party." The Soviet adviser made no denials but pointed out that both the Kuomintang and the Chinese Communists were using each other in their present collaboration and that the result of this mutual utilization would benefit the Kuomintang most. This, however, failed to convince the two skeptical Nationalist leaders.[26]

Having no illusion about the Chinese Communists himself, Dr. Sun Yat-sen, nonetheless, needed the Soviet alliance and wanted to unite all the revolutionary forces in China to achieve the national revolution. Furthermore, he felt that the interest of his Party was to a large degree safeguarded both by the Sun-Joffe statement and by the pledge made by the Chinese Communists through Li Ta-chao. According to Chiang Kai-shek's account, Dr. Sun considered the skeptical views expressed by Chiang on the future Sino-Russian relations as being "over-cautious and unsuitable, particularly in view of the revolutionary realities of the moment." Sun was of the firm belief that "in the circumstances, the only way to deter the Chinese

Communists from inciting class conflicts and sabotaging our
national revolution was to place them under the leadership of
Kuomintang and to subject them to our Party's unified direction." He thought that "the moment the Northward Expedition
came to its successful conclusion, the Three People's Principles could be implemented according to schedule, and that
by that time it would be too late for the Chinese Communists
to disrupt our national revolution even if they should so try." [27]
In order to allay his followers' fear and promote Party harmony, Sun frequently attempted to reconcile his ideas with
Communism and even went so far as to interpret the Soviet
revolution as an actual application of his Three People's
Principles. He did this in many of his speeches made during
1923-1924.[28] In his marginal comments on the accusing letter
against the Chinese Communist Party by Teng Tse-ju and
others in December 1923, Sun gave the following explanation:
"Essentially, there is really no difference between the Principle
of People's Livelihood and Communism. The Russian revolution, in its initial stage, only carried out the Principles of
Democracy and People's Livelihood. After six years of struggle
with foreign powers, it then realized that its utmost effort had
been really given to the Principle of Nationalism." [29]

Thus, in the interest of promoting the Chinese revolution
through the Soviet alliance, Dr. Sun chose to stick to his policy
of permitting the Chinese Communists to join the Kuomintang
even in the face of considerable dissension with the Party. This
policy was reaffirmed by the Second Plenum of the Central
Executive Committee of the Kuomintang in August 1924,
when the CEC passed resolutions to clarify the fundamental
position of the Party on the question of the Chinese Communists. First, the resolutions stated that in seeking the liberation
of the country, the Kuomintang must include in its fold all
genuine revolutionary elements, irrespective of party or class
lines. Then, it was pointed out that although the Chinese
Communist Party might be destroyed by force, no way was
found to destroy the Chinese proletariat, from which the Communist Party would be organized again. Therefore, the resolutions went on to declare, the attitude of the Kuomintang

towards the Communists "is to ask whether their conduct is in harmony with its principles and its platforms and nothing else, because everywhere and at all times the Kuomintang ought to govern all its members in accordance with its platform and regulations. Since the Communists have accepted the principles of the Kuomintang and are admitted to its membership, they ought to be governed as such." [30]

In short, in forming an alliance with each other, both the Kuomintang and the Communists, knowing their ultimate aims to be different, had to take pains to adjust themselves to the new orientation. However, they were held together, at least temporarily, by Dr. Sun's personal influence and by the presence of a common enemy, Western imperialism. Above all, they all stood to gain in working side by side for the Chinese revolution. This was the essence of the Kuomintang-Communist alliance, a marriage of convenience which was to last as long as their respective interests coincided.

Russia as the model

The immediate effects of the Moscow-Canton alliance were undeniably tremendous. In Canton, "learn from Russia" and "use Russian models" became the slogans of the day. At the First National Congress of the Kuomintang in January 1924, Sun Yat-sen frequently praised Russia's revolutionary methods, organizations, and tactics and urged his followers to use them as examples.[31] Upon learning of the death of Lenin, he adjourned the Congress for three days as a token of mourning, and praised the Soviet leader as "the saint and model of revolution." [32] In a reply to Chiang Kai-shek in October 1924, concerning the organization of a Revolutionary Committee, Sun wrote: "The Revolutionary Committee must be formed at once to meet all kinds of emergencies. It is unnecessary to include Hu Han-min and Wang Ching-wei on the Committee. *Today our revolution must follow the Russian pattern* and Hu Han-min has lost faith in this. . . . Neither is Wang Ching-wei a Russian-type revolutionary, and we can do without him. *Henceforth our revolution can never succeed unless we follow Soviet Russia as our model.* I am afraid that both Hu and Wang cannot bring themselves to accept this policy."[33]

Instrumental in the introduction of Soviet methods to the Kuomintang was Borodin, the man in whom Moscow's influence on Sun Yat-sen found its best expression. By way of reorganization, Borodin drafted a new constitution for the Kuomintang, closely following the pattern of the Bolshevik Party.[34] The constitution, approved by the First National Congress, provided for small local nuclei as the basic units of the Kuomintang. From them, the Party organization was pyramided through district and provincial organizations to a National Congress, designed to meet annually and to be the ultimate authority on policy. When the Congress was not in session, a Central Executive Committee and a Supervisory Committee were to direct and supervise Party affairs.[35] Although Sun was made president of the Party for life, the reorganization transformed the Kuomintang from a collection of followers of a national hero to a highly organized party of disciplined individuals, united by the acceptance of a common revolutionary program. It made democratic centralism the guiding principle of the Party. It laid special emphasis on Party discipline and solidarity. In a speech on January 20, 1924, before the First National Congress, Dr. Sun pointed to the direction of the change:

> The reason for the lack of solidarity in our Party in the past was not because of any enemy using great power to destroy us; it was entirely due to the fact that we destroyed ourselves; it was because our mind and discernment were too immature, often engendering senseless misunderstandings. . . .
> There is one thing of the greatest importance in a political party, that is, all party members must possess spiritual unity. In order that all members may be united spiritually, the first thing is to sacrifice freedom, the second is to offer ability. If the individual can sacrifice his freedom, then the whole party will have freedom. If the individual can offer his ability, then the whole party will possess ability. . . .
> The past failures of our Party were due to the fact that

while the individual member had freedom, the Party as a whole had none, and that while the individual member had ability, the Party as a whole was powerless. Herein lay exactly the failure of the Kuomintang. In our reorganization today we must first get rid of this shortcoming.[36]

Together with the Party, the armed forces of Canton were also reorganized on the Soviet model. Early in 1924, a military academy was established at Whampoa with Chiang Kai-shek as its head and Liao Chung-k'ai as the Party Commissar. Staffed by Russian experts and supplied with Russian arms and funds, the academy became the cadre of a powerful military machine that later brought most of China under Kuomintang control. Credit must be given to Borodin and Soviet military advisers, headed by General Bluecher (Galens), for the rise of the new Kuomintang army, well-trained in both revolutionary principles and military tactics.[37] With this newly-acquired military strength, Dr. Sun not only freed himself from previous dependence on some warlords, but was able to prepare a northern expedition for unifying the country.

Soviet influence, of course, was not confined to matters of organization alone. It extended to some of Sun's revolutionary techniques and programs as well. Among them were his stress on propaganda work and the introduction of Bolshevik methods of agitation into the Kuomintang. Between 1923 and 1924, Dr. Sun made a series of speeches, in which his followers' attention was called to the importance of propaganda.[38] He attributed the past failure of the revolution partly to the Kuomintang's neglect of propaganda, and he urged his comrades to make determined efforts to rectify this shortcoming. According to him, the effectiveness of propaganda was as great as that of military force, if not greater, because propaganda could win the people's hearts and make them willing to fight for the Party and its principles. Citing Russia to support this argument, he pointed out that the power of propaganda was a major factor in the success of the Soviet revolution and that its effect was felt in Russia as well as abroad. Consequently, not only did he place propaganda among the most important activities of the reorganized Kuomintang, but he had his followers undergo special training to learn propaganda techniques.

Another case of Soviet influence was Sun's advocacy of drastic and uncompromising measures to carry out the revolution. In a speech on January 23, 1924, Sun said that, in the past, the Kuomintang had frequently stopped halfway and made compromises with the warlords and bureaucrats, with the result that it suffered defeat even after the revolution had achieved initial success. From now on, he continued, the Kuomintang should work for a thorough revolution to overthrow the warlords internally and to oppose imperialist aggression externally. "We should never again repeat our old mistakes and make halfway compromises." [39] Writing to Chiang Kai-shek in October 1924, Sun again stressed the importance of taking drastic action as against maintaining the *status quo*. To create a new order, he declared, it was necessary to "use a sharp knife to chop the confused hemp." [40]

Turning to Sun's concrete programs, we find that his anti-imperialist campaign definitely bore a strong Soviet flavor. Although Dr. Sun had expressed resentment of foreign oppression on previous occasions, the adoption of anti-imperialism as a policy was undoubtedly the result of his contacts with the Russians.[41] A letter to Inukai Ki on November 16, 1923, indicated this trend. In the letter, Sun urged the Japanese premier to assist the Chinese revolution and to recognize the Soviet government. Playing up the evils of Western imperialism, he maintained that Japan should join hands with China and Russia to oppose the imperialist powers led by Britian and France, and their potential ally, the United States.[42] Then there was an incident late in 1923 which served to launch Sun's "get tough" policy with foreign powers. The incident involved the Chinese Customs Service in Canton—an internationally administered organ which collected funds and sent them to Peking. In December, Sun threatened to seize the Customs House unless the money were handed over to his government. Four powers—Britain, America, France, and Japan—promptly responded with a demonstration of naval forces in Canton harbor. However, Sun stood firm and implied that he might seek Russia's aid in resisting the four-power pressure.[43] In the end, a compromise was effected, but the stand taken by Sun over this issue won him the support of the people and marked only the beginning of a series of anti-imperialist agitations.

In January 1924, the Manifesto of the First Kuomintang Congress officially attacked the role of foreign powers in China with undisguised bitterness. The chaos of China was attributed to militarism and foreign imperialism, and the cooperation of these two was described as reducing China to the status of a semicolony. In its introductory statement, the Manifesto said:

> The fact that the militarists were unable to stand on their own feet drove them to establish close connection with the imperialists. The so-called government of the Republic, being under the control of the militarists, was utilized by them to court favor with the foreign powers so as to strengthen their own positions. The imperialists, in turn, utilized these militarists by means of loans to instigate civil war and thereby to safeguard their special privileges and spheres of influence in China. From this point of view, it is evident that the chaos in China has been caused by the imperialists, who have gained advantages through the militarists' bloody hands. Moreover, the internal strife has prevented the development of native industries and has enabled foreign goods to reign supreme in our own markets. Not only politically, but also economically, we are in danger of extermination. . . . The arbitrary rule of the militarists and the invasions of the imperialists are getting worse everyday, causing China to sink deeper and deeper into the hell of a semicolonial condition.[44]

In somewhat Russian fashion the Manifesto formally made anti-imperialism a very important part of Chinese nationalism. It demanded the abrogation of the unequal treaties and the abolition of foreign concessions, extraterritoriality, foreign control of customs, etc. It also offered friendship to those countries which would voluntarily renounce their special rights and privileges in China. Along the same lines, Sun Yat-sen blasted at imperialism in his lectures on the Principle of Na-

tionalism, delivered between January 27 and March 2, 1924.
He stressed the political aggression and economic pressure of
foreign powers and repeatedly used "racial extinction" or
"hypo-colony" to arouse the people to the danger of imperialism.[45] In spite of his rejection of class struggle within China,
Dr. Sun advocated "the Class War of the Nations" between
might and right, between the oppressors and oppressed—a
struggle in which he believed China and Russia would fight side
by side as allies.[46] This anti-imperialist attitude persisted until
Sun's death in 1925 and was frequently reiterated on occasions
like his "Manifesto on the Northern Expedition" in September
1924, and "Manifesto on Going to Peking" in November of
the same year.[47] One outstanding case was his quarrel with
the British in September 1924, over the latter's assistance to a
rebellious, semi-Fascist organization in Canton, known as the
Merchants' Volunteer Corps. In this dispute not only did Sun
emerge a victor, but he singled out Britian for attack as the
symbol of imperialism and served a general warning to all
foreign powers by saying: "Formerly the battle cry of the
revolution was the overthrow of the Manchu Dynasty. Henceforth, it will be the overthrow of the intervention of foreign
imperialism in China, so that the principal obstacle to the
achievement of the historical mission of the revolution can be
removed."[48] On this occasion the Executive Committee of the
Communist International threw its full weight behind Dr. Sun
and called upon British workers to prevent the imperialists
from "directing the muzzle of their guns upon the center of the
national liberation movement in China."[49]

If Sun's anti-imperialist campaign was influenced by Russia, the same was true of his bid for the support of peasants
and workers. Though long interested in China's economic and
social problems, Sun had not been able to reach the great
masses of the country with his revolutionary principles. It was
the Communists, first Maring and then Borodin, who advised
him to broaden the basis of the revolution by seeking active
support of peasants and workers. This policy was adopted at
the First National Congress of the Kuomintang in January
1924, and it, together with "Alliance with Russia" and "Ad-

mittance of Chinese Communists," constituted what were later known as Sun's "three great policies." [50] The Manifesto of the Congress, after enumerating certain measures designed to promote their interests, made a direct appeal to peasants and workers:

> Throughout China, from north to south, from the commercial cities to the villages, destitute peasants and exploited workers are found everywhere. Because their sufferings are so similar, and because their desire for emancipation is so pressing, both of them possess the powerful will to oppose imperialism. Therefore, it is beyond doubt that the success of the national revolution will depend upon the participation of the peasants and the workers of the whole country. The Kuomintang, on the one hand, is to help peasant and labor movements, and to raise the economic status of these two classes, in order to strengthen the national revolution; on the other, it invites the peasants and workers to join the Party to make continuous efforts for the promotion of the revolutionary movement. Inasmuch as the Kuomintang is engaged in the struggle against imperialism and militarism, which are the most dangerous enemies of the workers and peasants, to participate in the struggle of the Party is to struggle for the two classes' own interests.[51]

A similar tone was voiced by Sun's May Day speech in 1924, which urged the workers to organize themselves into large unions and to support the Nationalist government for the liberation of their nation and themselves.[52] So was his address of August 20, 1924, which not only advocated a "land to the tiller" policy, with Soviet Russia as the example, but also told the peasants that, being "the great majority of the Chinese population," they had a duty to participate actively in the national revolution.[53] Moreover, the Central Committee set up special departments to help organize the peasants and workers. As a result, the mass movement in China gained momentum and gave the Chinese revolution a new strength it never had before.

All in all, Dr. Sun's Russian alliance had tremendous effects on the revolution in China. It revitalized the Kuomin-

tang with Soviet methods, tactics, and organization; it introduced anti-imperialist propaganda as a very important factor
to Chinese nationalism; it broadened the basis of the Chinese
revolution with the peasants' and workers' movements. To Dr.
Sun, Soviet Russia became not only a living example of revolution, but also a trusted ally in the struggle against imperialism.

In November 1924, with his newly-strengthened position,
Sun left Canton for Peking to negotiate with Generals Tuan
Ch'i-jui and Feng Yü-hsiang for a plan to unite China and to
overthrow foreign imperialism. Unfortunately, he became ill in
the North and died at Peking on March 12, 1925. Up to the
time of his death, Sun's faith in the Soviet alliance remained
strong and was best shown in the following message sent to
the Central Executive Committee of the U.S.S.R. in his dying
hour:

Dear Comrades:
While I lie here in a malady against which men are
powerless, my thoughts are turned towards you and towards
the fates of my Party and my Country.

You are at the head of the union of free republics—that
heritage left to the oppressed peoples of the world by the
immortal Lenin. With the aid of that heritage the victims of
imperialism will inevitably achieve emancipation from that
international regime whose foundations have been rooted
for ages in slavery, wars, and injustice.

I leave behind me a Party which, as I always hoped, will
be bound up with you in the historic work of the final
liberation of China and other exploited countries from the
yoke of imperialism. By the will of fate I must leave my
work unfinished, and hand it over to those who, remaining
faithful to the principles and teachings of the Party, will
thereby be my true followers.

Therefore I charge the Kuomintang to continue the work
of the revolutionary nationalist movement, so that China,
reduced by the imperialists to the position of a semicolonial
country, shall become free.

With this object I have instructed the Party to be in
constant contact with you. I firmly believe in the continu-

ance of the support which you have hitherto accorded to my country.

Taking my leave of you, dear comrades, I want to express the hope that the day will soon come when the U.S.S.R. will welcome a friend and ally in a mighty, free China, and that in the great struggle for the liberation of the oppressed peoples of the world both those allies will go forward to victory hand in hand.

With fraternal greetings,
Sun Yat-sen [54]

Sun's rejection of Communism

The foregoing discussion demonstrates beyond any doubt how great an influence the Canton-Moscow alliance exerted on Dr. Sun's revolutionary tactics and programs, but it should not be taken as a proof of his conversion to Communism. To the extent that Soviet models of Party discipline, military organization, mass movements, and anti-imperialist propaganda met his needs in the struggle for national unification, he was both sincere and eager to learn from Russia and to have her as an ally. However, insofar as the underlying political philosophy behind the revolution was concerned, Sun clung to his Three People's Principles and did not embrace Soviet ideology.[55]

Since a detailed comparison of Sun's ideas and Communism will be attempted in the latter part of this study, we shall mention here only his major criticisms of Marx in his lectures on the Principle of People's Livelihood in August 1924, more than a year after the conclusion of the Moscow-Canton entente. First, he rejected the materialist interpretation of history by Marx; instead, he believed that mankind's struggle for existence, rather than the change in the methods of production, was the central force of history.[56] Second, he had no love for Marx's theory of class struggle. "Class war," he argued, "is not the cause of social progress, it is a disease developed in the course of social progress. The cause of the disease is the inability to subsist, and the result of the disease is war. What Marx gained through his studies of social problems was a knowledge of diseases in the social progress. Therefore, Marx can only be called a social pathologist; we cannot say that he is a social physiologist." [57] In Sun's opinion, society progresses through the adjustment of major economic interests, rather than through the clash of interests. Third, he criticized the Marxian theory of surplus value for having given "all credit for production to the labor of the industrial worker and overlooked the labor of other useful social factors." [58] Surplus value, according to Sun, "is the fruit not only of labor within the factories but of many useful and powerful factors in society working directly or indirectly and making a large or a small contribution towards the production or consumption of the manufactured commodities." [59] Using Ford factories as evidence, he further contradicted Marx's three essential conditions for increasing surplus value:

> Marx said that the capitalist would have to lengthen the working day; the Ford factories have shortened the working day. Marx said that the capitalist would have to reduce wages; the Ford factories have raised wages. Marx said that capitalist would have to raise the price of the manufactured product; the Ford factories have reduced the price of their product. Marx did not foresee these contradictions, so his conclusion was seriously and peculiarly false. All that Marx knew from his long study of social problems were facts in past history; he did not at all anticipate what would happen in the future.[60]

Finally, as explicitly as in his joint statement with Joffe of January 1923, Dr. Sun maintained on several occasions after his Russian alliance that neither Marxism nor Sovietism was applicable to the present political, economic, and social conditions in China, and that the answer to Chinese problems lay in the application of his Three People's Principles. In an interview with a Japanese reporter while on his way to Peking in November 1924, Sun explained that China and Russia were cooperating because they shared the same revolutionary objectives and traveled the same road. However, due to the difference of their national conditions, he continued, they should have different political systems. The future system for China should be the system of the Three People's Principles and the Five-Power Constitution.[61] In his lecture on the Principle of the People's Livelihood in 1924, Sun described the basic facts in China as follows:

> All of us have a share in the distressing poverty of the Chinese people. There is no especially rich class, there is only a general poverty. The "inequalities between rich and poor" which the Chinese speak of are only differences within the poor class, differences in degree of poverty. . . . There are no great rich among us, only differences between the fairly poor and the extremely poor.[62]

With this, he went on to ridicule the idea of applying Marxism in China:

> The youthful scholars to-day who are pinning their faith on Marxism, and who, as soon as socialism is mentioned, advocate Marx's way for the solution of China's social and economic problems are no different from young Cantonese in furs who cried, "Unless the wind shifts to the north, the people's health will be impaired!" They do not take it in that China now is suffering from poverty, not from unequal distribution of wealth. Where there are inequalities of wealth, Marx's methods can of course be applied; as a class war can be started to destroy the inequalities. But in China, where industry is not yet developed, class war and the dictatorship of the proletariat are unnecessary. So to-day we can take Marx's ideas as a guide, but we cannot make use of his methods. In seeking a solution for our livelihood problem, we are not going to propose some impracticable and radical method and then wait until industry is developed. We want a plan which will anticipate dangers and forearm us against emergencies, which will check the growth of large private capital and prevent the social disease of extreme inequality between the rich and the poor. Such a plan will rightly solve our immediate social problems and will not be like first wearing furs and then hoping for the north winds.[63]

All these statements spoke in no uncertain terms of Dr. Sun's rejection of Communism as an ideology, despite the Canton-Moscow alliance. It is true that at times he identified his Principle of People's Livelihood with Communism. Nevertheless, this seeming contradiction can be explained partly as his attempt to reconcile the Kuomintang to the alliance with the Communists, on the theory that their ideologies were not incompatible and should not constitute an obstacle to their collaboration.[64] Another explanation is that most of Sun's lectures and writings were unsystematic and improvised propaganda pieces, and therefore could not avoid certain inconsistencies and contradictions. In the preface of *San Min Chu I*, Sun admitted:

> In these lectures I do not have the time necessary for careful preparation nor the books necessary for reference. I can only mount the platform and speak extemporaneously, and so am really leaving much that was in my former manuscripts. Although I am making additions and corrections before sending the book to the press, yet I realize that in clear presentation of the theme, in orderly arrangement of the discussion, and in the use of supporting facts, these lectures are not at all comparable to the material which I had formerly prepared. I hope that all our comrades will take the book as a basis or a stimulus, expand and correct it, supply omissions, improve the arrangement, and make it a perfect text for propaganda purposes.[65]

It should be noted that even in his occasional identification of the *Min-sheng* Principle with Communism he often drew a distinction. For instance, in his second lecture on the Third Principle, while calling the *Min-sheng* Principle, Communism, he nonetheless declared: "I can put my distinction today between communism and the *Min-sheng* Principle in this way: communism is an ideal of livelihood, while the *Min-sheng* Principle is practical communism. There is no real difference between the two principles—communism and *Min-sheng*—the difference lies in the methods by which they are applied." [66] In the same lecture, he also said: "The great aim of the Principle of Livelihood in our Three Principles is communism— a share in property by all. But the communism which we propose is a communism of the future, not of the present." [67] In fact, the word "communism" Sun used seems to be rather misleading and quite different from the one generally used by modern writers. What he had in mind was not Marxian Communism with its dogmas of dialectical materialism and class struggle, but some type of utopian communism as envisaged by ancient thinkers like Plato or Confucius. The ideal of the *Min-sheng* Principle, which Sun referred to as "communism," is actually the Great Commonwealth of Confucius. Sun made the following statement at the end of his second lecture on the Third Principle:

> We cannot say, then, that the theory of communism is different from our *Min-sheng* Principle. Our Three Principles of the People mean government "of the people, by the people, and for the people"—that is, a state belonging to all the people, a government controlled by all the people, and rights and benefits for the enjoyment of all the people. If this is true, the people will not only have a communistic share in state production, but they will have a share in everything. When the people share everything in the state, then will we truly reach the goal of the *Min-sheng* Principle, which is Confucius' hope of a "great commonwealth." [68]

Furthermore, a study of an unpublished manuscript of *San Min Chu I,* personally revised by Dr. Sun, throws new light on the relationship between the *Min-sheng* Principle and Communism.[69] In the published version of the Three People's Principles, there is a passage in Sun's introductory remarks on *Min-sheng:* "And now I shall use the phrase *Min-sheng* to describe one of the greatest problems that has emerged in the West during the past century or more—socialism. The Principle of Livelihood is socialism, it is communism, it is utopianism." [70] In the revised version, however, the same passage reads: "Nevertheless, the words *Min-sheng* as I now use them refer to a major problem which arose in foreign countries in past decades. What is this problem? It is socialism. So the principle of *Min-sheng* is used to take the place of socialism. Also, it is used to encompass all the problems of socialism." [71] This shows that Sun did not mean to equate his Third Principle with Communism. What he really had in mind was to conceive the *Min-sheng* Principle as a superior form of economic theory capable of embracing socialism and Communism.

Judging from the evidence available, there is no reason to

believe that, in his efforts to learn from Russia, Sun Yat-sen ever went so far as to make any drastic change of the basic principles he formulated over the years under the combined influences of Chinese and Western cultures. Even in reorganizing the Kuomintang on the Bolshevik model, he does not seem to have meant to transform the former into a Party characterized with the same degree of rigidity and sternness as the latter, for he was, after all, a man of warm personality and considerable Confucian background. In a conversation with Tsou Lu at the time of the reorganization, he credited affection—or rather, brotherly love for each other—with having held together the several hundred thousand Kuomintang members scattered over China and abroad. "Today in remolding the Party," he stressed, "we must keep our previous affection while adopting Soviet methods of organization. In this way we shall have the benefit of the Soviet system without its shortcomings and shall be better off than Russia is." [72]

Notwithstanding his new anti-imperialism campaign, Dr. Sun never followed the Leninist dogma of identifying imperialism with capitalism. Notwithstanding his enthusiasm for Russia, he never hesitated to welcome whatever assistance he could possibly get from other foreign sources. More than half a year after he concluded the agreement with Joffe, Sun was contemplating a possible collaboration with Germany. Writing a letter to Teng Chia-yen in Germany on August 18, 1923, Dr. Sun suggested a blueprint for China and Germany to cooperate: using Chinese raw material and manpower, together with Germany's machinery and science, to develop China's resources, to reform her administration, and to strengthen her defense. Should China become rich and strong as a result of German aid, Sun promised, she would use all her power to help free Germany from the bond of the Treaty of Versailles.[73] True, this letter was written before the arrival of Borodin; but even Borodin failed to persuade Sun to relinquish this type of thinking completely. In January 1924, when he was reorganizing the Kuomintang on the advice of Borodin, Sun sent a telegram of congratulations to the new labor government in England in which he urged the leaders of the British Labour

Party to adopt a new policy of stopping aid to Chinese militarists and reactionaries, and of providing the democratic and liberation movement in China with ample opportunities for free
development.[74] In one of his lectures on the Principle of
People's Livelihood, delivered almost one year after Borodin
came to Canton, Dr. Sun talked about the necessity to "borrow
foreign capital to develop our communication and transportation facilities, and foreign brains and experience to manage
them." [75] This sounded like his 1919 plan for the International
Development of China. Late in 1924, stopping off in Japan
on his way to Peking, Sun had interviews with reporters and
made several public lectures, including the famous Pan-Asiatic
speech on November 29. In all of them, he appealed to Japan
to help China and other Asian nations to free themselves from
foreign domination and oppression.[76] In his will, dated March
11, 1925, the Kuomintang leader instructed his followers to
"ally ourselves in a common struggle with those peoples of
the world who treat us on the basis of equality." [77] This naturally included Soviet Russia, but it also made equality a
condition for China's continued alliance with Moscow. Moreover, this kept open the door for cooperation with any Western
power that would approach China on the basis of equality.
Unfortunately, during his lifetime the West continued its
"gun boat" policy in China and failed to give Sun any friendly
response.[78]

Moreover, Dr. Sun certainly differed with the Russians in
his approach to the questions of Outer Mongolia and the
Chinese Communists—two issues which had all the potentialities of causing a rift between Moscow and Canton, but which
were submerged during his lifetime in the joint efforts of both
sides to keep the alliance. Sun had always considered the
Mongols as one of the five races constituting the Chinese
nation. Despite his endorsement of the principle of self-
determination,[79] he never approved Outer Mongolia's separation from China. Still less would he approve its becoming a part
of the U.S.S.R. It should be recalled that in their joint statement of January 1923, Sun had Joffe pledge that "it is not and
never has been the intention of the present Russian govern-

ment to pursue an imperialistic policy in Outer Mongolia or
to cause it to secede from China." He is also reported to have
rejected a request from Ch'en Tu-hsiu and other Communist
leaders, in 1923, that he recognize the independence of Outer
Mongolia in the name of the Kuomintang.[80] In a speech on
January 20, 1924, before the Party delegates to the First
National Congress, he welcomed what he called the intention
of Outer Mongolia to seek reunion with China, and stressed
that his policy toward Mongolia, different from that of the
Peking government, was based on peace and principles rather
than on force.[81]

Regarding the Chinese Communist Party, Sun's attitude
was a combination of expediency and distrust. As we have
seen, the admittance of individual Communists into the Kuomintang was prompted by Sun's desire to conclude a Soviet
alliance and to enlist every possible support for the Chinese
revolution. He made it no secret, however, that he intended
to keep the Chinese Communists subordinate to the policy
and discipline of his Party. He is reported to have told Maring
many times that the Chinese Communists, as members of the
Kuomintang, must obey its discipline or face expulsion. He
also warned that he would oppose Soviet Russia immediately,
if the latter should support the Chinese Communists.[82] In his
marginal comments on a letter addressed to him in December
1923 by some anti-Communist Kuomintang members, Sun
pictured the Chinese Communists as a group of young students
who wanted to monopolize Russian friendship and assistance
so as to compete with the Kuomintang. The experienced and
learned leaders of Russia, he observed, had not been fooled
by these youngsters and had ordered them to join the Kuomintang for the purpose of a united action. "If Russia wants to
cooperate with China," he said, "she will only cooperate with
our Party and not with Ch'en Tu-hsiu. If [Ch'en and his fol-
lowers] disobey our Party, we must expel them." [83]

Tensions and mutual suspicions between the Chinese Communist Party and the Kuomintang existed before Dr. Sun's
death, even though the Communists, after entering the Kuomintang, had professed to follow his leadership. The fact that

the Communists made every effort to keep their independence and to control the mass movement within the Kuomintang must have caused Sun's concern. Once he instructed the municipal Kuomintang organ at Canton to check their activities, and, as a result, the Communists bitterly attacked those responsible Kuomintang officials who carried out this order.[84] During the rebellion of the Merchant Corps in September 1924, a Communist leader took the occasion to criticize Sun's past mistakes and compromises, and urged him to declare war against British imperialism and to purge the Kuomintang of the "Right-Wing, counterrevolutionary Fascists." [85] In November 1924, when Dr. Sun went to the North to negotiate with the military leaders in Peking for the purpose of establishing a provisional government, the Chinese Communists viewed this move with disapproval and misgivings. Their official attitude was expressed in the Fourth Manifesto on the Current Situation in January 1925, which not only made sweeping demands of any proposed national assembly and provisional government, but also warned that the recent political changes in Peking "simply reflect, as in the past, conflicts between the Mukden and Chihli cliques and between Anglo-American and Japanese imperialism." [86] According to one report, Borodin on this occasion first made unsuccessful attempts to persuade Sun to go to Moscow and then instigated criticisms of Sun in the Chinese Communist organ *Hsiang-tao (The Guide Weekly)*.

Conclusion

Sun Yat-sen's alliance with Russia marked the entry of Soviet influence into China's politics and provided the Chinese Communists with an opportunity for development. In view of the circumstances under which the alliance was concluded, there is no reason to believe that Sun could have done otherwise. Frustrated in the Chinese revolution and ignored by the West, Sun was impressed not only by the Soviet regime's achievement, but also by its readiness to help China on the basis of full equality. The decision to ally himself with Russia was one of political necessity, a move to save his revolutionary work from bankruptcy.

The alliance was from the beginning a marriage of convenience from the standpoint of both Moscow and Canton. To the Russians, the Chinese revolution was a part of the world revolution, and cooperation with the Kuomintang could pave the way for eventual victory of Communism in China. As for Sun, he was prompted by the desire to use Moscow's aid to achieve the Chinese revolution according to his own programs. Not only did both sides differ in their ultimate objectives, their alliance was essentially a limited arrangement. There were a number of Kuomintang leaders who had serious misgivings about the sincerity of Russia. There also existed some issues like the Chinese Communist and Outer Mongolia, either of which had the potentialities of splitting the two allies.

Nevertheless, during Sun's lifetime the alliance remained on a firm ground. This was due partly to his personal influence and partly to Moscow's policies that won his confidence through assistance to Canton, a pledge not to impose Sovietism on China, and efforts to bring the Chinese Communists to accept the Kuomintang's leadership. In Sun's mind, Soviet Russia was China's trusted ally and a nation dedicated to "checking the strong and aiding the weak." It was his belief that Soviet leaders would sincerely cooperate with the Kuomintang rather than with the Chinese Communists. The unchanged policy of the West further served to convince him of the wisdom of the Soviet alliance.

In appraising the effects of the Moscow-Canton alliance, there is a general agreement that the alliance had a tremendous effect on Dr. Sun's revolutionary methods, organization, and tactics. The reorganization of the Kuomintang, the establishment of a new army, and the launching of the mass movement were among the obvious results. So far as Sun's revolutionary doctrine is concerned, we find that the impact of the Soviet alliance was also considerable. During the years between 1923 and 1925, Sun tried to give a more comprehensive explanation of his basic principles in a series of lectures and writings, among which were *"San Min Chu I"* (16 lectures), "The

Manifesto of the First National Congress of the Kuomintang," "Five-Power Constitution," and "The Outline of National Reconstruction." Some of his statements definitely showed evidence of the influence of the Bolsheviks. Most of the views, however, seemed to reflect ideas which he had expressed repeatedly in the past. In other words, Sun's Russian orientation brought some new additions and limited changes to his revolutionary theory but did not cause any basic ideological transformation. This can be seen from the following analysis of the Three People's Principles.

1. PRINCIPLE OF NATIONALISM

After Sun's alliance with Moscow he made anti-imperialism a very important part of Chinese nationalism. He spoke of the evils of foreign imperialism; he called for the abolition of unequal treaties; he talked about an international class war between the oppressing nations and the oppressed. Nevertheless, he never accepted the Communist theory of identifying imperialism with capitalism, and he was always willing to accept friendly assistance from the capitalist countries. The Manifesto of the First National Congress of the Kuomintang in 1924 formally incorporated the doctrine of self-determination by racial minorities into his Principle of Nationalism. But Sun never gave up his idea of uniting all the races in China to form a great Chung-hua nation on the basis of the ancient Chinese cultures.

2. PRINCIPLE OF DEMOCRACY

The successful experience of the Bolshevik dictatorship undoubtedly strengthened Sun's concept of the three-stage revolution and gave him a justification for the Kuomintang's tutelage. As a result of the Soviet alliance, the idea of one-party rule in a guided democracy took its final shape. Citing the Russian system as a model, Sun stated that the Kuomintang should place the Party above the state.[88] In the period of political tutelage, the Kuomintang would assume all the responsibilities for the state, unrestricted by any constitution.[89] It must be the center of all political power in order to crush both internal and external enemies and to overcome all the obstacles to the realization of its revolutionary program.[90] In spite of all this, however, there was no change in the ultimate objective of Sun's Principle of Democracy, namely, the formation of a constitutional government based on popular sovereignty. The ideal political system remained the five-power government advocated by Sun as early as 1906.

3. PRINCIPLE OF PEOPLE'S LIVELIHOOD

The *Min-sheng* Principle seemed to acquire a new importance following Sun's Soviet alliance. In the "Outline of National Reconstruction" this Principle was explicitly given priority over the others.[91] In several statements made in 1924, Dr. Sun appealed directly to the peasants and workers for their active support. On another occasion, he advocated a "land to the tiller" policy with Soviet Russia as the example. At other times, he spoke vaguely of the similarity between the Third Principle and "Communism." On the other hand, notwithstanding his Russian orientation Dr. Sun categorically rejected the dogmas of Marxism. The concrete proposals he offered, to bring economic justice to all classes in China, continued to be those of land reform and control of capital to be achieved through a peaceful and gradual process.

In the final analysis, the Moscow-Canton alliance represented a very important stage of the Chinese revolution. The influence of the Bolsheviks contributed much to vitalizing the Kuomintang and left its mark in varying degrees on Sun's revolutionary tactics and political doctrines. The premature death of Sun Yat-sen in March 1925 cut short the stage of his Russian orientation and prevented him from completing the ideological process of absorption and digestion. He left behind not only an incomplete revolution but also an ideology yet to be perfected. Between 1923 and 1925, Dr. Sun did not have time to develop a synthesis between the new Soviet influence and many other ingredients of his doctrine. Indeed, in his hasty attempts to reconcile what he learned from Russia with his basic beliefs, he introduced more contradictions into his not-too-coherent ideology and paved the way for the later contentions of his professed followers on doctrinal grounds.

Chapter 5

The Chinese Communists' Interpretations
of Sun Yat-sen's Doctrine

The untimely death of Sun Yat-sen in March 1925 was certainly both a personal tragedy and a tragedy for the Chinese revolution. It not only interrupted the career of this great revolutionary, who experienced more failures than successes in his lifetime and who died without seeing his work accomplished; it also deprived the unfinished Chinese revolution of a great leader and left the country in turmoil for many years to come.

Since Sun's death, there has been a great controversy over the interpretation of his doctrine, as each of the contending groups in China tried to make use of the name of the national hero to further its own cause. Most interesting of all was the attitude of the Chinese Communist Party. While always remaining faithful to Communism, the Chinese Communists often claimed that they, rather than the Kuomintang, were the inheritors of Sun's mantle, that they alone actually put Sun's ideas and policies into practice. This claim was supported by Madame Sun Yat-sen and was one of the Communists' most effective propaganda weapons in winning non-Communist support away from the Kuomintang during the period between 1937 and 1949. This, however, adds more confusion to the nature of Sun's principles as well as to the nature of Chinese Communism.

In order to clarify the confusion, we propose to examine the Chinese Communists' interpretations of Sun's doctrine along the following lines: How have they reconciled the Three People's Principles with Chinese Communism? What elements of Sun's program have received their special attention? What kind of criticism have they made of Sun? How is Sun regarded in the new People's Republic of China?

The Kuomintang-Communist split after Sun's death

The Kuomintang-Communist alliance concluded in 1923 was a marriage of convenience. The Kuomintang needed the Communists' assistance to achieve its revolutionary task in China, while the Communists wanted to develop their strength within the framework of the Kuomintang. Although from the beginning an eventual struggle for domination was anticipated, the alliance was held together by the personal influence of Sun Yat-sen and by the presence of common enemies—imperialism and warlords. The death of Sun in 1925 removed the very important cementing factor, and the alliance immediately showed signs of cracking. Some Right Wing leaders of the Kuomintang began to take open actions against the policy of collaboration with Communists.[1] Nevertheless, the Kuomintang-Communist united front was temporarily preserved in the face of an impending expedition against the Northern militarists.[2] It finally came to an end in the spring of 1927, when the Kuomintang armies under Chiang Kai-shek completed the first phase of the Northern Expedition by capturing Nanking. Suspicious of Communist treachery, Chiang struck first. With the support of the conservative elements of the Kuomintang, he instigated, in April, a bloody *coup d'état*, suppressing the Communists in Shanghai and in all other areas under his control.

When Wang Ching-wei's Left Wing group at Wuhan joined forces with Nanking in July, the breakdown of the Kuomintang-Communist alliance became complete. By the end of 1927, Russian advisers had left China, and the Chinese Communists had been driven to the countryside.

The split between the Kuomintang and the Communists was a great defeat for the Comintern's China policy, and it intensified Trotsky's feud with Stalin. In the end, Ch'en Tu-hsiu was made the scapegoat in China, and Trotsky was exiled from Russia. It is not our purpose here to be concerned with the details of events during these fateful years from 1925 to 1927.[3] Rather we are interested in the official explanations given for the split, by the Kuomintang and the Communists, particularly in their references to Sun Yat-sen.

According to the Kuomintang, the split was necessitated by the fact that the Communists violated their pledges and employed every "treacherous" act in the attempt to achieve their domination of China and to destroy the Kuomintang and its revolutionary work.[4] Chiang Kai-shek, in a manifesto to the people in 1927, justified the Party purge with an explanation of Sun Yat-sen's policy:

> It is true that Dr. Sun consented to admit the Communists into the Kuomintang as individuals, but not as a unit. So, speaking of it as the "alliance of the two parties" is a misinterpretation of the facts by the Communists. In his consent, Dr. Sun had two intentions: first, to prevent them from practicing the Communist ideals in China and to convert them intellectually to a belief in the *San-min* principles, and second, to afford them an opportunity to participate in the Nationalist revolution. But this was not done so that they might usurp the Party power and dictate the Party policy, disregarding the *San-min* principles.
>
> Dr. Sun's policy of cooperation with Russia was made possible only by the Soviet's "equal treatment of our people." It was not to invite Comrade Borodin purposely to hinder our revolutionary progress. The determining factor of whether or not the policy of cooperation with Soviet Russia is to be maintained does not lie with China, but the test is whether or not Soviet Russia can treat us as equals.

If Soviet Russia had not changed her policy, we could still have cooperated with her. In the world only principles dictate policies, policies never dictate principles.[5]

On the other hand, Madame Sun Yat-sen, along with a small number of the Left-Wing leaders of the Kuomintang, sided with the Communists in denouncing Chiang's "betrayal" of Dr. Sun's three policies of "Alliance with Soviet Russia," "Alliance with the Communists," and "Alliance with the Workers and Peasants." [6] In a public statement issued in July 1927, she had this to say:

> To guide us in the Chinese revolution, Sun Yat-sen has given us his Three Principles and his Three Policies. . . .
> Today there is much talk of policy. Sun defined Three Policies, which he decided were the only means by which his Three Principles could be carried out. But today it is being said that policies must be changed to fit the needs of the time. There is some truth in this statement, but change of policy should never be carried to the point where it becomes a reversal, so that a revolutionary party ceases to be revolutionary and becomes merely an organ, operating under the banner of revolution, but actually working in support of the very social structure which the party was founded to alter. . . .
> Sun Yat-sen's policies are clear. If leaders of the Party do not carry them out consistently, then they are no longer Sun's true followers, and the Party is no longer a revolutionary party, but merely a tool in the hands of this or that militarist. It will have ceased to be a living force working for the future welfare of the Chinese people, but will have become a machine, the agent of oppression, a parasite fattening on the present enslaving system.[7]

Before leaving for Moscow, Madame Sun made another statement on August 22 to urge the true followers of Dr. Sun to "rescue the real Kuomintang from the degradation of becoming a mere secretariat of the new militarist clique emerging out of the intrigues and disloyalties now afoot." According to her, real Nationalist success in the struggle with Chinese militarism and foreign imperialism depended upon the carrying out of

Sun's three policies. She was going to Moscow to explain to Soviet leaders that "though some have crossed over to reaction and counterrevolution, there are others who will continue true and steadfast to the Three Policies enunciated by him [Dr. Sun] for the guidance and advancement of the work of the revolution." [8]

The denunciation of Chiang Kai-shek by the Communists was, of course, even more vehement. In a resolution adopted on April 14, 1927, the Executive Committee of the Communist International stated: "With the greatest indignation and with utter hatred for the hangman, we declare Chiang Kai-shek a traitor, and an ally of the imperialist bandits, an enemy of the revolutionary Kuomintang, and enemy of the working class, and of the Communist International." [9] Stalin, in "Questions of the Chinese Revolution," published on April 21, 1927, pictured Chiang's *coup* as marking "the desertion of the national bourgeoisie from the revolution, the emergence of a center of national counterrevolution, and the conclusion of a deal between the Kuomintang Rights and the imperialists against the Chinese revolution." [10] The resolution of the Fifth National Congress of the Chinese Communist Party in May 1927 declared that Chiang Kai-shek, as the leader of the bourgeoisie, had led his class into an alliance with feudalism and imperialism in order to suppress the national revolution. [11] In a circular letter to all Party members on August 7, 1927, the Chinese Communists pointed out that the counterrevolutionary forces of the Kuomintang had betrayed the true, revolutionary principles of Dr. Sun Yat-sen. [12] In recollection, Mao Tse-tung later claimed that, after the 1927 purge, it was the Chinese Communist Party and the Chinese people who inherited Sun's revolutionary ideas and carried on the national revolution. [13] It should be noted, however, that between 1927 and 1936, while continuing to use some of Sun's slogans like "equalization of landownership," "land to the tiller," and "down with imperialism," [14] the Chinese Communists made no special efforts to reconcile their doctrine with the Three People's Principles. They were too busily engaged in various experiments in the

Chinese Soviets and in a life and death struggle against the Kuomintang.

The "New Democracy" and the "New Three People's Principles"

By the time the Chinese Communists established themselves in Northwest China in 1936, they had become, politically speaking, a mature and experienced group under the undisputed leadership of Mao Tse-tung. Judging correctly the national sentiment, and in conformity with the Comintern's line, they began to seek a *rapprochement* with the Kuomintang in the formation of a united front against Japan.[15] It was at this point that they once again emphasized the compatibility of Chinese Communism with the Three People's Principles. For instance, Mao Tse-tung, in an interview in 1936, stated that in the proposed anti-Japanese united front the Communists would support a parliamentary form of representative government, which should restore and once more realize Sun Yat-sen's final will and his three "basic principles." [16] The united front finally came into being after the Sian incident of December 1936, when the Chinese Communist leaders, apparently in accord with the advice of Moscow, played an important part in saving Chiang Kai-shek's life and securing his release from his two captors, Generals Chang Hsueh-liang and Yang Hu-ch'eng. While the details of the Sian incident are still obscured by the conflicting accounts, and while it is extremely doubtful that Chiang signed any agreement with the Chinese Communists, it seems quite certain that an informal understanding of some kind was reached between them. At any rate, beginning in 1937 the establishment of a *rapprochement* between the Kuomintang and the Chinese Commuists moved rapidly ahead.[17]

To reorient the rank and file of the Chinese Communist Party toward cooperating with the Kuomintang once again, Mao Tse-tung, in May 1937, explained to his followers the necessity of two-party collaboration and of joint striving for the realization of Dr. Sun's revolutionary Three People's Principles: ". . . what perfectly meets the historical need of the Chinese revolution and ought to be clearly grasped by every member of the Communist Party is that, reviving the spirit of

the Three People's Principles, the two parties resume their cooperation in foreign policy under the Principle of Nationalism
which aims at winning China's independence and liberation,
and in domestic policy under the Principle of Democracy
which aims at realizing democracy and freedom, and the
Principle of People's Welfare which aims at promoting the
people's welfare, and furthermore, jointly lead the people to
put these resolutely into practice." [18] While leaving no doubt
that the Communists would never abandon their ideal of socialism and Communism, Mao nevertheless emphasized that
they must accept, at the present stage, the Three People's Principles as the basis for the Kuomintang-Communist united
front.[19] This kind of reasoning was completely in line with the
theory advanced by Stalin in 1927 as stated in his letter to
Chugunov:

> The criticism of Sun Yat-sen that Lenin gave in 1912 is, of
> course, not out-of-date and retains its validity. But it was
> a criticism of the old Sun Yat-sen. Sun Yat-sen, after all,
> did not remain at a standstill. He went on developing, just
> as everything in the world develops. After October, and
> especially in 1920-1921, Lenin had a great respect for Sun
> Yat-sen, chiefly because Sun Yat-sen began to draw closer
> to the Chinese Communists and to cooperate with them.
> This circumstance must be borne in mind when speaking of
> Lenin and Sun Yat-senism. Does this mean that Sun Yat-sen
> was a Communist? No, it does not. The difference between
> Sun Yat-senism and Communism (Marxism) remains. If,
> nevertheless, the Chinese Communists cooperate with the
> Kuomintang party, the reason is that Sun Yat-sen's three
> principles—Democracy, Nationality, and Socialism—con-
> stitute a fully acceptable basis for joint work of Communists
> and Sun-Yat-senists within the Kuomintang party at the
> present stage of development of the Chinese revolution.[20]

In entering into the second entente with the Kuomintang,
the Central Committee of the Chinese Communist Party
pledged itself to the following four points in a manifesto issued
on July 15, 1937:

1. The *San Min Chu I* (Three People's Principles) enunciated by Dr. Sun Yat-sen is the paramount need of China today. This Party is ready to strive for its enforcement.
2. This Party abandons its policy of overthrowing the Kuomintang of China by force and the movement of sovietization and discontinues its policy of forcible confiscation of land from landowners.
3. This Party abolishes the present Soviet Government and will enforce democracy based on the people's rights in order to unify the national political machinery.
4. This Party abolishes the Red Army, reorganizes it into the National Revolutionary Army, places it under the direct control of the Military Affairs Commission of the National government, and awaits orders for mobilization to share the responsibility of resisting foreign invasion at the front.[21]

By way of explanation, Mao Tse-tung issued, on September 29, a statement entitled "The Urgent Tasks After the Announcement of Kuomintang-Communist Cooperation." [22] To show his Party's sincerity to fight for the realization of the Three People's Principles, he made it clear that, as Communism was to be implemented in a future stage of the revolution, the Chinese Communists did not dream of realizing Communism at present, but considered it necessary "to carry out the national revolution and democratic revolution as required by history." Then he went on to prove that all the past policies of his Party were in harmony with Sun Yat-sen's principles: "Never does a day pass but the Communist Party opposes imperialism—this means the thoroughgoing implementation of the Principle of Nationalism; the system of worker-peasant democratic dictatorship means nothing but the thoroughgoing implementation of the Principle of Democracy; the agrarian revolution means the thoroughgoing implementation of the Principle of the People's Welfare." Consequently, the question to him was not "whether the Communist Party believes in or is carrying out the revolutionary Three People's Principles, but whether the Kuomintang believes in them or is carrying them out." To amplify this argument, when interviewed by the British correspondent James Bertram on October 25, Mao pointed out that the Kuomintang had now carried out in part Dr. Sun Yat-sen's Principle of Nationalism, as shown in its resistance to Japan, but had carried out neither Sun's Principle of Democracy nor his Principle of People's Welfare (Livelihood). The war situation was so tense, declared the Communist leader, that it was high time for the Kuomintang to carry out fully the Three People's Principles before it was too late. "The duty of the Communist Party," according to him, "is to explain this tirelessly and in loud and urgent tones to the Kuomintang and the whole nation, and to persuade them to carry out fully and thoroughly and on a nation-wide scale the revolutionary Three People's Principles, the Three Cardinal Policies and Dr. Sun's Testament, so that the Anti-Japanese National United Front may be expanded and consolidated." [23]

Mao's statements launched a series of official expositions of Sun's doctrine by the Communists, who made the identification of their program with the Three People's Principles part of the united front strategy. Although the formation of the united front did not actually change the fundamental conflict between the Communists and the Kuomintang,[24] it did mark a shift to a moderate and less revolutionary line on the part of the Communists. It was during the resistance war against Japan that Mao Tse-tung's "New Democracy" emerged as the Party's most effective program to enlist non-Communist support and to pave the way for its victory in 1949—a program which included identification with Chinese nationalism, adoption of a moderate land reform, and cooperation with all revolutionary classes.[25] As a propaganda measure, the name of Sun Yat-sen was frequently referred to by the Communists in justifying their policies and in allaying people's fear. The general theme was that Sun's "new Three People's Principles," including his three policies of alliance with Soviet Russia, cooperation with the Chinese Communists, and support of workers and peasants, were the minimum program of the Communists for the "New Democratic" revolution, although, at the same time, it was stressed that the Chinese Communist Party continued to have Communism as the ultimate goal.

In a book entitled *Survey of the Three People's Principles,* written in 1939, Ch'en Po-ta, one of the leading Chinese Communist theoreticians, called Sun's principles "the continuation of the best traditional thought of our nation." [26] According to him, during the period between 1919, when Sun's Party adopted the name of the Chung Kuo Kuomintang, and 1924, when the Declaration of the First National Kuomintang Congress was issued, the Three People's Principles underwent a great change and acquired a new life. He pointed out two outstanding characteristics. First, the revolutionary Three People's Principles became united with the revolutionary three major policies, i.e., alliance with Russia, with the Communists, and with the workers and peasants. The latter became the former's soul as well as its revolutionary method. Second, new contents were added to the Three People's Principles. The Principle of Nationalism developed from the anti-Manchu movement before 1911 to anti-imperialism; from "Great Han-Chauvinism" to "freedom, equality, and free union for all peoples within China." The Principle of Democracy developed from restricted suffrage and indirect democracy to universal suffrage and direct democracy. The Principle of Livelihood developed from "equalization of landownership" to "land to tillers" and "labor legislation to improve the conditions of the workers." All these, in Ch'en's opinion, were the great developments of the Three People's Principles in the period between 1919 and 1924, and the Chinese Communists had contributed much to these developments in helping Dr. Sun.[27] He further maintained that the Chinese Communists had not only continued the great work of Sun's revolutionary principles, the first step of the Chinese revolution, but would eventually lead China to the second step of the revolution and the greatest undertaking of all—Communism.[28]

When Mao Tse-tung wrote *The Chinese Revolution and the Communist Party of China* in 1939, he again explained that what his Party pledged to strive for in 1937 were the new Three People's Principles of Dr. Sun, namely, the three major policies. "Under the new domestic and international conditions," he said, "they would not be revolutionary Three People's Principles if they exclude these three major policies." [29] It was, however, in his famous "On New Democracy" that Mao gave a more detailed treatment to Sun's doctrines.[30] Using the Manifesto of the First National Kuomintang Congress in 1924 as the dividing point, he divided the Three People's Principles into two categories, corresponding to two historical phases: before that Manifesto the Three Principles were the Three People's Principles of the old category—of the phase of the old colonial, semicolonial, bourgeois-democratic revolution, and of the old democracy; after that Manifesto they were transformed into the Three People's Principles of the new category—of the phase of the new colonial, semicolonial bourgeois-democratic revolution, and of the New Democracy. He considered the old Three People's Principles as being revolutionary only during the old period, as they reflected the historical peculiarity of that time.

> Russia was then an imperialist power, and, of course, there could be no policy of alliance with her; there was then no Communist Party in our country, and, of course, there could be no policy of cooperation with the Communists; the workers' and peasants' movement at that time, with its political significance not yet fully manifest, did not attract the people's attention, and, of course, there could be no policy of alliance with the workers and peasants.[31]

But with the advent of the new period, Mao stated, the old Three People's Principles became out-of-date and reactionary. Therefore, Dr. Sun, with the help of the Soviet Union and the Chinese Communist Party, "reinterpreted the Three People's Principles, thus endowing them with new historical features." These new Three People's Principles were based on Sun's three major policies of "Alliance with Soviet Russia," "Alliance with the Communists," and "Alliance with the Workers and Peasants," and were "the product of the era when the Chinese revolution has become part of the world socialist revolution." "It is only such Three People's Principles," Mao stressed, "that basically agree with the Communist Party's political program for the stage of democratic revolution or its minimum program." [32]

Accompanying this new interpretation of the Three People's Principles were the Chinese Communists' conspicuous efforts to identify their programs with Sun's during the Sino-Japanese war. For instance, in a propaganda outline issued in 1938, it was declared that one of the primary tasks of the Chinese Communist Party was "to establish a democratic republic based on national independence, democratic liberty, and the people's welfare," [33] a statement bearing a striking resemblance to the Principles of Nationalism, Democracy, and People's Livelihood, which Sun had advocated. In a speech on the youth movement delivered on May 4, 1939, Mao Tse-tung cited Dr. Sun's will to drive home the idea of "arousing the masses of the people." [34] On another occasion when he explained the "new democratic constitutionalism," Mao defined it, again citing Sun's words, as "something to be shared by all the common people and not to be monopolized by a few." [35] The fact that the Chinese Communists appreciated the tremendous propaganda value of Sun's name and wanted to utilize it to woo non-Communist elements in China can be best illustrated by the following passages from "Questions of Tactics in the Present Anti-Japanese United Front," a report Mao made at a Party meeting on March 11, 1940:

> In the struggle to develop the progressive forces, to win over the middle-of-the-road forces and to isolate the die-hard forces, the role of the intellectuals must not be overlooked and, as the die-hards are doing their utmost to win them over, it is a necessary and important policy for us to win over all progressive intellectuals and bring them under the influence of our Party.
>
> *In the matter of propaganda we should adhere firmly to the following program:* (1) *Carry out the Testament of Dr. Sun Yat-sen* by arousing the people to resist Japan to a man. (2) *Carry out the Principle of Nationalism* by resolutely resisting imperialism and securing the thorough liberation of the Chinese nation externally and the equality

of the nationalities internally. (3) *Carry out the Principle of Democracy* by granting the people absolute freedom to resist Japan and to save their nation, letting them elect their governments at all levels and setting up the revolutionary democratic political power of the Anti-Japanese National United Front. (4) *Carry out the Principle of the People's Welfare* by abolishing exorbitant taxes and miscellaneous assessments, reducing rents and interest, enforcing the eight-hour working day, developing agriculture, industry and commerce and improving the living conditions of the people. . . . *This is a program of the utmost simplicity and has become generally known among the people, but many Communists still do not know how to use it as a weapon to mobilize the masses of the people and isolate the die-hards.*[36]

Indeed, throughout the war the Chinese Communists' policies of resisting Japanese aggression, encouraging "self-government," and reducing land rents gave the impression that they were actually carrying out the program of the late founder of the Kuomintang.[37] This was exactly what Mao Tse-tung was trying to show Gunther Stein, when the latter interviewed him in 1944.[38] Numerous statements to the same effect were also made by other Communist leaders from time to time. In commemoration of the sixth anniversary of the resistance war, Kao Kang, a Central Committee member, stated on July 7, 1943, that Dr. Sun's Three People's Principles were truly realized in the border region and that "the record of construction in the border region points to the bright prospect for the establishment of a republic of the Three People's Principles in which all the people can enjoy freedom and welfare." [39] The editorials of the *Liberation Daily* also took special occasions to advance the theory that only the New Democracy, which was actually the Three People's Principles, could save China and that Chiang Kai-shek had betrayed everything Sun stood for.[40] Chou En-lai, in an interview with an American reporter in 1944, explained his Party's policy with the following words:

Our ultimate ideal is the socialist collectivism of Communism—which, however, I don't believe can be achieved in China for a long, long time to come. China's development

*will not proceed along the same lines as Soviet Ruissia's.
There will be stages.* For example, on the basis of individual
production we have adopted the mutual help or labor-ex-
change method, rather than an immediate and drastic establishing of collectivism. Second, from the principle of private
ownership we hope to move to the nationalization of big
enterprises—communication systems, banks, war industries.
Third, we shall progress from the reduction of rents and
interest to the stage of land owned by the tillers, and eventually to state ownership or nationalization of the land.
Fourth, on the basis of equal suffrage for all social classes,
we shall enable the majority—the laboring classes—to obtain the privilege of suffrage. The intention is to make rule
by a minority less likely. This is the spirit incorporated in
the one-to-three ratio system. Fifth, under conditions of
equality we shall strive for international peace and cooperation. *These five points summarize what we call our Democracy. They are also incorporated in the program of the
revolutionary* San Min Chu I *as interpreted by Dr. Sun Yat-
sen in the Manifesto of the First Congress of the Kuomintang in 1924.* [41]

Just before the end of the war Mao Tse-tung, in "On Coalition Government," again made a deliberate attempt to link his
program to Sun's. According to him, the New Democracy (the
minimum program of the Chinese Communist Party) and the
new Three People's Principles, although not completely identical, were consistent with each other in certain basic principles.[42] For one thing, he cited the similarity of their
approaches to the political system:

The New Democracy we uphold demands the expulsion of
imperialistic oppression and the overthrow of the feudalistic,
Fascist oppression. But after removing this oppression, we
do not propose to set up an old democratic political system.
Instead, we want to set up a political system based on the
United Front in which all democratic classes collaborate.
These views of ours are identical with those of Dr. Sun
Yat-sen. In the Manifesto of the First National Congress of
the Kuomintang, Dr. Sun Yat-sen said: "The so-called
democratic system in modern nations is often exclusively

controlled by the moneyed classes, and is therefore a tool
with which to oppress the common people. But the Kuomintang's democracy is meant for the general mass, and not for
a few." [43]

Then he pointed out that the Communists' views on the New
Democratic economy also conformed to the principles laid
down by Dr. Sun Yat-sen:

> On the question of land, Dr. Sun maintained that "every
> tiller should have his own land." On the question of industry
> and commerce, Dr. Sun said in the Manifesto mentioned
> above: "All native or foreign enterprises that are either of
> the nature of monopolies or on a scale beyond the means
> of private interests—for instance, banking, railways, ship-
> ping, etc.—should be managed and controlled by the state,
> so that private capital may not control the livelihood of the
> people. This is the essence of the restriction of capital."
> Our views on the present stage economy are in complete
> accord with those of Dr. Sun Yat-sen. . . .
>   Dr. Sun's principles and the experience gained in the
> Chinese revolution show that China's present economy
> should be managed partly by the State, partly by private
> concerns, and partly by cooperatives. Here "State" is not
> one "monopolized by a few" but a New Democratic State
> "of the common people." [44]

Moreover, with respect to such issues as the freedom of the
people, the people's army, and racial minorities, Mao likewise
quoted Dr. Sun's words in support of the New Democratic program.[45]

In short, Mao Tse-tung and the other Chinese Communist
leaders all interpreted Sun's doctrines in such a way as to make
them appear to be more truly Sun's followers than the Nationalists were. They claimed that they had contributed to the
development of the new, revolutionary Three People's Principles as represented in the Manifesto of the First National Kuomintang Congress of 1924, which included the three major
policies of alliance with Soviet Russia, cooperation with the
Chinese Communists, and support of workers and peasants.
They identified these new Three Principles with the New

Democracy, their minimum program in the stage of bourgeois-democratic revolution. Aside from stressing the importance of Sun's three major policies, they also made best use of some other elements of his program. Thus, anti-imperialism was used effectively by them to organize the people to fight the Japanese; the Principle of Democracy became the basis for their demand of a coalition government of all democratic classes; land reform became their key to popular support. All in all, it can be said that the Chinese Communists' manipulation of Sun's doctrine was one of the most subtle and successful propaganda lines in their competition for power with the Kuomintang during and after the war. The name of Sun Yat-sen undoubtedly added much to the attraction the New Democracy had to the various segments of the Chinese population.

The Communists' criticisms of Sun Yat-sen

In spite of their special tributes to Sun Yat-sen between 1937 and 1949, at no time had the Chinese Communist leaders indicated that they would substitute his doctrine for Communism. They merely stated that the Three People's Principles were consistent with their *minimum program* in the present stage of the Chinese revolution and repeatedly declared Communism to be the ultimate goal of the Chinese Communist Party.[46] As a matter of fact, their attitude toward Sun's doctrine was purely opportunistic and selective—taking whatever elements of it they considered revolutionary, to fit into their own strategy. In the meantime, they wanted to convey the idea, particularly to their Party members, that Sun's principles were inferior to Communism. This was, of course, fundamentally in agreement with the concept of Lenin, who in 1912 praised the genuine democratic spirit of Sun's program and yet was quick to criticize its "petty-bourgeois" errors.[47]

An interesting analysis of the relationship between the Three People's Principles and Communism was presented in 1937 in an article by Wang Chia-hsiang, head of the Political Department of the Eighth Route Army. Calling the Three People's Principles the program of the radical bourgeoisie, Wang explained that the acceptance of these principles as the com-

mon program of the united front by the proletariat did not
mean that the latter had no program of their own. On the contrary, he said, because of their special class and historical position, the proletariat offered a more thorough and resolute
program than that of the radical bourgeoisie.[48] To demonstrate
his point, he proceeded to compare the programs of the two
classes along the lines of nationalism, democracy, and economic policy.[49] First, on the national problem both the radical
bourgeoisie and the proletariat advocated "the overthrow of
imperialism and the striving for national independence." But
the proletariat of colonies and semicolonies followed "the theory of Marxism-Leninism to combine patriotism with internationalism"; their program of national liberation was not only
"resolute and thorough without any element of national doctrines of compromise and aggression," but also had "a thorough
idea and practice for solving the racial problems in the country." Second, on the problem of democracy both classes were
"in accord with each other in advocating the overthrow of
absolutism and the feudal and semifeudal rule so as to establish
a modern democracy." But there were differences. Regarding
the masses as Ah Tou,[50] the radical bourgeoisie did not emphasize the "popular type" revolution to establish democracy and
instead insisted on "a period of tutelage before the realization
of democracy." On top of that, due to the lack of an economic
and practical program as its basis, their political democratic
program was therefore considered to be very difficult to put
into effect. Quite differently, the political program of the proletariat in the national democratic revolution was characterized
by thoroughness and by an emphasis on the "popular-type"
revolution to realize democracy. Furthermore, it had "as its
economic basis for realizing democracy a thorough economic
program to wipe out all the feudalistic relationships." Third,
speaking of economic programs, the two classes were compared as follows. The Marxist-Leninists—the proletariat's representatives—realized that colonial and semicolonial countries
must go through the transitional stage of the bourgeois national
democratic revolution before arriving at the proletarian socialist revolution; therefore, they did not "attempt to practice any

socialist economic program in the national democratic revolution." But they firmly advocated "the complete expulsion of the economic influence of imperialism and the adoption of a thorough land program to eliminate the feudal land system." On the other hand, the radical bourgeoisie had the illusion that "China can avoid capitalism." They considered the Principle of People's Livelihood as socialism. In fact, it was merely "subjective socialism" and would "actually contribute to the development of capitalism." Moreover, although the radical bourgeoisie had a revolutionary land program, their methods of implementation were "those of reformists" and, hence, made "the realization of their land program extremely difficult."

In his essay "On New Democracy," written in 1940, Mao Tse-tung dealt directly with the prevailing question of the time: "Since you Communists have pledged to fight for the Three People's Principles, why don't you tuck away Communism for the time being?" His answer was a clear-cut statement of the superiority of Communism:

> Communism is at once the entire ideological system of the proletariat and a new social system. Different from any other ideological system or social system, it is the most perfect, the most progressive the most revolutionary and the most rational system since human history began. . . . Since the introduction of scientific Communism into China, people's vistas have been opened up, and the Chinese revolution has changed its physiognomy. Without the guidance of Communism, the democratic revolution in China cannot succeed, let alone the later stage of the revolution. This is the reason why the die-hards of the bourgeoisie are so noisily demanding that Communism be "tucked away." But in reality it should not be "tucked away": once Communism is "tucked away," China will perish. The whole world today depends on Communism for its salvation, and China is no exception.[51]

While insisting that the Three People's Principles and Communism were fundamentally consistent, Mao at the same time listed their differences:

(1) The difference in a part of the program for the stage of democratic revolution. The Communists' program for the whole course of the democratic revolution contains the planks of full realization of the people's power, the eight-hour working day and a thoroughgoing agrarian revolution, whereas the Three People's Principles do not. . . . (2) The difference between having and not having a stage of socialist revolution. Besides the stage of democratic revolution, Communism envisages a stage of socialist revolution; hence besides the minimum program it has its maximum program, i.e., the program for the realization of the social system of socialism and Communism. The Three People's Principles include only the stage of democratic revolution, but not the state of socialist revolution; therefore they contain only a minimum program and no maximum program; i.e., no program for building up a social system of socialism and Communism. (3) The difference in world outlook. The world outlook of Communism is dialectical materialism and historical materialism, and that of the Three People's Principles is the interpretation of history in terms of the people's livelihood, which in essence is dualism or idealism; these two are opposed to each other. (4) The difference in revolutionary thoroughness. The Communists' theory is consistent with their practice, i.e., Communists have revolutionary thoroughness. Followers of the Three People's Principles, with the exception of those who are completely loyal to the revolution and to truth, are not consistent in their theory and practice and their words contradict their deeds; that is to say, they lack revolutionary thoroughness.[52]

Perhaps the most elaborate commentary on the Three People's Principles ever to come from a Chinese Communist theoretician is Ch'en Po-ta's *On Sun Yat-senism*. Ch'en's book was published in 1946, at a time when the civil strife between the Kuomintang and the Chinese Communists had again broken out and a war of ideas was being waged by both sides.[53] Under the circumstances, Ch'en's criticisms of the doctrine of Sun Yat-sen were understandably more outspoken and detailed than any previous comments made by the Party leaders, including his own *Survey of the Three People's Principles* in 1939. Nevertheless, Ch'en still continued the thesis that Sun's new Three Principles were revolutionary and that their realization had to depend upon the Chinese Communist Party. Ch'en's comments on Sun Yat-senism can be divided into two major parts: those on the Three People's Principles themselves and those on Sun's criticisms of Marx. Since the latter part amounts to no more than a repetition of the familiar dogmas of Marx,[54] we shall deal with the former only.

In Sun's Principle of Nationalism, Ch'en pointed out several theoretical shortcomings.[55] First, Sun attributed the formation of a nation to five natural forces: blood kinship, common livelihood, common language, common religion, and common customs. Judging by Marx's teaching, Ch'en asserted, Sun was wrong in "confusing race with nation" and in "neglecting 'common territory,' one of the most important characteristics of a nation." Second, Sun talked about the "pressure of the population problem." According to Ch'en, "it is not the 'pressure of the population problem' that weakens a society or a nation; rather it is a certain social system or national pressure that creates the problem of 'underpopulation' or 'overpopulation.' " Third, Dr. Sun considered the loss of the national spirit as the chief cause for China's decline and consequently emphasized the importance of the ancient Chinese morality. But Ch'en would blame the "dark, decadent, and corrupt feudal system" for causing China's decline, inviting foreign invasion, and hindering the growth of the people's strength. "The problem of the national spirit," he said, "naturally can never be concretely understood if it is not viewed in connection with the social, economic, and political systems."

These theoretical weaknesses, asserted Ch'en, resulted in a number of errors when applied to practical policies. First, Sun's letter to the Governor of Hong Kong in 1900 [56] and his "Pan-Asiatic" speech in Japan [57] were cited as erroneous. Second, his attitude before 1924, regarding the relations between the Chinese and other racial groups in China, was one of "Han superiority" [58] and therefore a mistake. Third, his idea of using clan as a basis to build a great nation was passive and impractical, as the clan itself "is a conservative, backward, and feudalistic group." All in all, Ch'en found "the contradiction between

revolutionary nationalism and nationalism of compromise tendency" as "the characteristic of Sun Yat-sen's Principle of Nationalism."

As to Sun's Principle of Democracy, Ch'en listed its theoretical shortcomings as follows: [59] First, Sun divided men into
three classes according to their intelligence—the discoverers,
the promoters, and the operators.[60] But Ch'en maintained that
"the 'discoverers' are actually a product of the historical development of a certain society," and that "to regard the people,
the 'operators,' as those who do not see or perceive is contrary
to historical facts." The revolutionary vanguard, he continued,
"should first of all learn from the people and try as their duty
to awaken those who are backward." Sun's mistake here "lies
in drawing a rigid division between the discoverers and the
operators." Second, Sun advocated a separation of "political
power" and "governing power," i.e., a separation of the political sovereignty of the people and the administrative power of
the government.[61] This was called fallacious by Ch'en, who
claimed that in the light of history "the realization of democracy requires the unity of the People's power and the government's power," and that "the best government for the people
is the one directly managed by themselves." Third, Sun's attitude toward the people's fight for liberty was criticized for
being passive and mistaken. Sun thought that the Chinese people had too much individual freedom and had no need to fight
for it.[62] "The fact is," Ch'en stated, "that for several thousand
years the Chinese people under feudal and despotic control
have been deprived of not only the freedom of assembly and of
association, but also the freedom of thought." Sun compared
the Chinese people to "a rope of sand" to show that they had
too much freedom. But according to history, Ch'en pointed
out, the Chinese people became a rope of sand because they
formerly had neither the freedom of assembly and of association to unify their strength, nor the freedom of speech to communicate their opinions.

These theoretical shortcomings and mistakes of Sun Yat-
sen, said Ch'en, demonstrated one thing: on the one hand, Sun
believed in the strength of the people, and on the other, he had

no complete confidence in it. This lack of complete confidence in the people was particularly expressed in his practical programs of democracy. First, his idea of the "three-stage revolution" was cited as an example. "From a Marxist's point of view," Ch'en asserted, "a revolution, if expected to succeed, requires a revolutionary people's democratic dictatorship." The programs of military operation and of political tutelage suggested by Sun not only would "hinder this revolutionary people's democratic dictatorship," but also would be "used by the counterrevolutionaries to oppress the people." Second, Sun's Five-Power Constitution was similarly singled out as a proof of his failure to trust the people fully.[63] This constitution, according to Ch'en, would "increase rather than remedy the defects of the three-power constitution." The adoption of the old examination system could only "enable the sons of landed gentry and of bureaucrats to get appointed to do things like fraud, corruption, and exploitation of the people." Although Ch'en agreed to the need of the power of control, he maintained that such a power should not be separated from, and put above, the people so as to limit their right of suffrage. All told, he found "the contradiction between revolutionary democracy and democracy of compromise tendency" as "the special feature of Sun's Principle of Demcoracy."

With respect to Sun's Principle of People's Livelihood, Ch'en likewise pointed out the mingling of both progressive and conservative elements in its theory.[64] First, Sun was alleged to have enthusiastically hoped that the peasants would awaken, on the one hand, but to have wrongly estimated the landlords' position in the country and their consciousness, on the other. Second, Sun was criticized for his misunderstanding and misinterpretation of the class struggle, particularly concerning the situation in China. The problem of "equalization of land" and "land to tillers," maintained Ch'en, was originally "the problem of the struggle between the peasant class and the landlord class which has filled the pages of the several-thousand-year history of China." Consequently, to use the concept of "the fairly poor and the extremely poor" could not "explain the history and the actual truth." [65] Moreover, Ch'en found that Sun, on the one hand, actually admitted the existence of the class struggle by calling the peasants "the largest class in China" and by approving the international class war of the oppressed against the oppressing nations,[66] but, on the other hand, he denied in his theory the whole idea of class conflict. This was Sun Yat-sen's "contradiction."

These theoretical shortcomings, according to Ch'en, were reflected in the weaknesses of Sun's program of action for the land question. When he first put forth the principle of "equalization of land," Ch'en maintained, Sun did not link it to the practical problem of acquistion of land by the peasants. In fact, what he tried to solve then was merely the land problem in cities. Even when the slogan of "equalization of land" was later developed to that of "land to the tillers," Ch'en continued, the practical measure offered by Sun still had "an illusion of a subjective tendency to compromise." For one thing, Sun's idea of giving land to the peasants without incurring any loss to the landlords was described by Ch'en as highly impractical in a general historical situation. Also pictured as contradictory was Sun's advocacy of not changing the landlords' gains of the past, but only their possible gains in the future. In criticizing this position, Ch'en pointed out: "First, to change the landlords' possible gains in the future actually means to change their gains of the past, that is, to change their monopoly over the land; second, it is impossible to change the landlords' possible gains in the future without first changing their past gains." In short, Ch'en found "the contradiction between the revolutionary principle and the doctrine of compromise" to be "the characteristic of Sun Yat-sen's Principle of People's Livelihood."

From all this analysis, Ch'en concluded that Sun fundamentally belonged to the revolutionary democratic group and that the Three People's Principles based on the three great policies were the peak of his revolutionary democratic doctrine.[67] "Of course," Ch'en observed,

> in his thinking there was a complicated mixture of various revolutionary and conservative elements. On the one hand,

there was national revolutionary doctrine; on the other, there was also national reformism. On the one hand, there was radical bourgeois democracy; on the other, there was also bourgeois compromise-ism. On the one hand, there was the revolutionary principle of People's Livelihood; on the other, there was also the doctrine of the compromise of People's Livelihood. On the one hand, he enthusiastically sympathized with the oppressed toiling masses and was hostile to the exploiting system; on the other, he took a passive view toward the liberation struggle of the oppressed class.

The dual nature of Sun's thinking, from the standpoint of the background it represented, reflected the revolutionary awakening of modern China on the one hand and the trace of the backwardness of old China, on the other. It was beset, from the standpoint of the social basis, by the dual nature of the Chinese bourgeoisie as well as by that of the Chinese petty bourgeoisie. First, it reflected, on the one hand, the certain revolutionary nature of the bourgeoisie and their dependence on the peasants, and on the other, the certain distance between them and the people, as well as their connection with outmoded things. Second, it reflected the radical democracy of the peasants and the urban petty bourgeoisie and their objective demand for the development of capitalism; at the same time it also reflected the inadequacy of their awareness and the illusion of their subjective socialism concerning the equalization of property.[68]

All in all, Ch'en emphasized that Sun Yat-sen's thinking merely represented a particular period. As time always marches on without stop, true followers of Sun should, in accordance with the development of the revolutionary life, expand the practical and revolutionary essence of his ideas and at the same time overcome their retrogressive elements.[69] Throughout his book Ch'en drove home two important points. First, because of Sun's class background, his ideas were not infallible. Second, by stressing only the retrogressive aspect of the Three People's Principles, the members of the Kuomintang were the renegades of Sun Yat-sen. In contrast, the Chinese Communists would continue to improve Sun's doctrine and to

adopt its revolutionary elements in the struggle for the establishment of a new democratic China.

Sun Yat-sen's place in the People's Republic of China

The policy of stressing the "revolutionary" features of Sun's
doctrine—particularly the alliance with Soviet Russia—on the
one hand, and of rejecting its "reactionary" features, on the
other, was generally maintained by the Chinese Communists
after their victory over the Kuomintang in 1949. In an article
on "Internationalism and Nationalism," written just a few
months before his Party's complete victory, Liu Shao-chi
voiced the familiar thesis that the Three People's Principles of
Sun Yat-sen changed, after the October Revolution, from the
old democracy to the new democracy.[70] On Sun's revolutionary nationalism of 1924, Liu had this to say:

> Although the world outlook of Sun Yat-sen was even at
> that time still the world outlook of the bourgeoisie and the
> petty bourgeoisie, and although his nationalism was still a
> variety of bourgeois nationalism and preserved reactionary
> features (for instance, the conception of the so-called "blood
> tie," the "dominant race in the country," "Greater Asia,"
> etc.), nevertheless Sun Yat-sen endorsed the doctrine of
> national revolution, the doctrine of the "awakening of the
> masses and their unification with all the peoples of the world
> who regard them as equals for the general struggle"; he
> also proclaimed these three great principles: solidarity with
> the Soviet Union, with the Communist Party, and extension
> of support to the workers and peasants. This reflected the
> highly progressive nature of the nationalism of the revolu-
> tionary bourgeoisie in the colonial and semicolonial coun-
> tries during the new period of world socialist revolution.[71]

Mao Tse-tung's views on Sun Yat-sen were further expressed in his famous work *On People's Democratic Dictatorship*, published shortly before the establishment of the new
government of the People's Republic of China. According to
him, Sun Yat-sen had a different world outlook from the Chinese Communists and started out from a different class standpoint in observing and dealing with problems. But in the

second decade of the twentieth century, said Mao, on the problem of how to struggle against imperialism, Sun arrived at a conclusion which was fundamentally in agreement with that of the Chinese Communists. This common conclusion, as mentioned in Sun's will, was that to attain victory "we must awaken the masses of the people and unite ourselves in a common struggle with those peoples of the world who treat us on the basis of equality." [72] Twenty-four years having passed since Sun's death, Mao continued, Chinese revolutionary theory and practice, under the leadership of the Communist Party, had made big strides forward, fundamentally altering the face of China. The Chinese people, he declared, had accumulated vital and basic experiences along the following two lines:

1. Internally, the people must be awakened. This means welding the working class, the peasantry, the petty bourgeoisie and the national bourgeoisie into a united front under the leadership of the working class, and from this proceeding to the creation of a state of the people's democratic dictatorship, a state led by the working class and based on the alliance of workers and peasants.
2. Externally, we must unite in a common struggle with the peoples of all countries and with those nations which treat us as equals. This means allying ourselves with the Soviet Union, with every New Democratic country, and with the proletariat and broad masses in all other countries. This means forming an international united front.[73]

While giving new meanings to the words of Sun's will, Mao at the same time voiced some criticisms of the late Kuomintang leader. All this was, of course, designed to show the correctness of the New Democratic program. In Mao's opinion, Sun had been duped into dealing with the imperialist countries. He pointed out the futility of Sun's frequent appeal for aid from the imperialists, and he emphasized the fact that the only international aid Sun received was from the Soviet Union. From Dr. Sun's experience, Mao therefore drew the following conclusion: "Internationally we belong to the side of the anti-imperialist front, headed by the Soviet Union. We can only turn to this side for genuine and friendly assistance, not to the side of the imperialist front." [74] Moreover, Sun's idea to have the petty and national bourgeoisie "awakening the masses" or "helping the peasants and workers" was ridiculed as unrealizable. According to Mao, Sun Yat-sen's forty years of revolutionary work was a failure, because, in the era of imperialism, it was impossible for the petty and national bourgeoisie to lead any revolution to success. The twenty-eight years' experience of the Chinese Communist made it clear that the "people's democratic" revolution must be led by the working class through the Communist Party. [75]

With their victory assured, the Chinese Communists, in the fall of 1949, convened the Chinese People's Political Consultative Conference to establish the People's Republic of China and to bring into being the Central People's Government. [76] The new Republic was declared to be "a state of the People's democratic dictatorship, led by the working class, based on the alliance of workers and peasants, and rallying all democratic classes and various nationalities within the country." [77] As a gesture to the united front, three non-Communists were named Vice-Chairmen of the Central People's Government, two of whom were professed followers of Sun Yat-sen— Madame Sun Yat-sen and Li Chi-shen, Chairman of the Kuomintang Revolutionary Committee. [78] In the Common Program, which was the "minimum program" of the Chinese Communist Party, Sun's slogan of "land to the tiller" was specifically mentioned. [79] At the People's Political Consultative Conference his name was mentioned several times. In an opening speech before the Conference on September 21, 1949, Mao Tse-tung said: "For over a century, our predecessors have never paused in their unflinching and unswerving struggle, including the 1911 revolution led by Dr. Sun Yat-sen, the forerunner of the Chinese revolution, against foreign and domestic oppressors. Our predecessors instructed and requested us to fulfill their behest. We are doing it now." [80] Speaking before the same Conference, Madame Sun Yat-sen praised the Chinese Communist Party as the only party having the strength of the masses infused into its ranks. "As a result," she stated, "it is the surest guarantee that Sun Yat-sen's three principles—People's Nationalism, People's Democracy, and People's Livelihood—will be successfully carried out." To prove this point, she called attention to the fact that the Chinese Communists had given land to the tiller in the country-side, and that they were "in the process of putting solid flesh on the skeletal plans which Sun Yat-sen drew up for the industrialization of China." [81] Speaking on behalf of the Revo-lutionary Committee of the Kuomintang, Ho Hsiang-ning (Madame Liao Chung-k'ai) also said that "the revolutionary objectives of Sun Yat-sen—freedom, equality, regulation of capital, land to the tiller, and uniting with the nations in the world which treat us on a footing of equality—have been realized under the leadership of Chairman Mao Tse-tung." Then she went on to laud the superiority of Mao's program by saying: "It has been proved that the new democracy is more satisfactory and more thorough than the revolutionary Three People's Principles believed by us. We disciples of Sun Yat-sen and the revolutionary Three People's Principles must today become model new democratic workers and model vigorous executors of the common program of the PPCC." [82]

The fact that Sun Yat-sen's name should find a place of esteem in the People's Republic of China should occasion no surprise, at least as long as the Communist hierarchy wish to maintain the façade of the demorcatic united front. Since the formation of the New Republic, the Chinese Communists' attitude toward Sun's ideas has become increasingly opportun-istic and selective. They have prohibited the study of the Three People's Principles; [83] yet, at the same time, they have found it convenient to make use of Sun's name to support their own programs. Addressing the Sino-Soviet Friendship Association on October 5, 1949, Liu Shao-chi called attention to Sun's alliance with the Soviet Union in 1923-1925 and declared that the day Sun cherished—when the two great nations of Soviet Russia and China would march hand in hand to win victory—had now become a reality.[84] In presenting a Draft Agrarian Reform law to the National Committee of the People's Political Consultative Conference in June 1950, Liu again cited Sun's slogans of "equalization of land ownership" and "land to the tiller" to support his argument that agrarian reform should be carried out.[85] Commemorating the thirtieth anniversary of Dr. Sun's death on March 12, 1955, *Jen-min jih-pao* (The People's Daily), Peking, stated that the late Kuomintang founder was great because he was capable of resolutely adopting the three major policies, after which he "had abandoned the program of setting up a bourgeois republic and had accepted in its place the program of setting up a people's republic advocated by the Chinese Communist Party." As the best memorial to Dr. Sun, Tung Pi-wu, a top Communist leader, urged the Chinese people to fight to liberate Taiwan, fight in defense of world peace, and fight for the complete realization of socialist transformation.[86] Since 1949, books and newspaper stories have been published in Communist China about Sun Yat-sen, with emphasis always on his three major policies and the "betrayal" of his principles by Chiang Kai-shek.[87] Sun's portrait has appeared in parades along with those of Marx, Lenin, Stalin, and Mao Tse-tung. His articles and speeches have been included in propaganda materials to support the present Moscow-Peking alliance. The Sun Yat-sen Mausoleum in Nanking has been renovated and has become a place frequented by visitors.[88] Madame Sun Yat-sen has been given high positions in the Central People's Government and the Sino-Soviet Friendship Association, and has been active in leading the "peace" movement and good-will missions to foreign countries.[89] All this indicates a recognition by the Communist leaders that Sun's name still has a certain propaganda value both at home and abroad.

One most conspicuous instance in this regard was the elaborate celebration in Communist China in November 1956, on the nineteenth anniversary of Dr. Sun's birth. Throughout the country, memorial services and public meetings were held to honor the late revolutionary leader. Official statements and newspaper editorials paid high tribute to Sun's unique career. Even the Kuomintang members in Formosa were urged by Peking to return and to participate in the various commemoration activities. In a special article published on November 12, Mao Tse-tung acclaimed Dr. Sun for his great work in leading the democratic revolution and in developing the old Three People's Principles into the new Three People's Principles. Moreover, Mao pointed out that the Chinese people had not only brought to fruition the democratic revolution left unfinished by Dr. Sun, but had developed it further into a socialist revolution.[90] At the commemoration meeting on November 11, Chou En-lai declared that the democratic-revolutionary ideas of Dr. Sun had exercised a strong influence on the Chinese revolution in its first stage, as well as on many Asian countries engaged in democratic revolution today. Noting that "Taiwan was still suffering aggression at the hands of the United States," the Communist premier urged all patriots and followers of Dr. Sun Yat-sen to strive jointly for the "peaceful liberation of Taiwan." [91] For the occasion an edition of *Selected Works of Sun Yat-sen* was published in Peking, containing speeches, letters, interviews, the "Three People's Principles," the "Plans for National Reconstruction," etc. Arranged chronologically, the collection stressed the later period of Sun's revolutionary activities, particularly his Russian orientation.[92] Another book, *The Great Sun Yat-sen,* was also compiled, including some thirty-six commemorative articles written by Sun's widow and professed followers. The general theme was that the greatness of Dr. Sun lay in his ability to "adapt himself to the trends of the world and meet the needs of the masses" by bringing forward the enlightened policy of alliance with the Communists.

Thus, the Chinese Communists made special efforts in 1956 to put on a big show on the occasion of the ninetieth anniversary of Dr. Sun's birth. This was done at a time when they were pursuing a seemingly moderate policy, symbolized by such slogans as "Peaceful liberation of Taiwan" and "Let all flowers blossom and all schools contend." Sun's name apparently fitted well into the picture and was exploited to the fullest possible extent.

Whatever the propaganda efforts of Peking, it should be noted, however, that, as a "radical bourgeois," Sun's place in Communist China is bound to be secondary. At no time has he been treated as the true equal of such proletarian leaders as

Lenin, Stalin, and Mao Tse-tung. There are indications that
his name is being gradually pushed into the background as
time goes by. For instance, at the first session of the National
People's Congress in September 1954, when Communist
China's Constitution was adopted, Sun Yat-sen was conspicu-
ously less frequently referred to than at the Chinese People's
Political Consultative Conference in 1949. With the exception
of some special occasions, such as the ninetieth anniversary
of his birth, the annual commemoration of Dr. Sun has been
officially performed only by the Kuomintang Revolutionary
Committee, and not in the same manner as the historical figures
of international Communism have been honored in Communist
China. Furthermore, even his professed loyal disciples have
openly shown more enthusiasm for Communism than for his
teachings. When a prominent Indian journalist interviewed
Madame Sun at her Shanghai office in 1952, he found por-
traits of Stalin, Lenin, Marx, Engles, Mao Tse-tung, and Chu
Teh on the walls but none of Sun Yat-sen.[93] At the third
plenum of the second Central Committee of the Revolutionary
Committee of the Kuomintang on January 10, 1953, a report
delivered by its Central Standing Committee called for remolding of ideology inside the Party to conform to the Common
Program and encouraged Party members to make a further
study of the theories of Marxism-Leninism and the thought of
Mao Tse-tung. Yet no mention was made of Sun's Three People's Principles.[94] At a meeting commemorating the thirtieth
anniversary of Sun's death in March 1955, Li Chi-shen, Chairman of the Revolutionary Committee of the Kuomintang,
stated "with pride" that "the Chinese people, under the leadership of the Chinese Communist Party and Chairman Mao
Tse-tung in the past thirty years, have not only realized the
ideals for which Dr. Sun Yat-sen fought all his life but have
even done far better." Disciples of Dr. Sun Yat-sen, continued
Li, would consistently follow the leadership of the Chinese
Communist Party and would continue to play their role in
the great cause of socialist construction as well as in the struggle against enemies both at home and abroad.[95] In an article
celebrating the ninetieth anniversary of Sun's birth in Novem-

ber 1956, Madame Sun also declared that what had been achieved in the Chinese People's Republic had surpassed anything ever dreamed of by her late husband. In memory of Dr. Sun, she concluded, "we should do our best to appreciate his fighting spirit by learning from his ardent patriotism, his revolutionary firmness, and his determination to learn from the Soviet Union; we should carry forward our efforts under the leadership of the Chinese Communist Party and Chairman Mao Tse-tung to build socialism and world peace." [96]

Summary

The Chinese Communists have been interpreting Sun Yat-sen's doctrine to their advantage from 1925 to the present time. This was particularly true during the period between 1937 and 1949, when their claim of being Sun's true followers had a great appeal to various segments of the Chinese population. In seeking to justify this claim, they were able to capitalize on the vagueness of his principles and the fact of his alliance with Soviet Russia.

Throughout all these years, the Communists' tactical line toward Sun Yat-sen and his doctrine has been generally consistent, and can be summarized as follows: They regard the Manifesto of the First National Congress of the Kuomintang in 1924 as marking the transition from Sun's old Three People's Principles to the new Three People's Principles. According to them, only the latter, which are based on the three major policies of "Alliance with Soviet Russia," "Alliance with the Chinese Communists," and "Alliance with the Workers and Peasants," are Sun's genuine, revolutionary Three People's Principles. The Chinese Communists not only identify their minimum program, the New Democracy, with these new Three Principles, but they also make use of Sun's slogans of "down with imperialism" and "land to the tiller" to support their policies. On the other hand, while paying special tribute to Dr. Sun, they are always quick to point out his shortcomings. In their opinion, Sun's world outlook was limited by his bourgeois background, and there were both revolutionary and reactionary features in his thinking. They criticize Sun for the tendency to compromise, the concepts of "Greater Asia" and "Pan-Hanism," the suggestion to revive ancient morality, the lack of complete confidence in the people, the insistence upon political tutelage, the denial of class war, and the reformists' type of economic program. As true followers of Sun, they claim, they have adopted the revolutionary aspects of his doctrine, i.e., the famous three policies, and discarded its retrogressive elements.

Although their general theme has remained the same, the Chinese Communists, in interpreting Sun's doctrine, have shifted the emphasis from time to time, to suit the changing conditions of their fortunes. In the early stage of the united front, 1937-1941, they emphasized Sun's three major policies and, at the same time, made efforts to justify their programs along the line of the Principles of Nationalism, Democracy, and People's Livelihood. From the deterioration of the united front with the Kuomintang to their final victory in the civil war, 1941-1949, their attitude became more selective—stressing only what they called Sun's revolutionary ideas, such as the three major policies, and criticizing the "reactionary" elements of the Three People's Principles. Since the formation of the People's Republic, this attitude has become more apparent. They have prohibited the study of the Three People's Principles, but they have continued to stress Sun's three major policies, particularly the alliance with Soviet Russia, as a means of supporting their "lean to one side" policy. To the extent that Sun's name still has propaganda value he will continue to be quoted. There is no doubt, however, that his role in Communist China is only secondary and will become even less important as time passes. It is quite possible that eventually the name of Sun Yat-sen, like those of Hung Hsiu-ch'üan, Ch'ü Yuan, Confucius, and other historical figures of old China, will serve no more than decorative purposes in the new Chinese People's Republic.[97]

Chapter 6

Comparison of Sun Yat-senism
and Chinese Communism

The preceding chapter has shown how skillfully the Chinese
Communists have interpreted Dr. Sun's doctrine to support
their own programs. In order to clear the confusion about the
true nature of Sun Yat-senism and of Chinese Communism,
a careful and objective comparison of these two ideologies
seems to be necessary. Some perspective may be gained through
comparing Sun's doctrine and Chinese Communism along the
following major lines: ideological basis, nationalism and internationalism, elite government, democracy, land reform, and
general economic policy.

Ideological basis

Undoubtedly the most important difference between Sun Yat-
senism and Chinese Communism lies in their fundamentally
divergent ideological bases. The former is based on Western

democracy and Confucianism; the latter is based on Marxism-Leninism. According to Dr. Sun, the principles which he had held in promoting the Chinese revolution were "in some cases copied from our traditional ideals, in other cases modeled on European theory and experience, and in still others formulated according to original and self-developed theories." [1] Sun never advocated wholesale Westernization. By fusing Chinese and Western thought, he tried to construct a solution specifically for China. Although he expressed some doubts about the applicability in China of Western representative systems, he was fundamentally a believer in democracy and popular sovereignty. Throughout his writings and speeches, he often made references to such liberal thinkers of the West as Rousseau, Montesquieu, Jefferson, Henry George, and Maurice William. [2] Time and again he attributed his Three People's Principles to President Lincoln's classic phrase—"government of the people, by the people, for the people." For instance, in a speech on "The Three People's Principles" in 1921, Sun stated:

> The principles of President Lincoln completely coincide with mine. He said: "A government of the people, elected by the people and for the people." These principles have served as the maximum of achievement for Europeans as well as Americans. Words which have the same sense can be found in China. I have translated them: "nationalism, democracy, and socialism." Of course, there can be no other interpretations. The wealth and power of the United States are a striking example of the results of great men's teachings in that country. I am glad to observe that my principles, too, are shared by the greatest political minds abroad and are not in contradiction to all the world's democratic schools of thought. [3]

The Chinese Communist Party, on the other hand, boasts that it "guides its entire work by the teachings which unite the theories of Marxism-Leninism with the actual practice of the revolution—the thought of Mao Tse-tung—and fights against any dogmatist or empiricist deviations." [4] Like Dr. Sun, Mao Tse-tung is opposed to wholesale Westernization, and he wants to Sinonize Marxism to meet China's realities. In his "On New Democracy," he states:

> So-called "wholesale Westernization" is a mistaken view-point. China has suffered a great deal in the past from the formalist absorption of foreign things. Likewise, in applying Marxism to China, Chinese Communists must fully and properly unite the universal truth of Marxism with the specific practice of the Chinese revolution; that is to say, the truth of Marxism must be integrated with the characteristics of the nation and given a definite national form before it can be useful; it must not be applied subjectively as a mere formula. Formula-Marxists are only fooling with Marxism and the Chinese revolution, and there is no place for them in the ranks of the Chinese revolution.[5]

In contrast to Sun, Mao is a foe of Western democracy and a faithful student of Marx, Engels, Lenin, and Stalin. His fundamental ideas are firmly based on the Marxist dogma of class struggle and dialectical materialism. He accepts the standard Bolshevik interpretation of Chinese society as "feudal." His program of agrarian reform and New Democracy for China corresponds basically with the Leninist-Stalinist theories of revolution in semicolonial areas. In other words, Chinese Communism developed by Mao Tse-tung is a legitimate and genuine development of Marxism-Leninism, an ideology quite different from the democratic principles of the West, which contributed much to Sun Yat-senism.

Of particular interest in this connection are the different interpretations of history by Sun Yat-sen and the Chinese Communists. Coinciding with the view of Maurice William, Sun advocated the "livelihood," or social interpretation of history. In a lecture on his Third Principle, he declared:

> Livelihood is the center of government, the center of economics, the center of all historical movements. Just as men once misjudged the center of the solar system, so the old socialists mistook material forces for the center of history. ... We can no longer say that material issues are the central force in history. We must let the political, social, and economic movements of history gravitate about the problem

of livelihood. We must recognize livelihood as the center
of social history.[6]

Just as he rejected Marx's materialistic interpretation of history, so did he criticize the corollary Marxian theory of the
class war. According to Sun, mankind's struggle for continuous
existence is the cause of social progress, while class war is
merely a disease developed in the course of social progress.
Since Marx was concerned with nothing but the disease, he
can only be called a social pathologist.[7] In contrast to Sun's
view, Chinese Communism follows the materialist interpretation of history by Marx. For example, in "On New Democracy"
Mao Tse-tung states: "Any given culture (culture as an
ideological form) is a reflection of the politics and economy
of a given society, while it has in turn a tremendous influence
and effect upon the politics and economy of the given society;
economy is the basis, and politics is the concentrated expression of economy."[8] Indeed, the contradiction between the
livelihood interpretation of history and the materialist interpretation of history is one of the fundamental differences between Sun Yat-senism and Chinese Communism. Comparing
these two ideologies Mao has this to say:

> The world outlook of Communism is dialectical material-
> ism and historical materialism, and that of the Three Peo-
> ple's Principles is the interpretation of history in terms of
> the people's welfare, which in essence is dualism or idealism;
> these two are opposed to each other.[9]

From the standpoint of philosophical background, another
important difference between Sun Yat-senism and Chinese
Communism is their relationship with Confucianism. With all
the influence of the West upon Sun's thinking, both his admirers and critics agree that he had an unshakable faith in
China's traditional culture and derived many of his ideas from
Confucianism.[10] "The greatness of Sun Yat-sen," wrote Richard
Wilhelm, the greatest of German Sinologues, "rests upon the
fact that he has found a living synthesis between the fundamental principles of Confucianism and the demands of modern
times, a synthesis which, beyond the borders of China, can

again become significant to all humanity." [11] In his sixth lecture on the Principle of Nationalism, Sun proposed, together with the adoption of Western science, the revival of the ancient Chinese morality and the recovery of the ancient Chinese learning as the necessary steps to restore the national standing of China.[12] He listed China's old virtues as loyalty, filial devotion, kindness, love, faithfulness, justice, harmony, and peace.[13] As for the ancient learning, he especially praised China's political philosophy for having a deep, all-embracing logic not found in the West. By way of example, he quoted a passage from *The Great Learning:* "Search into the nature of things, extend the boundaries of knowledge, make the purpose sincere, regulate the mind, cultivate personal virtue, rule the family, govern the state, pacify the world." [14] Moreover, in another lecture he declared that the goal of his Principle of People's Livelihood was the Confucian ideal of "the Great Commonwealth": "When the people share everything in the state, then will we truly reach the goal of the *Min-sheng* Principle, which is Confucius' hope of a 'Great Commonwealth.' " [15] All this demonstrates the fact that Sun incorporated certain Confucian concepts into his doctrine and thought of himself "as a rebuilder and not as a destroyer of the ancient Chinese culture." [16]

Chinese Communism, on the contrary, rejects Confucianism and the feudal culture of old China. This, however, is not to say that the Chinese Communists have no relations with Confucianism at all. For one thing, the tradition of Confucian paternalism has certainly provided them with a convenient ancient foundation on which to build a "democratic dictatorship." Many Communist leaders, in their youth, were exposed to the influence of Confucian teachings in one form or another. Some writers maintain that Mao Tse-tung has been under the strong influence of Confucianism.[17] Liu Shao-chi in his *On the Training of a Communist Party Member* even quotes Confucius and Mencius to support his arguments.[18] But the fact remains that Confucianism as an ideology has no place in the New Democracy. Liu Shao-chi, in the same book, criticizes the methods and ways of self-cultivation and study expounded by *The Book of Poetry, The Great Learning,* and Sung Neo-Confucians as unadoptable for a Communist, because they are mostly "idealistic, formal, abstract, and separated from the social actuality." [19] Mao Tse-tung in "On New Democracy" calls the old Chinese culture semifeudal and says that the struggle between the old and new cultures is a life and death one.[20] The semifeudal culture in China, he explains, "is a reflection of semifeudal politics and economy and has as its representatives all those who, while opposing the new culture and new ideologies, advocate the worship of Confucius, the study of the Confucian canon, the old ethical code and the old ideologies." [21] As for the new culture, he defines it as "the anti-imperialist, antifeudal culture of the broad masses of the people under the leadership of the proletariat." [22]

> It opposes imperialist oppression and upholds the dignity and independence of the Chinese nation. It belongs to our own nation, and bears our national characteristics. It unites with the socialist and new-democratic cultures of all other nations and establishes with them the relations whereby they can absorb something from each other and help each other to develop, and form together the culture of the world; but it can never unite with the reactionary imperialist culture of any nation, for it is a revolutionary national culture.[23]

Since 1949, "love for the fatherland and the people, love of labor, love of science, and taking care of public property" have become the new morals of the Chinese People's Republic.[24] Old Confucian virtues like filial devotion and love of family are completely out of place in Communist China.

Nationalism and internationalism

Although anti-imperialism and nationalism are important factors in both Sun Yat-senism and Chinese Communism, national and international problems are approached by the two ideologies from different standpoints and with different emphasis. Dr. Sun attributed the development of a nation to five natural forces—blood kinship, common language, common livelihood, common religion, and common customs.[25] The Chinese Communists, on the other hand, follow the Marxist definition of a nation and criticize Sun for confusing the race with the nation.[26] According to Ch'en Po-ta, a nation is "characterized by its common language, common territory, its common economic life, and the common psychological expressions of its life revealed by its common culture." [27] In other words, the Chinese Communists replace the element of blood kinship, suggested by Sun, with that of common territory as an essential basis for a nation. Naturally, with their antireligious bias, they do not accept Sun's listing of a "common religion" as a binding force in national development.

Sun Yat-sen proposed to develop Chinese nationalism out of the deep-rooted family and clan sentiments.[28] "If we are to recover our lost nationalism," he said, "we must have some kind of group unity, large group unity. An easy and successful way to bring about the unity of a large group is to build upon the foundation of small united groups, and the small units we can build upon in China are the clan groups and also the family groups." [29] In contrast, the Chinese Communists regard those social organizations of old China as "feudalistic" and a great obstacle to the growth of national unity and real patriotism. In place of old virtues, Communist China is promoting the public spirit of the people on the basis of the new "Five Loves." Deliberate efforts have been taken to shatter the "feudal" social relationships and sentiments by dividing parents and children, husbands and wives, brothers and brothers.

On the problem of national minorities, the principles of racial equality and of self-determination are accepted both by Sun Yat-senism and by Chinese Communism. Yet, at the same time, Sun wanted to weld the five races in China into a great Chung-hua nation, through cultural assimilation, while the Chinese Communists are adopting a policy of respecting the cultural developments of all nationalities, on the one hand, and keeping them within the bounds of the "People's Democratic Dictatorship" by political means, on the other. Ever since 1912, Dr. Sun had advocated the equality of the five races.[30]

With equal consistency, he also had suggested the assimilation of Manchus, Mongols, Mohammedans, and Tibetans by the Chinese (Han) to form a new nation. In a lecture on the Three People's Principles in 1921, Sun spoke of Pan-Hanism and said that the positive kind of nationalism for China meant following the example of the United States of America to mingle and unite all the races together, with the Chinese (the Han People) as the center, to constitute a single Chung-hua nation.[31] After his alliance with Soviet Russia in 1923, he formally adopted the principle of self-determination. In the Manifesto of its First National Congress of 1924, the Kuomintang declared that "it recognizes the right of self-determination of all the races within China and that it will organize a free and united Chinese Republic, based on the free association of various races, after the success of the revolution against imperalism and warlords." [32] The acceptance of the principle of self-determination, however, did not mean that Sun was, at heart, in favor of the secession of the Mongols or the Tibetans from China.[33] He never gave up the idea to "unite all the races in the country to form one great Chung-hua nation," [34] and the basis of such a union was the ancient Chinese civilization, the superiority of which he emphatically expounded in his sixth lecture on the Principle of Nationalism.[35] All in all, politically, Sun recognized the rights and equality of national minorities, but culturally, he envisaged the evolution of all races in China into a single nation as in the case of the United States or Switzerland. The assimilation he had in mind was to be voluntary and peaceful; the final goal was the formation of a great Chung-hua nation, with the disappearance of all the names of individual nationalities.

The Chinese Communists have frequently attacked the concept of Pan-Hanism as reactionary and have endorsed the nationality policy Dr. Sun enunciated in the 1924 Manifesto of the First National Congress of the Kuomintang.[36] They describe China as a country of multiple nationalities.[37] Their policy toward the minorities has been clearly set forth in the Common Program of the CPPCC (Chinese People's Political Consultative Conference) of 1949 and in the Constitution of the People's Republic of China of 1954. According to these documents, all nationalities in China are equal; there should be no discrimination and no oppression; regional autonomy as well as freedom to keep and develop native languages, customs, and habits are guaranteed to national minorities.[38] Before 1949, the Chinese Communists officially endorsed the right of national self-determination and the independence of Outer Mongolia. But since 1949, they have shown no tendency to allow Tibet, Sinkiang, or Inner Mongolia to go free in the name of the principle of national self-determination. The Chinese Constitution, as a matter of fact, does not provide the right of secession for the national minorities. The familiar argument is that, with the country "liberated," the interests of the national minorities lie not in separation but in cooperation to construct the united New China.[39] The revolt in Tibet early in 1959, for instance, was ruthlessly suppressed by the Communist forces. Peking claimed that the victory over the rebellion was a mortal blow to "the Tibetan clique of traitors and foreign imperialism" and that it greatly strengthened not only "the cause of national unity and solidarity among the nationalities" but also "our national defense in the southwestern part of our country." [40]

Throughout Communist China some three hundred national autonomous units, of the country level and above, have been established. The largest among them are the five Autonomous Regions (Inner Mongolia, Sinkiang Uighur, Tibet, Ningsia Hui, and Kwangsi Ch'uang). In all these units, the national minorities are supposed to enjoy a considerable amount of self-government, particularly in cultural spheres. The Preamble of the Constitution further guarantees that, in the course of economic and cultural development, special attention will be paid to the needs and characteristics of the different nationalities. On the other hand, it should be noted that the Chinese Communists exercise strong control over the national minorities through the activities of the Nationalities Affairs Commission, the training of Party cadres from the minorities, and other organizational devices. The Constitution makes it clear that national autonomous areas are inaliena-

ble parts of the People's Republic of China. It also stresses
the unity of China's nationalities, and their sharing of a common goal. Their unity is founded "on ever-growing friendship
and mutual aid among themselves, and on the struggle against
imperialism, against public enemies of the people within the
nationalities, and against both dominant-nation chauvinism
and local nationalism." [41] Their common objective is the building of a "socialist" society. According to Liu Shao-chi, the
state has a duty to help all nationalities within the country,
step by step, to take "this path to happiness." Because of their
advanced experience, he feels, the Han people are under a
special obligation to assist all the brother nationalities to
achieve material and cultural advancement along the road of
"socialist transformation." [42] Any resistance to the central
control, or any move for separatism by the national minorities,
is viewed by Peking as intolerable. A Vice-Chairman of the
Nationalities Affairs Commission has stated: "Only by uniting
themselves in the big united family of the motherland, can the
various nationalities of China construct socialism and resist
imperialism. Any nationality, if it attempts to secede from the
big family of the motherland, is bound to leave the socialist
road and follow the imperialist and colonial road." [43] Mainland newspapers have frequently warned the minority peoples
against "local nationalism" and "Rightist tendencies." In the
light of all these, it seems clear that the Chinese Communist
nationality policy, which grants regional autonomy and cultural freedom to national minorities and, at the same time,
develops political control to keep them in the orbit of the
"People's Democratic Dictatorship," bears much closer resemblance to the Soviet approach than to Dr. Sun's program
of cultural assimilation. In fact, the Communist policy appears
to have more propaganda and practical value than Dr. Sun's,
in that it lets minority peoples speak different languages but
only on the same thing—Marxism-Leninism.

Insofar as the factor of anti-imperialism is concerned, it
is unquestionably one of the most important elements which
Sun Yat-senism and Chinese Communism have in common.
After his alliance with Soviet Russia in 1923, Sun waged a

vigorous anti-imperialist campaign.[44] He repeatedly stressed the political and economic oppression of foreign imperialism; he spoke of China as a hypo-colony of the imperialist powers; he called for the abolition of unequal treaties to restore China's independence; he envisaged an international war between the oppressing nations and the oppressed; until his death, he regarded the Soviet Union as a trusted ally of China in the struggle against imperialism. The Chinese Communists have frequently quoted Dr. Sun to support their anti-imperialist propaganda. Mao Tse-tung, in *The Chinese Revolution and the Communist Party of China,* also speaks of the unequal treaties and the other devices of the imperialist powers designed to turn China into their semicolony and colony.[45] He and other Communist leaders divide the world into two opposing camps and justify their alliance with Soviet Russia as in complete accordance with Sun's policy of working hand in hand with Soviet Russia and of combating imperialism.

Nevertheless, the analogy should not be carried too far. For all the influence the Russian alliance might have had upon his anti-imperialist policy, Sun never accepted Lenin's theory of imperialism. At no time did he identify imperialism with capitalism; still less did he regard imperialism as "the latest stage in the development of capitalism." [46] For him the chief criteria for differentiating friends from foes among the nations of the world, be they capitalist or Communist countries, were their foreign policies toward China. It has been noted that Sun's alliance with Moscow in 1923 was made out of political necessity rather than ideological affinity.[47] In addition to Russia, he placed Germany in the group of oppressed nations and considered her a possible ally. [48] He even urged Japan, in 1924, to help China fight foreign imperialism.[49] Moreover, Sun never wrote off the West completely and always hoped for the international development of China through foreign aid.[50] As late as 1924, he appealed to the United States to call a peace conference in Shanghai for the purpose of limiting armaments and stopping civil wars in China.[51] In the second lecture on the Principle of Livelihood, delivered in August 1924, he emphasized the necessity of borrowing foreign capital to promote Chinese industry.[52] To him, there was no contradiction in fighting imperialism, on the one hand, and in inviting foreign capital for a just and honorable economic development of China, on the other.

In contrast, the Chinese Communists' approach is very dogmatic. They follow the Leninist thesis that imperialism is the dying form of capitalism.[53] Along the ideological line, they divide the world into two camps: the imperialist camp composed of the United States and her allies, and the anti-imperialist camp made of the U.S.S.R., the People's Democracies of Europe, and the proletariat and masses of all other countries.[54] For China, there is no choice but to "lean to one side"—to ally with the Soviet camp. Mao Tse-tung justifies this policy by saying:

> The forty years' experience of Sun Yat-sen and the twenty-eight years' experience of the Chinese Communist Party have convinced us that, in order to attain victory and consolidate it, we must lean to one side. According to these experiences, the Chinese people must lean either toward the side of imperialism or toward that of socialism. There can be no exception to this rule. It is impossible to sit on the fence; there is no third road. . . . We also oppose illusions about a third road. Not only in China but throughout the world, without exception, one leans either toward imperialism or toward socialism. Neutrality is merely a camouflage; a third road does not exist.[55]

The fight between the two camps is to the bitter end. There cannot be any compromise. With a man-eating tiger, said Mao, one can only choose between killing it and being eaten.[56] He ridiculed the idea of seeking assistance from the capitalist countries and cites Sun's futile attempts as an example. According to his thesis, China can look for genuine friendly aid only from the "anti-imperialist front" headed by the Soviet Union and not from the "imperialist front." [57]

Finally, a comparison must be made between Sun Yat-senism and Chinese Communism on the basis of their points of emphasis regarding nationalism and internationalism. There is no doubt that internationalism played a considerable role in

Dr. Sun's thinking. He spoke of the divine obligation of the Chinese nation to "rescue the weak and lift up the fallen." [58] He advocated the "Pan-Asian Doctrine," based on *wang-tao* (way of right), to fight for the liberation of the oppressed people of Asia.[59] He set as his final goal a world governed by the universal rule of equality and fraternity.[60] Nevertheless, in no uncertain terms he put nationalism before internationalism. To him, to stress internationalism or cosmopolitanism before solving China's national problems was not only impractical but dangerous.[61] He maintained that the Chinese must establish their own nationalism first if they wanted to talk cosmopolitanism: " 'Those desiring to pacify the world must first govern their own state.' Let us revive our lost nationalism and make it shine with greater splendor, then we will have some ground for discussing internationalism." [62] In other words, first things should come first. Sun's main concern was the survival of the Chinese civilization and the perpetuation of the Chinese nation. Only after China became strong would Sun suggest that she take the responsibility of helping the oppressed people in Asia and throughout the world. In the end, he envisaged the future emergence of a world of justice with China as its center and the traditional Chinese morality as its basis.[63] The following passage from his sixth lecture on the Principle of Nationalism is quite illustrative:

> If we want to be able to reach this ideal [governing the state and pacifying the world] in the future, we must now revive our national spirit, recover our national standing, unify the world upon the foundation of our ancient morality and love of peace, and bring about a universal rule of equality and fraternity. This is the great responsibility which devolves upon our four hundred millions.[64]

While Sun Yat-senism is essentially nationalistic, Chinese Communism appears to be more internationally oriented. This is, of course, not to say that the Chinese Communists lack or neglect the sentiment of nationalism. During the Sino-Japanese war, they identified themselves with Chinese patriotism to organize resistance. In the Korean war, the Chinese "volun-

teers" used the slogan of "Aid Korea, Protect our Homes." [65]
"Love for the Fatherland" is at present one of the new morals
in the Chinese People's Republic. When Mao Tse-tung was
once asked whether "the Communists are Chinese first or
Communist first," he replied: "Without a Chinese nation there
could be no Chinese Communist Party. You might just as
well ask 'what is first, children or parents'?" [66] With a strong
nationalistic undercurrent, the Chinese Communists often
boast of the significance of their own Party and Mao Tse-tung's
thought in the world-wide "liberation" movement. [67] In spite
of their denunciation of the feudalistic Confucian tradition,
they too take pride in pointing out the glorious past of China.
"In the five thousand years of Chinese history," Mao Tse-tung
writes, "many national heroes and revolutionary leaders have
been produced; in addition, we can boast of many revolutionary military leaders, statesmen, writers and thinkers. Consequently, the Chinese people possess a glorious revolutionary
heritage and fine historical traditions." [68] Liu Shao-chi also
claims that the Chinese Communist Party has carried on the
finest traditions of many progressive men of thought and
action in Chinese history. [69] Since its establishment, the Peking
government has made such efforts to exalt China's valuable
heritage as the commemoration of Ch'ü Yuan, an ancient
patriot-poet, and the issuance of special postage stamps in
memory of ancient Chinese inventions. [70] At times, Mao Tse-
tung sounds as nationalistic as Sun Yat-sen or Chiang Kai-
shek, particularly when he speaks of the humiliation China
suffered at the hands of the imperialist powers. In *The Chinese
Revolution and the Communist Party of China,* Mao makes the
following statement: "In defeating China in war, the imperialistic powers took many Chinese dependent states and a part of
her territories. Japan took Korea, Taiwan, the Ryukyu Islands,
the Pescadores Islands, Port Arthur. England seized Burma,
Bhutan, Nepal and Hong Kong. France occupied Annam; and
even an insignificant country like Portugal took Macao." [71]
His aspirations to regain China's past glory and even to surpass
the greatest emperors known in Chinese history are well expressed in his most famous poem, "The Snow":

O wait for the pure sky!
See how charming is the earth
Like a red-faced girl clothed in white!
Such is the charm of these mountains and rivers
Calling innumerable heroes to vie with each other in pursu-
ing her.

The Emperors Shih Huang and Wu Ti were hardly lettered,
The Emperors T'ai Tsung and T'sai Tsu were barely
chivalrous,
For a whole generation Genghis Khan was a favorite of
Heaven,
But he knew only how to bend his bow at the eagles.
All have passed away—only today are there men of great
feeling.[72]

On the other hand, the Chinese Communists are dedicated
internationalists, as any true Marxists should be. They put
nationalism within the framework of internationalism and consider national questions from the context of the world revolution. Mao Tse-tung, for example, often calls the Chinese
revolution a "glorious and important part of the world revolution," and gives credit to the October Revolution in Russia for
helping the Chinese Communists to use the world outlook of
the proletariat as the means of determining their actions.[73]
Following the conclusion of the Soviet-German Non-Aggres-
sion Pact of 1939, Mao praised the pact, as did all Communists the world over, as the victory of Stalin's peace policy:
"The pact has shattered the schemes for instigating a Soviet-
German war on the part of the international reactionary bourgeoisie represented by Chamberlain, Daladier, and others,
smashed the encirclement of the Soviet Union by the German-
Italian-Japanese anti-Communist bloc, consolidated peace between the Soviet Union and Germany, and ensured the further-
ance of socialist construction in the Soviet Union." [74] In a
report to the Central Committee of the Chinese Communist
Party during the war against Japan, he made the following
statement on the question of "patriotism and internationalism":

Can a Communist, who is an internationalist, be at the
same time a patriot? We hold that he not only can but also

ought to be one. The specific content of patriotism is determined by historical conditions. There is the "patriotism" of the Japanese aggressors and of Hitler, and there is our own patriotism. Communists must resolutely oppose the so-called "patriotism" of the Japanese aggressors and of Hitler. The Communists in Japan and Germany are all defeatists in the wars of their respective countries. It suits the interests of the Japanese and German people to ensure by every means that the Japanese aggressors and Hitler are defeated in their wars, and the more complete the defeat, the better. . . . China's case is different because she is a victim of aggression. The Chinese Communists must therefore combine patriotism with internationalism. We are at once patriots and internationalists, and our slogan is to fight in defense of the motherland against the aggressors. For us defeatism is a crime, and to win the War of Resistance is a duty that we cannot shirk. For only by fighting in defense of the motherland can we defeat the aggressors and achieve national liberation. And only by achieving national liberation will it be possible for the proletariat and the toiling masses to achieve their own liberation. The victory of China and the defeat of the imperialists invading China will also be a help to the people of foreign countries. The patriotism is simply an application of internationalism in the war of national liberation.[75]

The same subject was given a most elaborate treatment by Liu Shao-chi in an article, "Internationalism and Nationalism," published in 1949. According to him "bourgeois nationalism" and "proletarian internationalism" are not only different but the opposite of each other. Based on capitalist exploitation, bourgeois nationalism is the vehicle by which the bourgeoisie attempts to perpetuate its special class interests at home and to enslave other nations abroad.[76] Proletarian internationalism, on the contrary, opposes any system of exploitation or oppression and is intimately linked to the real patriotism of the masses of people in all countries.[77] Its approach to national questions is "based on the vital interests of the masses of the people in a given country, and at the same time on the general interests of all the masses throughout the world, on the interests of all mankind." [78] In accordance with proletarian internationalism, said Liu, the Communists elsewhere must unite with the Soviet Union and all other revolutionary forces for the common struggle against imperialism and for the liberation of all the oppressed peoples of the world.[79]

There is little doubt that the Chinese Communists have been faithfully working in that direction, particularly since their conquest of the mainland of China. Their close cooperation with Moscow in practically all fields and their great enthusiasm to "learn from Russia" sometimes are beyond the comprehension of Western observers. Special efforts have been undertaken in Communist China to promote "ideological education on internationalism and Soviet experience." [80] The Sino-Soviet Alliance has been presented as "an invincible force in the consolidation and defense of peace in the Far East and the whole world." [81]

Peking's devotion to internationalism was best demonstrated in the 1956 Polish and Hungarian crises. Confronted with a serious challenge within the Soviet empire, the Chinese Communists threw their full weight behind Moscow to save the situation. They advanced a far-reaching thesis in a document entitled "More on Historical Experience of Proletarian Dictatorship." [82] According to this thesis, Communist nations may use "different roads to socialism" but should never deviate from the principle of the dictatorship of the proletariat; "great-nation chauvinism" must be avoided in relations between Communist states, but small nations should not develop bourgeois nationalism to threaten the solidarity of the Communist world. Since 1956, Peking has continued to stress the necessity for all Communists to support the unity of the "socialist camp" led by the Soviet Union in a struggle against the "imperialist camp." [83] It has further taken the lead in waging an ideological war against Titoism and other "dangerous" forms of revisionism and national Communism, in the interest of upholding proletarian internationalism.[84]

In addition to their "fraternal collaboration" with the Russians to preserve the unity of the Communist world, the Chinese Communists have shown strong internationalism in their efforts to promote "people's revolutions" beyond China's boundaries. Since 1949, Peking has consistently portrayed itself as the vanguard of the oppressed peoples of Asia, and the leader in their struggle for liberation. It has tried to spread Communism in the area through the tactics of subversion, infiltration, and direct military intervention. It also has made efforts to woo the uncommitted nations by way of "peace" propaganda, political trading, and "no-string" economic assistance. All this indicates that Chinese Communism, unlike the bourgeois nationalism of Sun Yat-sen, puts great emphasis on proletarian internationalism and has as its driving force not a desire to spread the traditional Chinese civilization but a religious dedication to promote the world-wide Communist movement.

Elite rule and democracy

One of the most important and interesting comparisons that can be made between Sun Yat-senism and Chinese Communism is that which relates to their theories of revolution and the political system. In general, the two ideologies resemble each other in their paternalistic character and elitist views of government, but they differ sharply in the questions of the ruling party and the ultimate objective. They both often refer to democracy, but their interpretations of the word are quite different.

Sun Yat-sen divided the revolutionary process in China into three periods: a period of military operations, a period of political tutelage, and a period of constitutional government.[85] He was emphatic on the necessity for the period of political tutelage, during which the Kuomintang should exercise one-party rule to educate and train people in the preparation for democracy. The Chinese Communists, on the other hand, divide the Chinese revolution into two stages: the New Democracy and Socialism-Communism. They do not formally provide a period of political tutelage, as they claim that, in the People's Republic of China, democracy is already established and the people are enjoying their rights of self-government.[86] In actuality, however, the "New China" is going through a period of tutelage, during which the Chinese Communist Party exercises a dictatorship in the name of the people to prepare the country for the final stage of Communism.

On the basis of intellect rather than of property, Dr. Sun divided human beings into three groups: those who see and perceive first (the discoverers), those who see and perceive later (the promoters), and those who do not see or perceive (the operators).[87] According to him, the cooperation of the three groups is necessary for social progress, and the enlightened few (an aristocracy of intellectuals) must lead the ignorant masses. He believed in the sovereign right of the people but had little confidence in their intelligence and ability. Comparing them to Ah Tou, an incompetent ruler during the period of the Three Kingdoms, Sun maintained that the people should let the government be run by men of special talent and skill.[88] He reconciled the concept of elite rule with the principle of democracy by advocating a separation of sovereignty *(ch'üan)* and ability *(neng)*. "The foundation of the government of a nation must be built upon the rights of the people, but the administration of government must be entrusted to experts." [89] With a clear division of the political sovereignty of the people and the administrative power of the government, he contended, China would find it possible to have both democracy and a very strong government.

> The political power will be given into the hands of the people, who will have a full degree of sovereignty and will be able to control directly the affairs of state; this political power is popular sovereignty. The other power is government, and we will put that entirely in the government organs, which will be powerful and will manage all the nation's business; this political power is the power of government. If the people have a full measure of political sovereignty and the methods for exercising popular control over the government are well worked out, we need not fear that the government will become too powerful and uncontrollable.[90]

In view of the unpreparedness of the Chinese people to exercise their sovereign power, however, Dr. Sun advocated especially a period of political tutelage to train them first. In his opinion, it was utterly necessary for the Kuomintang to institute one-party rule during this period to purge the people of their "slave psychology" and to teach them how to use their political rights.[91] The paternalistic role Sun assigned to his Party is well illustrated in the following passage:

> The Kuomintang bore this infant [the Chinese people], and is obliged to nurse it like a mother and train it, and only by training the people can it carry out its parental duty. And for this the period of preparatory training is necessary, so that the child can be given experience and trained up to years of discretion, up to the moment when it can take over power itself.[92]

The concept of elite rule is also inherent in the ideology of the Chinese Communist Party but is based on different premises. Using economic status as a criterion, the Chinese Communists have classified the people of China as follows: the landlord class, the bureaucratic capitalist class, the national bourgeoisie, the petty bourgeoisie, the peasantry, and the working class.[93] The first two classes are the enemies of the Chinese revolution, and the rest are its driving forces, so explains the Party doctrine. The working class, acting through the Communist Party, must lead all the other revolutionary classes to establish a "democratic dictatorship" in China, because it is the most far-sighted, just, unselfish, and consistently revolutionary class.[94] According to the dogma, without the leadership of this select group—the working class and the Communist Party—no Chinese revolution, democratic or socialist, can ever have a chance to succeed.[95] While advocating a form of elite rule, the Chinese Communists at the same time stress the necessity of "uniting with the masses" and "learning from the masses." They seem to be more aware of the potential power and capabilities of the masses than Dr. Sun Yat-sen. Mao Tse-tung, for instance, has the following advice to give to his Party:

> Our comrades must not assume that the people cannot understand what they themselves have not yet understood. Often the people overtake us. . . . Every comrade should be

made to understand that as long as we rely upon the people, have confidence in their inexhaustible creative power, trust them, and join forces with them, no difficulty will be too great to be overcome and no enemy will be able to crush us, but, on the contrary, we shall be able to crush our enemies.[96]

Liu Shao-chi states that the Communists can learn much from the people as the latter's "knowledge and experience are the most abundant and most practical and their creative power is the greatest." [97] Also illustrative is a quotation from the leading editorial of *Jen-min jih-pao,* January 3, 1951: "We depend upon the building up of direct relationships between the leadership of the Party and the masses of the people. It is imperative for the Communists to keep in incessant touch with the masses in order to gain invincible might." All this shows how keenly the Chinese Communist Party appreciates the importance of winning the support of the broad masses, but does not in any way indicate its willingness to change or relax its undisputed role. According to the Party's mass line, in their revolutionary struggle the masses of the people are "in urgent need of far-sighted and steadfast leaders and guides," and such a leadership can be provided only by the Communists, who are "the vanguard of the masses" and "the harbingers of enlightenment, the only people capable of helping the less enlightened." [98] Although the dogma speaks of "learning from the masses," it emphasizes that the Party must exercise correct leadership to educate the people untiringly, in a revolutionary spirit, for the purpose of awakening and developing their consciousness. Although it states that the Party must understand the views and needs of the masses, the Party is assigned a role which alone can interpret the views of the people, determine their "correctness," make final decisions, and mobilize and organize the masses to carry out these decisions as well as to supervise their execution.[99] In short, the Chinese Communist Party, like the Kuomintang, acts as a self-appointed ruling elite for China, but it has a more subtle program to take the masses into its fold and to rule through them.

So far as the problem of individual liberty is concerned,

there is a parallel between Dr. Sun's view and that of the Chinese Communists. Quite different from the general concept of Western liberalism, both put a special premium on the interests of a group (be it a nation or a class) and subordinate to the group the interests and freedom of the individual. It was Sun's belief that the Chinese people had had too much personal freedom rather than too little. In the face of foreign imperialism, he argued, what was at stake in China was the liberty of the nation and not the liberty of the individual.[100]

> If we apply it [liberty] we shall become a sheet of loose sand; on no account must we give more liberty to the individual; let us secure liberty instead for the nation. The individual should not have too much liberty, but the nation should have complete liberty. When the nation can act freely, then China may be called strong. To make the nation free, we must each sacrifice his personal freedom. . . . China is the colony of all the nations and the slave of all. In fact, we are now slaves to over ten masters; our national freedom is terribly restricted. If we want to restore China's liberty, we must unite ourselves into one unshakable body; we must use revolutionary methods to weld our state into firm unity. Without revolutionary principles we shall never succeed. Our revolutionary principles are the cement. If we can consolidate our four hundred millions and form a mighty union and make the union free, the Chinese state will be free and the Chinese people will be really free.[101]

While Sun favored the curbing of individual freedom in the interests of the nation, the Chinese Communist Party demand an absolute and unconditional subordination from the individual. "The interests of the revolution and the Party above all" is the highest principle for every Party member to understand and to carry out. The "Party spirit" calls for the individual to sacrifice everything, including his own life, without the slightest hesitation, in the interests of the revolution, the class, and the Party.[102] Liberalism has no place whatsoever in Chinese Communism, as evidenced in the following words of Mao Tse-tung:

> In a collective organization, liberalism is completely harmful. It acts as a corrosive agent which causes the dissolution

of unity, the loosening of relations, the cessation of work, divergence of opinion, and the loss of tight organization and discipline among the revolutionary rank and file. It prevents a deep penetration of policy and causes a split between the Party organization and the masses which the Party leads; it is a most injurious and evil tendency.

The source of liberalism is the egotism of the petty bourgeoisie, which places the interests of the individual first and the interests of the revolution second. It is as a result of this that liberalism is produced in thought, politics, and organization.[103]

The discussions above have shown the similarities between Sun Yat-senism and Chinese Communism in matters like elite rule and individual freedom, and their differences in such questions as the classification of the people and the designation of the ruling class. What needs to be further discussed here is how these two ideologies differ fundamentally, in their ultimate political aims and in their genuine attitudes toward democracy. With all his paternalistic views about the Chinese revolution, Dr. Sun, at heart, was mainly concerned with the rights of the people. His scheme of strong government and party rule was only the means with which to achieve his final end—democracy. In answering the charge that his proposed political tutelage bore a strong resemblance to enlightened depotism, Sun said that "enlightened despotism has as its end an absolute monarchy, whereas our period of preparation and training has as its end the creation of a republic. This constitutes a colossal difference between them." [104] He advocated democracy for China on the ground that it was an ideal cherished by the ancient sages, a general trend of the modern world, and the only remedy for China's ancient civil strife.[105] He looked upon the people as the sovereign of the state, and government officials as their chauffeurs, guards, cooks, physicians, carpenters, or tailors.[106] Critical of the imperfections of the representative system of government, Sun suggested a form of direct democracy which combined both Western and Chinese methods. According to his device of separating sovereignty *(ch'üan)* and ability *(neng)*, the people should have four rights of suffrage, initiative, referendum, and recall to control the government directly; and the government should be equipped to function efficiently with five powers, namely, legislative, judicial, executive, examination, and control.[107] "Such a government," stated Sun, "will be the most complete and the finest in the world, and a state with such a government will indeed be of the people, by the people, and for the people." [108] Admittedly, one may criticize Sun's ideas as being utopian and sometimes contradictory, but no one can question his sincerity in attempting to build up a political system based on popular sovereignty.

The Chinese Communists, on the other hand, have as their final objective the realization of Communism in China. They often speak of democracy, but they interpret the word quite differently from its generally accepted meaning. The People's Republic they have established in China is described by the 1954 Constitution as "a people's democratic state led by the working class and based on the alliance of workers and peasants." [109] The government they have instituted is a hierarchy of "people's congresses" based on the principle of "democratic centralism." [110] The political basis of the New China is still the People's Democratic Dictatorship, which, as prescribed by Mao Tse-tung in 1949, is a dictatorship exercised by the "people"—the proletariat, the peasantry, the petty bourgeoisie, and the national bourgeoisie—over the "reactionaries"—the landlords, the bureaucratic capitalists, and the lackeys of imperialism.[111] Democracy for the people and dictatorship for the reactionaries constitute the People's Democratic Dictatorship, so says the dogma. However, in actuality there is little "democracy" but plenty of "centralism" and "dictatorship" in Communist China.[112] "Democratic centralism" really means the concentration of power at the top, and the People's Democratic Dictatorship really means the dictatorship of the Communist Party. The power to define the people and the reactionaries rests solely with the Party leadership, which controls the country through the combined methods of force and persuasion and grants to individuals some "democratic" rights, merely as a matter of convenience. The dictatorship is by no means benevolent, and the power of the state is clearly defined as an instrument of oppression.[113] Ideologically and institutionally, Chinese Communism is totalitarian. Whatever slogans it may use, it is inherently dedicated to promote, and to maintain, a dictatorship of the Communist Party in China. In terms of regimentation and control, Peking already matches Moscow in efficiency and thoroughness. Democracy as understood in the West and by Dr. Sun is indeed out of place in the New China. The following observation by an Indian journalist is very illustrative.

> The New Democracy is democracy only in name, and the coalition is only a façade. The people of China have no voice in the formation of policy. The mass is given the thrill of taking up the cry of the leader and thus participating in the execution of policy but the individual remains inchoate. He functions only as a model, as a cry-raiser. China is a totalitarian dictatorship in which the Communists are its temporal and spiritual rulers.[114]

Land reform

Our study would be incomplete if no comparison were made between Sun Yat-sen's Principles of People's Livelihood and Chinese Communism. In fact, such a comparison is imperative, in view of some ambiguous and seemingly contradictory statements Sun made regarding his Third Principle, and in view of the Chinese Communists' claim that they have truly implemented it. We have already discussed the fundamental difference between Sun's livelihood interpretation of history and Marx's materialist interpretation of history. We have also pointed out that although Sun, at times, identified the Principles of People's Livelihood with Communism, he either said this out of expediency or meant utopian Communism and not Marxism. In his first lecture on the *Min-sheng* Principle, he rejected completely all the Marxist dogmas of materialism, class struggle, and surplus value.[115] What needs to be done here is to compare the two concrete policies of Sun's Third Principle—equalization of land ownership and regulation of capital—with the land and general economic policies of the Chinese Communists, and to find out where these two ideologies agree and where they differ in their approaches to China's economic and social problems.

Land reform undoubtedly is the program that has played a most prominent role in the Chinese revolution, and that has received great attention from both Sun Yat-senism and Chinese Communism. The agrarian policy of Sun Yat-sen and that of the New Democracy resemble each other in advocating "redistribution of land," "land to the tillers," and the undertaking of public works by the state. Since the organization of the T'ung Meng Hui in 1905, Sun always included the policy of "equalization of land ownership" as a part of his platform. In a speech before the Peasant Movement Training School in 1924, he suggested that China should imitate Soviet Russia's policy of "land to the tillers" to achieve a just solution of the peasant question.[116] In his third lecture on the Principle of Livelihood, he said that the state, besides liberating the peasants, should teach them seven new methods to increase production: use of machinery, use of fertilizers, rotation of crops, eradication of pests, manufacturing, transportation, and prevention of natural disasters.[117] The Manifesto of the First National Kuomintang Congress of 1924 gave a clear expression of Sun's land policy by enumerating certain measures designed to promote the interests of the peasants:

> China is an agricultural country, and of all the classes of people, the peasantry is the class that has suffered most. The Kuomintang's policy is that the state will provide land for cultivation to those landless peasants who have fallen into the status of tenants. The state will also provide irrigation systems and devise colonization schemes to increase the use of more land. For those peasants who have to borrow money at high rates of interest and are in debt for life, the state will establish farmers' banks to facilitate rural credits.[118]

In spite of policy shifts from time to time, the Chinese Communists, before their coming to power, consistently employed Sun's slogans for agrarian reform to win the support of the peasants. In the early years of the war against Japan, they limited their land policy to the implementation of the Kuomin-tang's law of rent and interest reduction. In "On New Democracy," written in 1940, Mao Tse-tung announced an agrarian program basically following Sun's idea:

> The [New Democratic] republic will adopt such necessary measures to confiscate the land of landlords and distribute it to those peasants having no land or only a little land, carry out Dr. Sun Yat-sen's slogan of "land to the tillers," abolish the feudal relations in the rural areas, and turn the land into the private property of the peasants. In the rural areas, rich peasant economic activities will be tolerated. This is the line of "equalization of land ownership." The correct slogan for this line is "land to the tillers." [119]

After the establishment of the People's Republic of China, the Chinese Communists vigorously enforced the policy of "land redistribution." The Agrarian Reform Law of 1950 declared, as its general principles, the abolition of the feudal land ownership system and the establishment of the system of peasant land ownership.[120] Throughout the land reform period (1950-1953) Peking's favorite slogan was "land to the tillers." Furthermore, the Chinese Communists, like Dr. Sun, have frequently advocated various measures to improve the quantity and the quality of agricultural production. They have paid special attention to such projects as irrigation and reclamation works, modernization of rural transport, preventive measures against natural calamities, new agricultural techniques, and promotion of subsidiary industries.[121]

We have noted certain similarities between Sun Yat-senism and Chinese Communism in their emphasis of land reform and advocacy of equal distribution of land ownership. But there are some fundamental differences in their land policies that deserve further study. For instance, Sun's land policy was reformist in nature, while the Chinese Communist program is inherently revolutionary; Sun's motivation was primarily economic, while the Chinese Communists have more political motives; Sun had "land to the tillers" as his final objective, while the Chinese Communists have collectivization and communization of agriculture as their ultimate goal. Thus, there are basic differences both in aims and in methods of implementation.

One of the major purposes of Sun's agrarian reform was to relieve the peasants of suffering, promote their interests, and provide them with an incentive to increase food production. In his opinion, although China had no big landlords, the majority of the peasants were exploited by small landlords and could barely keep themselves alive. In order to correct this unjust situation and to increase food production, he said that "we must make laws regarding the rights and interests of the farmers; we must give them encouragement and protection and allow them to keep more of the fruit of their land." [122] The Manifesto of the First National Kuomintang Congress made it clear that the main aim of Sun's land policy was to enable the peasants to enjoy the true happiness of life.[123]

So far as the Chinese Communists are concerned, their land reform was also intended to liberate the peasants and to increase agricultural production, but the emphasis was more on the building up of the national economy than on the improvement of individual farmers' livelihood. According to Liu Shao-chi, the basic aim of agrarian reform stemmed from the demands of production and was not designed purely to relieve poor peasants.[124] To be more specific, the primary purpose of the reform, as provided by the Agrarian Reform Law, was "to set free the rural productive forces, develop agricultural production, and thus pave the way for New China's industrialization." [125] In accordance with this announced purpose, the Chinese Communists had combined land distribution with intensive campaigning for increased production, and had urged the peasants to redouble their efforts to help build the national economy. Since the completion of land reform in 1953, they have taken a series of steps—planned purchase and supply of grain, and collectivization—to press the peasants to produce more in support of the industrialization plan. "To the Communists," comments one qualified observer, "the agrarian reform must be considered a failure if, after the redistribution of land, the peasants settle down to seek a better livelihood and forget their obligations to the state program of production and the manifold tasks of the proletarian revolution." [126]

In proposing land reform, Dr. Sun, too, had the purpose of winning the support of the peasants. He appreciated their numerical strength and naturally wanted their help in promoting the revolution. In a speech before the Peasant Movement Training School in 1924, he warned that if the peasants, being the great majority of the Chinese people, failed to participate in the revolution, then the revolution would be without a foundation and would have no chance of real success. He therefore called attention to the importance of awakening the peasants, organizing them, and securing their cooperation with the government.[127] In line with his policy, the Manifesto of the First National Congress of the Kuomintang contained a special appeal to the peasants.[128]

Compared to Dr. Sun, the Chinese Communists unquestionably had a more prominent political motive underlying their land reform. They knew the great potentialities of the peasantry as a political force and used agrarian reform accordingly as an effective instrument to win its support. Mao Tse-tung has described the peasantry as "the natural and most reliable ally of the proletariat and the main force of the Chinese revolution." [129] "Whoever wins the support of the peasants," he once declared, "will win China; whoever solves the land question will win the peasants." [130] With evident political considerations, the Chinese Communists throughout the years have shifted their agrarian program back and forth between right and left in response to changing conditions.[131] Immediately after their victory on the mainland of China, political expedience called for a shift to the policy of preserving the rich peasant economy as a necessary step to secure the support of the rich peasants to boost farm production. This policy change was explained by Mao Tse-tung on June 6, 1950:

> . . . there should be a change in our policy toward the rich peasants, a change from the policy of requisitioning the surplus land and property of the rich peasants to one of preserving a rich peasant economy, in order to help the early restoration of production in the rural areas. This change is

also favorable for isolating the landlords and protecting the middle peasants and small "renters-out" of land.[132]

However, with its power consolidated and its program of "socialist transformation" begun, the Peking regime then moved quickly to eliminate the rich peasant economy, the principal obstacle to the socialization of agriculture. Liu Shao-chi said in 1954: "We consider that rich peasant economy is capitalist economy in the countryside; the rich peasants are the last remaining exploiting class in the countryside." [133] The Constitution of 1954 (Article 8) declared that the policy of the state toward a rich peasant economy was "to restrict and gradually eliminate it."

Another important aim of Sun's land program was to avert a violent type of social revolution by taking preventive measures against the emergence of great landlords.[134] According to Sun, China, while having small landowners, had yet no such big landowners as existed in Europe; but, in view of the changes brought about by the impact of the West, it would be wise for her to take certain steps to prevent the rise of big landowners before the land problem became too serious to solve.[135] The method he proposed was truly a peaceful and moderate one. The landowners would evaluate their land themselves, and the government would impose taxes accordingly; the government might purchase the land at the declared value; if the land were to go up in value, the unearned increment should go to the community.[136] This was what he called the method of equalization of land ownership—"a Communism of the future, not of the present." It did not involve confiscation or nationalization of land. In fact, the landlords had nothing to fear, as Sun assured them that "those who have had property in the past will not suffer at all by it." [137] His intention to pursue land reform gradually and to avoid harsh measures against the landowning class was further expressed in his famous "land to the tillers" speech in 1924. Although he suggested in the speech that China should follow Russia's example of letting the cultivators own the land, he ruled out the Russian radical method of confiscation, on the ground that he did not want to provoke the small landowners in China to revolt. Instead, he favored peaceful means of organizing the peasants and taxing the landowners; he would confiscate the latter's land only when they failed to pay taxes.[138] All in all, in land reform he sought class cooperation rather than class struggle, and his program was designed to "promote the interests of the peasants while making the landlords not suffer." [139]

The Chinese Communist land reform, on the other hand, had a prominent political objective of promoting the social revolution by waging a class war against the landlords and other "feudalistic" and "capitalist" elements in the countryside. According to Liu Shao-chi, agrarian reform "is a systematic and fierce struggle." [140] In this struggle, the landlords, as a class, were the target for liquidation in the early years of the Peking regime. The Agrarian Reform Law of July 1950 provided for the confiscation of the landlords' land and of other means of production, to be distributed among the poor peasants.[141] In carrying out the agrarian reform, the first task the Communists undertook was to differentiate the class status of the various elements in the rural population in conformity with the decisions adopted by the Government Administration Council in August 1950.[142] From the Communist point of view, the determination of class status was a necessary step to arouse class consciousness and to sharpen class antagonism in rural areas, so that the peasants could be whipped up to engage in a fierce struggle against the landlords. The struggle took many forms, among which were "accusation" meetings, "speak bitterness" meetings, and public trials of the "despots." All people, including the "bourgeois" intellectuals, were urged to take active part in these various forms of struggle, as an important training for waging the class war. After the struggle against the landlords had been successfully completed by the middle of 1953, a new class war against the rich peasants was waged in Communist China to push forward the movement of agricultural cooperation. Calling the latter struggle a struggle between socialism and capitalism, a resolution of the Central Committee of the Chinese Communist Party in 1955 stated that in this drive "not only will an acute struggle be waged

against the rich peasants and speculative merchants, but the
peasants themselves will be constantly educated in the struggle." [143] Judging from all this, agrarian reform in Communist
China, in contrast to Sun Yat-sen's moderate land program,
should be regarded as a violent warfare and a revolution, cal-
culated not only to liquidate the landlords, the rich peasants,
and other capitalist elements in the countryside but to shatter
the feudal traditions of China and to remold Chinese rural
society in accordance with Marxism-Leninism.[144]

Lastly, the land policies of Sun Yat-sen and the Chinese
Communists are different in their ultimate objectives. In his
agrarian reform program, Sun accepted the system of private
ownership of land, with nationalization to be applied only to
the unearned increment of land values. His final aim was to
enable the cultivators to own the land by way of land redistribution. "When the *Min-sheng* Principle is fully realized and the
problems of the farmer are all solved, each tiller of the soil will
possess his own fields—that is to be the final fruits of our efforts." [145]

The Chinese Communist land program, however, goes far
beyond this. Its goal has always been the collectivization of
agriculture in a socialist economy. In order to achieve this goal,
three stages were originally devised: (1) the initial step of
agrarian reform (redistribution of land); (2) the transitional
stage of organizing mutual-aid teams and "semisocialist" producers' cooperatives; (3) the final stage of forming "socialist"
producers' cooperatives or collective farms. As early as December 1951, the Central Committee of the Chinese Communist
Party decided to guide the peasants, step by step, along the
road of socialism, by means of mutual aid teams and cooperatives. After the successful completion of land reform in 1953,
the Central Committee further passed a resolution late that
year on the development of agricultural producers' cooperatives:

> . . . the isolated, scattered, conservative, and backward
> individual economy limits the development of the produc-
> tive forces of agriculture, and an ever greater contradiction

between individual economy and socialist industrialization is making itself felt. It has become more and more evident that the small-scale agricultural production cannot satisfy the demand of the broad peasantry to improve their living conditions, nor can it meet the increasing need of the entire national economy. To further raise the productive forces of agriculture, the most fundamental task of the Party in its rural work would be to educate the peasants through measures most acceptable and understandable to them and stimulate them to gradually get organized and carry out the socialist reform of agriculture. . . . According to the nation's experiences, the concrete way for the gradual organization of China's peasants is to organize them through temporary mutual-aid teams which operate a simple form of collective labor, and year-round mutual-aid teams which have certain division of labor among their members on the basis of collective labor and with a small amount of property owned in common; then through agricultural cooperatives in which the members pool their land as shares and there is unified management and more property owned in common; and finally to agricultural cooperatives of a higher form (or collective farms) with collective peasant ownership which is entirely socialist in character. This is the path laid down by the Party for the gradual, step-by-step socialist transformation of agriculture.[146]

Despite peasant discontent and resistance Mao Tse-tung decided in July 1955 to accelerate the process of collectivization. He set a target date of 1957 for completion of the process and emphasized the inseparability of "socialist industrialization and the socialist transformation of agriculture." [147] Following his decision, a vigorous campaign was carried out in Communist China to extend agricultural cooperatives. The results were such that the entire program was drastically foreshortened. By 1957, all the 120 million peasant households of China had been changed from individual economy to collective economy.[148] In the summer of 1958, Peking moved one step further by ordering an all-out drive for communization of the entire rural population, with the announced purpose of increasing production and developing industry and resources. Since then, all the collectives in the country have been reorganized into some 26,000 large-scale people's communes.[149] Thus, in a short span of time the Chinese Communists, once called "agrarian reformers," have now successfully eliminated the system of private ownership of land and made all the peasants laborers for the state. Under the commune system, all means of production and all labor belong to the commune; every commune member receives a fixed wage; family and individual household living virtually disappears. The commune system in China is indeed the most radical communization step taken by any country in the Communist bloc. The tightness and intensity with which it is regimenting the Chinese people has no modern precedent and has even stunned East European Communists.[150]

Economic policy

From a comparison of the land policies of Sun Yat-senism and Chinese Communism we may proceed to compare the general economic policies of these two ideologies. To begin with, it must be pointed out that there are certain resemblances between the policy of "regulation of capital" in Sun's *Min-sheng* Principle and the moderate economic program in Mao Tse-tung's New Democracy, as they both seem to favor the coexistence of public and private enterprises, the restriction of private capital, the expansion of the state's economic activities, and the planned industrialization of the country.

In Sun's program, a mixed economy of state capitalism, private enterprise, and cooperatives was proposed. Private capital was allowed to operate, but it must be controlled so that it would not become so powerful as to dominate the economic life of the people and cause social unrest. The method of control took the forms of levying heavy income and inheritance taxes on individuals and of developing state capital through public ownership of principal industries.[151] Sun divided the spheres of state action and private initiative in economic activities along the following lines: "All matters that can be and are better carried out by private enterprise should be left to private hands which should be encouraged and fully protected by liberal laws. . . . All matters that cannot be taken up by private concerns and those that possess monopolistic character should be taken up as national undertakings." [152] Included in the latter category were banks, railways, steamship lines, natural resources, and the like.[153] Special emphasis was laid upon the development of the state enterprises of communications, mining, and manufacturing as an important means to increase the national wealth and to promote the welfare of the people. According to Sun:

> If these three great industries—communications, mining, and manufacturing—should all begin to thrive in China, our annual income from them would be very great. If the industries are carried on by the state, the rights and privileges which they bring will be enjoyed by all the people. The people of the whole nation will then have a share in the profits of capital and will not be injured by capital, as in foreign countries, where large capital is in private hands.[154]

It was his firm belief that the state had the duty to guarantee and improve popular livelihood, and in the *Min-sheng* Principle he committed his government to perform a number of functions for the masses—functions such as supplying food, clothing, shelter, and means of travel,[155] organizing cooperative societies,[156] establishing factory and labor legislation, and providing education, old-age pensions, unemployment relief, public hospitals, etc.[157]

Similar to Dr. Sun's program of "regulation of capital," the Chinese Communist economic policy in the transitional stage of the New Democracy also called for the maintenance of a mixed economy, with the state controlling private enterprise and leading the way to the advancement of the people's material welfare. In 1940, Mao Tse-tung described this policy as follows:

> Big banks and big industrial and commercial enterprises shall be owned by this [new-democratic] republic. "Enterprises, whether Chinese-owned or foreign-owned, which are monopolistic in character or which are on too large a scale for private management, such as banks, railways, and air

lines, shall be operated by the state so that private capital
cannot dominate the livelihood of the people: This is the
main principle of the control of capital." This was also a
solemn statement contained in the Manifesto of the First
National Congress of the Kuomintang during the period of
the Kuomintang-Communist cooperation; this is the correct
objective for the economic structure of the new-democratic
republic.[158]

Meanwhile, in his opinion, the state should not confiscate other
forms of private property nor forbid the development of capitalist production that "cannot dominate the livelihood of the
people," because Chinese economy was still very backward and
needed to utilize anything contributing to its development.[159]
In his work "On Coalition Government" in 1945, Mao further
asserted: "The task of our New Democratic system is . . . to
promote the free development of private capitalist economy
that benefits and does not control the people's livelihood, and
to protect all proper private property." [160] In line with this
policy, the Common Program of 1949 (Article 30) provided
that the People's Government should encourage the operating
of all private enterprises beneficial to the national welfare and
people's livelihood. At the same time, the prominent role assigned to the state in the New Democratic economy was well
reflected in the recognition of state-owned enterprise as the
leading force and in the long list of the government's economic
ministries that covered trade, food, heavy industry, light industry, and ten other fields.

While the economic policies of both Sun Yat-sen and the
Chinese Communists have been shown to resemble each other
in their advocacy of the expansion of the state's economic role
and the control of private capital, they differ more significantly
in their ultimate objectives, methods of implementation, and
attitudes toward private business. In proposing his economic
program, Sun definitely aimed at some form of socialism but
not in the Marxian sense of the word. As he emphasized in
San Min Chu I, the "Communism" the *Min-sheng* Principle
was trying to achieve was "a Communism of the future, not of
the present," "a very different thing from what is called in the

West 'nationalization of property,' confiscation for the government's use of private property which the people already possess." [161] In other words, his final goal was the attainment of a limited collectivism which would involve the common ownership of all the principal agencies of production and, at the same time, protect individuals' rights to own property. The methods he proposed to implement his policy were essentially peaceful ones, such as social and industrial legislation, nationalization of transportation and communications, direct taxation, and cooperative societies.[162] No outright confiscation of property nor class warfare was contemplated. According to him, in China, where there was no especially rich class but a general poverty, class war and the dictatorship of the proletariat were unnecessary.[163] On the subject of class war, he once wrote:

> Class war is a struggle between labor and capital. This war is at present raging at its full height in all the highly developed industrial countries. . . . China, however, owing to backwardness of her industrial development, which is a blessing in disguise, in this respect, has not yet entered into the class war. Our laboring class, commonly known as coolies, are living from hand to mouth and will therefore be only too glad to welcome even any capitalist who would put [up] a sweat shop to exploit them.[164]

As to the solution to China's economic problem, Dr. Sun emphasized the increase of production rather than the distribution of wealth. Although he wanted China to avoid the evils of Western capitalism through preventive measures against the rise of great capitalists, he had no fixed prejudice toward private business *per se* and never advocated its elimination. Interviewed by John Brailsford in 1922, he stated: "While there are many enterprises that can be undertaken by the state with advantage, others can only be managed effectively under competition." [165] In a Labor Day speech in 1924, he also declared that the Chinese workers were oppressed not by the Chinese capitalists but by foreign imperialism, and that their problem would not be solved through the destruction of the Chinese capitalists.[166]

Chinese Communist economic policy, on the other hand, has as its final goal the attainment of socialism and Communism in a strict Marxian sense. As mentioned before, Mao Tse-tung has divided the Chinese revolution into the stage of the New Democratic Revolution and the stage of the Socialist Revolution.

> The nature of these two revolutionary processes are different, and unless we complete the first revolutionary stage we cannot complete the second revolutionary stage. The Democratic Revolution is the necessary preparation for the Socialist Revolution, and the Socialist Revolution is the necessary tendency of the Democratic Revolution. The ultimate aim of all Communists is to strive for the accomplishment of a socialist and Communist society.[167]

In the first years (1949-1952) of the Chinese People's Republic, when the New Democratic phase of the revolution was still in the process of completion, the Peking regime needed the capital and managerial skills of the bourgeois class and showed some toleration for the continued operation of private enterprise. However, its basic prejudice against the bourgeoisie has never been concealed. In 1949, Mao Tse-tung welcomed the national bourgeoisie as an ally but warned that "the national bourgeoisie cannot serve as a leader of the revolution and should not occupy a major position in the state administration. This is because the social and economic status of the national bourgeoisie has determined its weak character, its lack of foresight and of sufficient courage. In addition, quite a few members of this class fear the masses." [168]

In 1952, the Communists struck a severe blow at the business and commercial interests with the "Three-anti" and "Five-anti" campaigns.[169] Marked by drastic measures, both campaigns were openly labeled as a fierce class war against the "rotten" bourgeoisie. They succeeded in breaking the economic backbone of the business class and created favorable conditions for the socialist transformation of private industry and commerce. The program of socialization undertaken by Peking has consisted of two major stages: state capitalism (joint state-private enterprise) and socialism (state-owned enterprise). The drive to implement this program gained momentum in 1953 with the launching of the Five-Year Plan and was further intensified in the latter part of 1955. By the end of 1956, the socialist transformation of private business in China was virtually completed. According to Chou En-lai, "The year 1956 saw the basic completion of the socialist transformation of private ownership of the means of production in our agriculture, handicrafts, and capitalist industry and commerce. . . . Some 70,000 private industrial enterprises have come under joint state-private management. Nearly two million big, small, and medium-sized commercial establishments have been turned into state-private stores, cooperative stores, and cooperative groups or straight into state stores. This is a great socialist revolution, changing the old system of private ownership of the means of production which has lasted several thousand years into a system of public ownership." [170]

Economically speaking, private businessmen no longer exist today in the People's Republic of China. Ideologically, however, Peking still sees the existence of some contradictions between the proletariat and the bourgeoisie, between the socialist way and the capitalist way. The rectification campaign has been officially designed to resolve such contradictions and to wage a relentless struggle against the "reactionary ideas" of the "bourgeois rightists." [171]

Finally, it must be pointed out that both Sun Yat-senism and Chinese Communism put equal emphasis on the industrialization of China by state planning, but Mao's industrial program is patterned after Soviet practices, while Dr. Sun's was oriented toward the West for assistance. The latter's program, better known as "The International Development of China," was a colossal plan which called for the modernization of the Chinese economy with the aid of a vast international loan. Among other things, it provided for the development in China of a communications system, of commercial harbors, and of heavy and light industries.[172] In outlining this ambitious program, Sun asked the Western powers to supply China with capital and experts. It was his desire to make international capitalism create state socialism in China.[173] While Sun should be given credit for his farsightedness in expounding some ideas similar to those motivating the Point Four and other international assistance programs in the mid-twentieth century, the fact remains that his plan never had a chance to materialize because of the lack of response from the West and other unfavorable conditions.

The Chinese Communists, on the other hand, in their industrial program look to the Soviet Union for inspiration and help. Since 1953, they have launched their Five-Year Plans to transform China from an agricultural into an industrial nation on the model of Soviet Russia. The essence of these plans is to build heavy industry as a foundation for national power and to achieve the industrial revolution in record time. One Communist writer explains this policy in the following words:

> The keynote of socialistic industrialization is the development of heavy industry; this will provide a firm foundation for the industrialization of the country and the modernization of China's national defense. Only when China possesses her own heavy industry can she provide other branches of industry, communications, and transport, as well as agriculture, with the equipment needed for their development and reorganization.
>
> The capitalist countries began with development of light industry, and the process of industrialization in these cases took from fifty to one hundred years. The socialist industrialization of the Soviet Union, on the contrary, began with the creation of a heavy industry and was successfully achieved in about ten years. In carrying out the socialist industrialization of their country, the Chinese people will follow the example of the Soviet Union, and will certainly complete their task in a comparatively short space of time.[174]

For their industrial program the Chinese Communists have been aided by Moscow in terms of practical experience, plant equipment, and technical advice. They have shown every determination to accelerate the pace of industrialization through forced domestic saving and other sacrifices required of the Chinese people. According to their claims, the First Five-Year Plan was a great success, and China expects to "catch up with Britain" as a major industrial power by the end of the Fourth Five-Year Plan (1973).[175] There is no doubt that Peking's industrial program has been making progress and may succeed in transforming the economic structure of the country substantially within a short span of time, but this Soviet type of forced industrialization without the people's consent is certainly something quite different from the program advocated by Sun Yat-sen.

Chapter 7

Conclusion

More than a century has passed since China was forced to open her doors to the outside world. Internal weakness and external pressures brought about the collapse of the old order of affairs, and launched China upon a new and turbulent era. The revolution which overthrew the decadent Manchu dynasty, in which Dr. Sun Yat-sen played a decisive role, achieved its negative objectives, but it did not lead to the achievement of Dr. Sun's positive goals. Instead of being able to devote his last years to the creation of the kind of political, economic, and social order for which he had been working for half a century, Dr. Sun was forced to fight for the very survival of his Party and his ideas, under the most discouraging and adverse circumstances. At last, through the dangerous—but to his mind necessary—expedient of an alliance with the Soviet Union, the international Communist movement, and the fledgling Communist Party of China, he was able to give new strength to the Kuomintang, both as a party and as an instrument for furthering the revolution. And at the time of his death, he felt that he was strong enough either to work with or to control his dangerous allies and to compel the warlords who controlled the fainéant Chinese regime in Peking to agree to his terms either by negotiation or by the use of force. In the hurly-burly of political intrigue and unceasing struggle, he had little time to formulate his program for China into a systematic ideology or to lead his country out of the stage of military domination to that of political tutelage, with the end purpose of paving the way for true constitutional government, adapted to China's peculiar needs and circumstances.

With the decline of Confucianism in China in the twentieth century, the most powerful ideologies that have influenced the leaders and educated groups of modern China have been Sun Yat-senism and Communism. As has been noted again and again, Sun Yat-senism was not a coherent ideology, in that it was never given systematic and completely consistent formulation; and Communism, in its Chinese setting, arose under very special conditions and developed certain peculiar features which have led many hopeful observers to conclude that it has somehow become a different and less dangerous brand of Communism.

Of particular interest is the precise relationship of Sun Yat-senism and Communism, in its Chinese version or in its international aspects. This is a subject of great importance, for the two ideologies have flourished together and, in various ways, have influenced all of the leaders of modern China. The Chinese revolution of the twentieth century was engineered by followers of Sun Yat-sen, and, for a time, it seemed quite likely that the revolution would continue to be directed by Dr. Sun and his associates, along lines that he had charted; yet, after his untimely death in 1925, before he had been able to lay even the foundations for the China he was striving to create, his followers and co-workers split in many directions, and out of the civil conflict, external aggression, and divided purposes which marked the history of China for the next quarter of a century, something very different from a *San Min Chu I* republic emerged.

We have seen that in ideological terms the differences between Sun Yat-senism and Chinese Communism are far more significant than the similarities. Yet we have also seen that the two ideologies have often been linked, that Dr. Sun himself often identified his ideas with those of Communism (although he usually had in mind a pre-Marxian type of "Communism"), and that the Chinese Communists have made effective use of Dr. Sun's name. Moreover, Sun Yat-senism and Communism have coexisted in China for more than a generation, sometimes apparently in close relationship. The most diverse claims have been made by followers of Dr. Sun, and Sun's own rather enigmatic views on Communism and on the Chinese Communists have been a source of unending confusion. There can be no question that, even unwittingly, he gave "aid and comfort" to the Communists—thereby providing the Comintern with a favorable climate for its first great test of applying its strategy for identifying Communism with Asian nationalism and with anti-imperialism as a vehicle for gaining footholds in Asia, and giving the Chinese Communists an opportunity to make the same identification and to establish deeper roots in China by their association with the revolutionary movement and with its deeply respected leader. In a sense, therefore, Sun Yat-sen did China a great disservice by helping Communism to become entrenched in China and by making it respectable. He was, as has been noted, one of the first Asian leaders, perhaps the very first, to fall victim to the fallacy of the "united front." He was, in short, "soft" as far as Communism was concerned. Since his time, a long list of non-Communist Asian leaders, for reasons peculiar to their own mental conditioning and to the conditions with which they have had to deal, have also, consciously or unconsciously, given aid and comfort to the Communists.

In fairness to Dr. Sun, it should be pointed out that his collaboration with the Communists, Chinese or otherwise, was intended to serve his own purposes, and that he was well aware of the risks he was taking. To be sure, he was rather sympathetically disposed toward the Soviet Union. He was greatly impressed with the Russian revolution of 1917, and by the policies and professions of the Bolshevik leaders in the years immediately following. As a specialist in revolutions, trying to lead a revolutionary movement which had succeeded in its negative objective of overthrowing the Manchu dynasty but which seemed to be failing in its positive aims, he followed, with something akin to hypnotic fascination, the progress of a revolution which seemed to be motivated by many of the same aims and which, most important of all, seemed to be succeeding. Quite naturally, he felt that China could learn a great deal from the Bolshevik example. This feeling must have grown with the increasing deterioration of his own movement, and with his failure to obtain needed support, or even sympathetic understanding, from the Western powers or from Japan. Rebuffed, as he thought, by those countries which in his opinion should have given him aid and encouragement, and receiving flattering attention and definite offers from the Russians and the Comintern, it is hardly surprising that, in a time of desperation and dire need, he should form an alliance with those who were ready, for their own reasons, to offer him concrete assistance. For Dr. Sun, the alternative must have seemed to be the complete failure of his life's work, and the dangers of associating with such dubious allies must have seemed to be relatively slight. After all, Dr. Sun had confidence in his own destiny, if he could create the minimum conditions in which to operate; and he did not have those apprehensions regarding the consequences of collaboration with Communists which others have come to hold as a result of bitter experience.

The success of the Communists in China, however, can be attributed only in part to Dr. Sun's willingness to collaborate with them, and it by no means follows that if he had lived, the future course of China would have been as satisfactory from the Communist point of view. Given the desperate position in which Sun found himself in the early 1920's, the impression which the Russian revolution made upon him in its early phases, his "rejection" by the West, and the effective ex-

ploitation by the Soviet Union and the Comintern of the opportunity which the situation in China afforded to them, Dr. Sun's
willingness to enter into the much-discussed alliance may be
easily understood, even if its consequences may be regretted.

The nature of the Kuomintang-Soviet alliance, and especially its effects upon the subsequent development of Communism in China, should also be clearly understood. It was
significant in that it marked the entry of Soviet influence into
the Chinese revolution and paved the way for the future
development of the Chinese Communist Party. However, it
should not be equated with the present Peking-Moscow alliance. For one thing, Sun allied himself with Russia out of
political expediency rather than out of doctrinaire conviction.
For another, in contrast with Mao Tse-tung's policy of "leaning
to one side," the Russian alliance did not prevent Sun from
continuing the search for other outside assistance nor from
openly criticizing the Marxian dogmas. While the alliance had
tremendous effects on the organization and revolutionary
tactics of the Kuomintang, it had rather limited influence on
Sun's ideology. During Dr. Sun's lifetime, the hold of the alliance was quite strong, because there was a conspicuous absence
of other alternatives, and because it was to the mutual interest
of the Kuomintang and the Communists to keep this alliance.
It is conceivable that, with their ultimate objectives being
different, Canton and Moscow could have parted company
even before Sun's death, if the immediate and objective conditions for the alliance had changed. The same speculation,
nevertheless, cannot be safely applied to the present relations
between Soviet Russia and Communist China, for their ideological ties are so strong that, allowing for the existence of
some conflicts, the leaders of both countries would go all out
to accommodate their differences and to maintain a united
front against the hostile capitalist world.

From Dr. Sun's point of view, the Soviet alliance was "a
marriage of convenience," forced upon him by his own desperate circumstances and by the lack of any hopeful alternatives. One can only speculate on the extent to which the
policies and attitudes of Western states were responsible for

the experiment of the "united front." Among the great "might-have-beens" of modern Chinese history must be listed the question: Would the evolution of modern China have been fundamentally different if the Western powers had adopted a more helpful and sympathetic attitude toward Dr. Sun's revolutionary movement, and had given him concrete assistance in his time of greatest need? If we ever try to answer the hypothetical question of how the West "lost" China, probably we can find part of the answer in the China policy of the West in the 1910's and 1920's. It was in those years, so some would argue, that the West missed a golden opportunity to influence the direction of the Chinese revolution through cooperating with Sun Yat-sen. In his efforts to unify and build China anew, Sun sought whatever assistance he could get, to strengthen his party and to make possible the realization of his program. His personal background and democratic outlook pointed naturally to the West, particularly to the United States, as the source from which he expected to receive help. Even his favorable attitude toward Japan was largely based on the hope that she could serve as a useful model for other Asian nations in the process of Westernization. However, the response of the Western powers to Sun's overtures and expectations was a negative one. Some still treated the Chinese Republic as they had the Manchus, and refused to give up their imperialistic designs. Others, including the United States, insisted on supporting the "legitimate" government in Peking under a strong man like Yüan Shih-k'ai, or under his warlord successors. This type of unimaginative and shortsighted approach on the part of the Western powers did much to drive Sun into the Russian arms, and helped to open China to Communist penetration.

In the light of this bitter lesson, and in the face of the present Soviet competition for the good will of the people in underdeveloped areas, the West in general, and the United States in particular, would perhaps be well-advised to adopt a bold policy of helping and guiding revolutionary movements in these areas, instead of trying to preserve the *status quo* or to support outmoded and reactionary leaders. But the difficulties in carrying out such a policy are indeed monumental. It is hard for established democracies of the West to work with revolutionary movements in Asia. In the first place, in many instances this would involve the bypassing, or even the flaunting, of the regimes in power. If they are indigenous regimes, however unsavory they are, they have the advantage of being the recognized governments of the countries, or, if they are not recognized, they at least wield the effective instruments of power and control the channels of communication. If they are foreign-controlled regimes, the foreign powers in control are probably some of the Western states themselves. In the second place, it is often difficult, if not impossible, to identify real revolutionary movements, or to distinguish those that have real strength and promise for the future from those that rise and fall like the tides.

Again the case of Sun Yat-sen and the Kuomintang in its early days provides useful lessons. From the vantage point of a generation later, one might assume that there could be no doubt in the 1910's and 1920's that here was a real revolutionary movement which was seeking to create a free, united, and democratic China; that its leader was the outstanding Chinese of his time, indeed "the George Washington of modern China"; and that the movement had a real chance of success, if it were encouraged and assisted in the right way. The fact is, however, that this was not the opinion held by the policy-makers of the Western governments at this time. They took a dim view of Dr. Sun and his movement; they gave it little chance to succeed; they still officially recognized the regime in Peking, against which the Kuomintang was in revolt from the time of the split between Dr. Sun and Yüan Shih-k'ai.

If, therefore, in what, from the vantage point of time, might seem to be a clear example of a true revolutionary movement which held the future of China in its hands, the mirror into which Western statesmen looked seemed so unclear, how much more difficult must it be in the even more confused circumstances of most Asian areas to discover the revolutionary movements which should be aided. The close association of Asian nationalist movements with Communism, in some particularly vulnerable parts of Asia, creates further problems and dilemmas, although it may well be that sympathetic aid to indigenous nationalist efforts at the right time may forestall such links with the Communists.

It may be that to the extent that the West "lost" China, it did so as a result of its own misreading of the signs of the times and of the true course of events in that vast country; but it must be added that this was by no means wholly due to Western myopia or paralysis, for even to Chinese the signs were not clear, and no one could really foretell in which direction the country was moving. If the basic choices for China were determined in the 1910's and 1920's, few of those living at that time were aware of this fact, and the subsequent course of Chinese history is no clear proof of it.

Whatever Sun Yat-sen's personal limitations and whatever the imperfections of his program, his name has symbolized, in the minds of many people both inside and outside China, a popular revolution designed to enhance China's international status and to provide the Chinese people with a genuine democracy, a modernized economy, and a decent livelihood. The Chinese Communists have appreciated the magic of Sun's name and have successfully manipulated it to their advantage. Capitalizing on Sun's alliance with Moscow and on the vagueness of his writings and statements, they have managed to give a new interpretation to his doctrine, one which will fit into their own program in any given situation. As a rule, they have played up Sun's three major policies as outlined in the First National Congress of the Kuomintang. They also have made use of his slogans of "down with imperialism" and "land to the tiller" to support their policies. Posing as true followers of Dr. Sun, the Chinese Communists have stressed only what they call his revolutionary ideas and dismissed the "retrogressive" elements of his doctrine.

During the years of their rise to power, the Communists' claim of being Sun Yat-sen's true followers added much to the propaganda value of the New Democracy. Between 1937 and 1949, this claim had a great appeal to various segments of the Chinese population. Even today, the name of the founder of the Kuomintang still has a place in the Chinese People's Republic, although its value is diminishing in proportion to the growing prestige and strength of the new regime. On the other hand, as long as Formosa is to be "liberated," and as long as neutral nations in Asia are to be wooed, it is safe to predict that Peking will continue to use both Sun's name and those identified with him, such as his widow, as a convenient device to help create a democratic façade to lessen the general fear of Chinese Communism.

In the early years of their careers as Communists, before their ideological conditioning had been fully developed, and before they had gone through the long and tough struggle for survival and, later, for control of the machinery of the state, Mao Tse-tung, Chou En-lai, and other top leaders of the present People's Republic of China came under the influence of Sun Yat-sen, one of the greatest of the non-Communist revolutionaries of modern Asia. In a formative period of their own development, these Communist leaders learned a great deal from the successes and failures of Dr. Sun, and from the influence of his personality, his example, and his ideas. Later, they tried to use Sun's programs, or their interpretations of these programs, in competing with the Kuomintang under Chiang Kai-shek, who also claimed to be the rightful follower and heir of Dr. Sun. In many ways, therefore, Sun Yat-sen influenced the future leaders of New China, although his teachings did not deflect them from the very different ideological path which they chose to follow. Sun's example may have opened Mao's eyes to the possibilities of developing a more flexible program to suit the peculiar needs and circumstances of China. Certainly, Maoism has seemed to be more flexible than most other brands of Communism, although it may be that this flexibility was introduced largely for tactical reasons. As we have observed, since their coming to power, and with the consolidation of their control over the country, the Chinese Communists, still led by those who have followed more flexible policies in the past, have tended to act in a more doctrinaire and inflexible manner. In other words, they have tended to act like Communists the world over under roughly similar circumstances. However much they were influenced by Sun Yat-sen, they have, in general, used him for their own purposes rather than accepted his ideas and example in their inmost hearts.

It is also clear that Dr. Sun was favorably inclined toward Bolshevik Russia and many features of Communism, but that the points of similarity between his ideas and Communism can be explained largely under the heading of coincidence. While he often seemed to talk the language of the Communists, he was really talking about different things in a different way. The Russian example undoubtedly influenced him, and he was also intrigued with many aspects of Communist doctrine; but he consciously and emphatically rejected the basic premises on which Communism rests, whatever the garb it may assume in different places at different historical periods. Whether his letter to the Central Executive Committee of the CPSU in the last hours of his life was actually written or dictated by him, or whether it was concocted by the pro-Communist group which surrounded him on his deathbed, is really a matter of little consequence. The letter undoubtedly reflected, although perhaps too uncritically, his hope that China and the Soviet Union would maintain close relations for mutual benefit, and that they would march together along the path of political, economic, and social freedom, a path to which the Communists perpetually point as of their own creation, even while they are marching in a diametrically opposite direction. The worst charge that can be levied against Dr. Sun in this connection is that he was naïve about Communism, or was too hopeful regarding its future evolution. The same charge could be levied against many of the other non-Communist leaders of our time, who have been in a less desperate position than Dr. Sun and who have had the opportunity of studying the lessons of later experience with the Communists.

However much Sun Yat-sen was influenced by the Communists and by Communism, he never even came close to becoming a Communist himself. Indeed, he showed a remarkable understanding of the basic fallacies of the Communist creed, even while he felt it to be to his advantage to work closely with those who espoused it. There is little basis for believing that he changed his basic principles to any substantial degree as a result of this close association; and some commentators have insisted that, in the last months of his life, his repudiation of Communism went even further than is generally believed.

Both Sun Yat-senism and Communism aim at translating foreign ideologies into practical programs applicable to the conditions and requirements of China, but they differ fundamentally in their respective philosophic foundations. Throughout his revolutionary years, Sun Yat-sen tried to work out an organic synthesis of Western democracy and Confucian traditions. Illustrative of these efforts are his ideas of a Five-Power Constitution and of promoting Chinese nationalism by associating it with the family, the clans, and the ancient virtues of China. Unfortunately, Sun did not have sufficient time and assistance to digest all he wanted to absorb in order to produce a working synthesis, nor did he have the opportunity to experiment with his program and to perfect it accordingly. Still worse, after his death his program became stagnant because his followers either paid only lip service to it or considered it as an eternal truth above and beyond the realm of criticism and modification. Nevertheless, Sun's efforts undoubtedly have a great historical significance in that they represent the first serious attempt of an Asian statesman to adapt Western democratic concepts and practices to the special environment and traditions of his country. The pattern which he had in mind was by no means clear, even to himself, and it would have been too much of a mixed system—combining in uncertain proportions elements of a controlled democracy and state socialism—to please a Western devotee of political and economic liberalism. But, at the same time, it did point in the direction of greater political freedom, and it was based on a radically different premise from the totalitarianisms that have mushroomed so alarmingly in the twentieth century.

Chinese Communism, in contrast, is based on Marxism-Leninism and openly rejects Confucianism and other "feudal" traditions of old China. However, it has its roots in China, and, under Mao Tse-tung's leadership, it has designed special tactics to apply its doctrine to the Chinese situation. The expounding of Chinese nationalism, the concentration on the peasantry, and the offer of the New Democracy have all illustrated the adaptability of Chinese Communism in operation. There is no doubt that this ability to tailor Marxism-Leninism to the cloth of China has been a major reason for the success of the Chinese Communists. Since their victory over the Kuomintang in 1949, however, they have shown signs of losing their flexibility. Their doctrinaire approaches to foreign affairs, to industrial development, to agricultural collectivization, and to the bourgeois class indicate partly their new confidence and partly the inherent limitations on freedom of thought or of action in the Communist system.

What should be crystal clear, but nevertheless needs to be stated for the record in view of the deliberate efforts of the Chinese Communists to distort the picture, is that Communism is not the logical end result of the kind of revolution that Dr. Sun Yat-sen was championing for his country. Sun Yat-senism did not become fused into Communism, nor does the Communist victory in China represent the inevitable outcome of the revolution to which Dr. Sun devoted his life. The failure of the Nationalists to carry on the revolution and to adhere to the principles and programs outlined by the founder of the Party is not due to any deficiencies in Sun's efforts or teachings; rather, it is due to later developments which imposed too heavy a burden on the Nationalist regime and to the inner failures of that regime. If, as seemed quite probable in the 1930's and early 1940's, the Nationalists had been successful in consolidating and maintaining power in China, they could have claimed, with much more validity than they were able to do, that they were guiding the Chinese revolution along the path charted by Sun Yat-sen. But neither Nationalists nor Communists can fairly claim to be the sole heirs to Dr. Sun's mantle, and the legacy and the hopes which he bequeathed to his country far transcend any group or any individual leaders.

In this profound sense it is still true that the revolution which Dr. Sun Yat-sen envisioned for China is not yet complete; indeed, for the moment at least, it has been diverted into different channels, leading to the kind of China that is a gross perversion of Dr. Sun's hopes and dreams. There is obviously a great gulf between the ideas and principles of the man who has been called "the kindest of all the revolutionaries of mankind," who believed in the Confucian traditions of harmony, the golden mean, and the Ta Tung, and the leaders of the New China of today, who boast of their dedication to a doctrine which emphasizes the idea of class struggle rather than of harmony and which they regard as "a hammer which we use to destroy the enemy." Nothing could be more contrary to the essence and spirit of Sun Yat-senism than Communist China's new system of communes, a system of socio-economic organization which is destroying the Chinese family and regimenting the Chinese people with a severity and ruthlessness that appalls even many Communists in other lands.

Sun Yat-sen envisioned a very different future for his country. The China for which he worked and dreamed can hardly be created under the totalitarian rule of Communists, however deep their roots may be in the Chinese scene. Communism, and not Sun Yat-senism, may yet prove to be a passing phase, rather than the climax, of the Chinese revolution.

NOTES

Chapter 1: Introduction

1. An unusually penetrating treatment of this neglected subject is presented in Shen-Yu Dai, *Mao Tse-tung and Confucianism* (Unpublished doctoral dissertation, University of Pennsylvania, 1953).

2. "On New Democracy," Mao Tse-tung, *Selected Works* (New York: International Publisher, 1954), Vol. III, p. 155. There are several English translations of this famous essay, written by Mao in 1940. On the basis of checking with the original Chinese text, Mao Tse-tung, *Hsin min-chu chu-i lun* [*On the New Democracy*] (Yenan: Chieh-fang she, 1946), we prefer the English translation in *Selected Works*.

3. "On New Democracy," pp. 132-134.

4. *Ibid.*, p. 134.

5. Sun Yat-sen, "Autobiography," *Tsung-li ch'üan-shu* [*Complete Writings of President Sun*] (Taipeh: The China Culture Service, 1953), Vol. 5, pp. 128-129. English versions of Sun's autobiography are available in Sun Yat-sen, *Memoirs of a Chinese Revolutionary* (London: Hutchinson & Co., 1927), chapter VIII, and in Leonard Shihlien Hsü, *Sun Yat-sen: His Political and Social Ideals* (Los Angeles: University of Southern California Press, 1933), pp. 44-82

6. R. R. Palmer, *A History of the Modern World* (New York: Knopf, 1952), p. 772.

7. K. M. Panikkar, *Asia and Western Dominance* (New York: John Day, 1954), p. 364.

8. Carsun Chang, *The Third Force in China* (New York: Bookman Associates, 1952), p. 69.

9. S. Radhakrishnan, *India and China* (2nd ed., Bombay: Hind Kitabs, 1947), pp. 27, 29.

10. Wolfgang Friedmann, *An Introduction to World Politics* (London: Macmillan, 1951), p. 198.

11. M. N. Roy, *Revolution and Counterrevolution in China* (Calcutta: Renaissance Publishers, 1946), p. 336. For a similar view from a very different source, see Chang, *op. cit.*, p. 65.

12. Nathaniel Peffer, "One of Asia's Three Great Moderns," *Asia*, August 1924, pp. 591, 593.

Chapter 2: Sun Yat-sen and the West

1. Paul M. A. Linebarger, *The Political Doctrines of Sun Yat-sen* (Baltimore: Johns Hopkins Press, 1937), p. vi.

2. *Tsung-li ch'üan-shu* [*Complete writings of President Sun*] (Taipeh: The China Culture Service, 1953), Vol. 5, p. 90. The Three Dynasties refer to the Hsia, the Shang, and the Chou, which form the ancient period of China's history. The Two Hans stand for the Western Han Dynasty (206 B.C.-9 A.D.) and the Eastern Han Dynasty (25-220 A.D.). Tang was the founder of the Shang Dynasty (1766 B.C.), and Wu was the founder of the Chou Dynasty (1122 B.C.).

3. Professor Linebarger gives this point an excellent treatment in *op. cit.*

4. Chang Ch'i-yün, *Tang-shih kai-yao* [*Outline of the History of the Chinese Nationalist Party*] (Taipeh: Central Reform Committee, 1951), Vol. I, p. 11.

5. James Cantlie and C. Sheridan Jones, *Sun Yat-sen and the Awakening of China* (New York: Fleming H. Revell, 1912), pp. 202-203.

6. The text of the letter is in *Tsung-li ch'üan-shu* [*Complete Writings of President Sun*], Vol. 10, part I, pp. 1-26. An English excerpt is in Ssu-yü Teng and John K. Fairbank, *China's Response to the West* (Cambridge: Harvard University Press, 1954), pp. 224-225.

7. Chang Ch'i-yün, *op. cit.*, Vol. I, p. 20.

8. Stephen Chen and Robert Payne, *Sun Yat-sen: A Portrait* (New York: John Day, 1946), p. 48.

9. Sun Yat-sen, "Autobiography," *Tsung-li ch'üan-shu* [*Complete Writings of President Sun*], p. 99.

10. For the text of the Manifesto, see *Chung-shan ch'üan-shu* [*Complete Writings of Sun Yat-sen*] (Shanghai: Ming-li Bookstore, 1936), Vol. IV, pp. 1-3. An English translation is in Teng and Fairbank, *op. cit.*, pp. 227-229.

11. Sun Yat-sen, *Fundamentals of National Reconstruction* (Chungking: Chinese Ministry of Information, 1945), p. 92.

12. *Tsung-li ch'üan-shu* [*Complete Writings of President Sun*], Vol. 7, part I, pp. 28-29.

13. *Ibid.*, pp. 30-34.

14. Madame Sun Yat-sen once described her husband in the following words: "Dr. Sun came from the people. He came from the peasantry. His father was a farmer, and the people of his district were farmers. Dr. Sun was poor. . . . Many times Dr. Sun has told me, it was in these early days, as a poor son of a peasant family, that he became a revolutionary. He was determined that the lot of the Chinese peasant should not continue to be so wretched, that little boys in China should have shoes to wear and rice to eat. For this ideal he gave forty years of his life." Carsun Chang, *The Third Force in China* (New York: Bookman Associates, 1952), pp. 53-54.

15. For an excellent discussion of this subject, see Harold Schiffrin, "Sun Yat-sen's Early Land Policy," *The Journal of Asian Studies*, August 1957, pp. 549-564.

16. Chen and Payne, *op. cit.*, p. 23.

17. Sun Yat-sen, *Kidnapped in London* (Bristol: J. W. Arrowsmith, 1897), p. 55.

18. Lyon Sharman, *Sun Yat-sen: His Life and Its Meaning* (New York: John Day, 1934), p. 310.

19. *Ibid.*, p. 148.

20. *Ibid.*, p. 310.

21. Sun Yat-sen, *San Min Chu I*, trans. Frank W. Price, ed. L. T. Chen (Shanghai: The Commercial Press, 1928), pp. 176-177. The Chinese text of Sun's Three People's Principles is in *Tsung-li ch'üan-shu* [*Complete Writings of President Sun*], Vol. 1. Another English version is given in Paschal M. d'Elia, S. J., (ed.), *The Triple Demism of Sun Yat-sen* (Wuchang: Franciscan Press, 1931).

22. For his discussion of Darwin's theory, see Sun Yat-sen, *Memoirs of a Chinese Revolutionary*, (London: Hutchinson & Co., 1927), pp. 96-100.

23. Sun Yat-sen, *San Min Chu I*, pp. 379-407. For a more detailed discussion, see *infra*, chapter IV.

24. *Ibid.*, p. 383. For more discussion of Sun's relations with William, see *infra*, chapter IV.

25. Sun Yat-sen, *Memoirs of a Chinese Revolutionary*, pp. 36-37.

26. *Tsung-li ch'üan-shu* [*Complete Writings of President Sun*], Vol. 7, part I, pp. 213-214.

27. *The Public* (Chicago), April 12, 1912, p. 349.

28. See Tsui Shu-chin, "The Influence of the Canton-Moscow Entente upon Sun Yat-sen's Political Philosophy," *The Chinese Social and Political Science Review* (Peiping), April-October 1934, pp. 360-361, note 67, pp. 371-376; Linebarger, *op. cit.*, pp. 136-137; also Schiffrin, *op. cit.*

29. *Tsung-li ch'üan-shu* [*Complete Writings of President Sun*], Vol. 7, part I, pp. 143-144.

30. Sun Yat-sen, *San Min Chu I*, p. 269.

31. *Ibid.*, pp. 271-272.

32. *Ibid.*, p. 234.

33. *Ibid.*, p. 181.

34. Sun Yat-sen, *Fundamentals of National Reconstruction*, p. 21.

35. Sun Yat-sen, *San Min Chu I*, p. 214.

36. *Ibid.*, p. 293.

37. Sun Yat-sen, *Memoirs of a Chinese Revolutionary*, pp. 128-130.

38. *Ibid.*, pp. 135-136.

39. *Tsung-li ch'üan-shu* [*Complete Writings of President Sun*], Vol. 7, part I, pp. 141-142.

40. Sun Yat-sen, *Fundamentals of National Reconstruction*, p. 92.

41. Sun Yat-sen, "China's Next Step," *The Independent* (New York), July 13, 1912, p. 1315.

42. Sun Yat-sen, *San Min Chu I*, pp. 327-334.

43. See his speech on "Five-Power Constitution" in 1923, in Sun Yat-sen, *Fundamentals of National Reconstruction*, pp. 11-26; also his speech on "Adoption of the Five-Power Separation System to Remedy the Defects of

the Three-Power Government," in *Tsung-li ch'üan-shu* [*Complete Writings of President Sun*], Vol. 7, part I, pp. 354-356.

44. Sun Yat-sen, *San Min Chu I*, p. 278.

45. A proclamation issued in 1907, quoted in T'ang Leang-li, *The Inner History of the Chinese Revolution* (New York: E. P. Dutton & Co., 1930), p. 116.

46. *Chung-shan ch'üan-shu* [*Complete Writings of Sun Yat-sen*], Vol. III, p. 57.

47. See Sun Yat-sen, *Memoirs of a Chinese Revolutionary*, pp. 169, 174; *Tsung-li ch'üan-shu* [*Complete Writings of President Sun*], Vol. 7, part I, pp. 148-149, 249-250.

48. Sun Yat-sen, "Autobiography," p. 107.

49. *Ibid.*, pp. 109-111.

50. *Tsung-li ch'üan-shu* [*Complete Writings of President Sun*], Vol. 10, part I, p. 267.

51. Sun Yat-sen, "Autobiography," p. 122.

52. Tsui Shu-chin, *op. cit.*, pp. 140-141.

53. Sun Yat-sen, "Autobiograpry," pp. 127-128.

54. *Tsung-li ch'üan-shu* [*Complete Writings of President Sun*], Vol. 5, pp. 159-160.

55. *Ibid.*, Vol. 10, part I, pp. 617-620.

56. *Ibid.*, Vol. 10, part II, pp. 658-659.

57. *Ibid.*, Vol. 8, pp. 123-125.

58. *Ibid.*, Vol. 7, part I, p. 415.

59. Department of State, *Papers Relating to the Foreign Relations of the United States, 1921* (Washington: Government Printing Office, 1936), Vol. I, p. 336.

60. For a detailed discussion of Sun's relations with Japan, see Marius B. Jansen, *The Japanese and Sun Yat-sen* (Cambridge: Harvard University Press, 1954).

61. Sun Yat-sen, "Autobiography," p. 104.

62. *Ibid.*, p. 100.

63. *Ibid.*

64. Sun Yat-sen, *Memoirs of a Chinese Revolutionary*, p. 114.

65. Sun Yat-sen, *San Min Chu I*, pp. 15-16.

Chapter 3: The Background of Sun Yat-sen's Soviet Alliance

1. For instance, many Kuomintang leaders have tried to minimize the significance of this alliance and to blame Communist conspiracy for its eventual breakup. Chiang Kai-shek, in *China's Destiny* (New York: Macmillan Co., 1947), pp. 93-100, makes no mention whatsoever of the Soviet role in the reorganization of the Kuomintang in 1924. On the other hand, the Chinese Communists, supported by the Left Wing of the Kuomintang, claim that, as a result of Soviet contact, Sun's old Three People's Principles were transformed into new Three People's Principles based on the three policies of "alliance with Soviet Russia," "alliance with Chinese Communists," and "alliance with the workers and peasants." See Mao Tse-tung, "On New Democracy," *Selected Works* (New York: International Publishers, 1954), pp.

134-141; Ch'en Po-ta, *San-min chu-i kai-lun* [*Survey of the Three People's Principles*] (Chungking: Sheng-huo Bookstore, 1939); and Chao Yuan-ming (ed.), *Lun San-min chu-i* [*Concerning the Three People's Principles*] (Darien: Ta-chung Bookstore, 1946). Among the interesting works of individual scholars on the same subject are: Maurice William, *Sun Yat-sen Versus Communism* (Baltimore: Williams & Wilkins, 1932), in which an American scholar tries to prove that his book saved Sun from falling prey to Bolshevism; Tsui Shu-chin, "The Influence of the Canton-Moscow Entente upon Sun Yat-sen's Political Philosophy," *The Chinese Social and Political Science Review* (Peiping) April-October, 1934, in which a Chinese scholar maintains that the alliance, while having tremendous influence on Sun's tactics, had no influence at all on his social and economic ideas.

2. For his views expressed in 1912, see *Tsung-li ch'üan-chi* [*Complete Collected Works of President Sun*] ed. Hu Han-min (Shanghai: Min-chih Bookstore, 1930), Vol. II, pp. 8-12.

3. For the text of the constitution, see *ibid.*, Vol. IV, pp. 31-37.

4. *Ibid.*, Vol. II, pp. 164-172.

5. For the speeches he delivered in 1912 on "state capitalism" and "regulation of capital," see *ibid.*, pp. 98-122.

6. Sun Yat-sen, *The International Development of China* (New York: G. P. Putnam's Sons, 1922), pp. 11, 236-237.

7. *Tsung-li ch'üan-shu* [*Complete Writings of President Sun*] (Taipeh: The China Culture Service, 1953), Vol. 7, part I, p. 64.

8. Sun Yat-sen, "The Chinese Republic," *The Independent* (New York), September 19, 1912, p. 664.

9. Claude A. Buss, *The Far East* (New York: Macmillan, 1955), p. 150.

10. "History of the Chinese Revolution," Sun Yat-sen, *Fundamentals of National Reconstruction* (Chungking: Chinese Ministry of Information, 1945), p. 46.

11. According to a Kuomintang member's account, Sun found no support of his principle of the Three Stages from the prominent Party leaders with the exception of Wang Ching-wei. T'ang Leang-li, *The Inner History of the Chinese Revolution* (New York: E. P. Dutton & Co., 1930), pp. 92-93.

12. Sun Yat-sen, *Memoirs of a Chinese Revolutionary* (London: Hutchinson & Co., 1927), pp. 147-148.

13. Stephen Chen and Robert Payne, *Sun Yat-sen: A Portrait* (New York: John Day, 1946), p. 121. It has been said that Sun resigned from the presidency in 1912 mainly because the Party members "would not abide by their revolutionary oath and would not submit to the guidance of their leader." See Sun Yat-sen, *Memoirs of a Chinese Revolutionary*, pp. 123-124, and Tsou Lu, *Chung-kuo Kuo-min-tang shih lüeh* [*A Brief History of the Kuomintang*] (Chungking: The Commercial Press, 1945), p. 56.

14. For some detailed discussion of Sun's efforts to reorganize his Party, see T'ang leang-li, *op. cit.*, chapter IX; Tsou Lu, *op. cit.*, pp. 62-100.

15. At the First National Congress of the Kuomintang in 1924, Dr. Sun admitted that the infiltration of the counterrevolutionaries into the Party undid the accomplishments of the revolution. Because of its defective methods, he said, the Party unknowingly let the counterrevolutionaries join it to carry out the work of sabotage. *Chung-shan ch'üan-shu* [*Complete Writings of Sun Yat-sen*] (Shanghai: Ming-li Bookstore, 1936), Vol. III, p. 107. At

a reunion conference of the Kuomintang in 1923, Sun stated that "while there are many who are devoted to the Party work and really struggle for its principles, the majority look upon the joining of our Party as a short cut to high government position." *Ibid.,* p. 60.

16. Leonard Shihlier Hsü, *Sun Yat-sen: His Political and Social Ideals* (Los Angeles: University of Southern California Press, 1933), pp.14-16.

17. T. C. Woo, *The Kuomintang and the Future of the Chinese Revolution* (London: Allen & Unwin, 1928), pp. 35-37.

18. In October 1922, Sun sent Hsu Ch'ien and Wang Ching-wei to woo Generals Wu P'ei-fu and Chang Tso-lin respectively. Both made statements in the press to the effect that Sun welcomed the backing of strong men like Wu or Chang in his work to advance the interest of China (*Shen Pao,* October 19, 1922; *Ming Kuo Daily,* October 10, 1922). Yeh Hu-shêng, *Hsien-tai Chung-kuo ko-ming shih-hua* [*A History of the Modern Chinese Revolution*] (Peking: K'ai-ming Bookstore, 1951), p. 9.

19. Tsui Shu-chin, "The Influence of the Canton-Moscow Entente," pp. 110-112. A leading Kuomintang theoretician writes that, before 1911, Dr. Sun, although devoted to the anti-Manchu movement, never overlooked the oppression of foreign powers. Because it was impossible to make war simultaneously against the Manchus and foreign powers under the existing circumstances, he goes on to say, Sun decided to start first with the anti-Manchu movement. See T'ao Pai-ch'uan, *San-min chu-i yü Kung-ch'an chu-i* [*The Three People's Principles and Communism*] (Chungking: Pai-lu Publishing Co., 1946), p. 12.

20. Sun Yat-sen, *Memoirs of a Chinese Revolutionary,* p. 221. A Communist author criticizes Sun's decision to woo "the sympathies of the imperialists" as a great mistake. Instead, Sun should have returned home at once to "unify democratic forces and to lead the revolution." This mistake was made, according to the author, because Sun had had no direct struggle with imperialism and his illusions about it still persisted. Chou Chê, *Sun Chung-shan* [*Sun Yat-sen*] (Peking: San-lien Bookstore, 1950), pp. 31-32.

21. *Chung-shan ch'üan-shu* [*Complete Writings of Sun Yat-sen*], Vol. IV, p. 5.

22. *Tsung-li ch'üan-chi* [*Complete Collected Works of President Sun*], Vol. II, pp. 8-12.

23. *Ibid.,* pp. 24-26.

24. In his lecture on the Principle of Democracy, Sun said: "Europeans and Americans once thought that if they could attain to representative government, they would be absolutely satisfied. After our revolution in 1911, did we not attain to representative government? What benefits of democracy did the people really obtain? You all know that our representatives have all become mere 'swine'; if there is money to be had they will sell themselves, divide the booty, and covet more gain. They are despised by the whole nation. No nation which uses a representative system of government can avoid some of its abuses, but in China representative government has led to intolerable evils. . . . So the hope of foreigners that representative government will insure the stability and peace of the state is not to be trusted." Sun Yat-sen, *San Min Chu I,* trans. Frank W. Price, ed. L. T. Chen (Shanghai: The Commercial Press, 1928), pp. 277-278.

25. A Kuomintang member charges that "what the West wanted was not a

China strong enough to withstand foreign aggression, but a strong man in China dependent on their support." T'ang Leang-li, *op. cit.*, p. 116.

26. For Wilson's policy toward Yüan Shih-k'ai, see Tien-yi Li, *Woodrow Wilson's China Policy, 1913-1917* (New York: Twayne Publishers, 1952), chapter V.

27. *Ibid.*, p. 144.

28. Department of State, *Papers Relating to the Foreign Relations of the United States, 1921* (Washington: Government Printing Office, 1936), Vol. I, pp. 339-340.

29. *Ibid.*, 1913, pp. 128-129.

30. *Ibid.*, 1921, Vol. I, p. 325.

31. *Ibid.*, 1922, Vol. I, p. 724.

32. *Ibid.*, 1921, Vol. I, p. 324.

33. *The Teachings of Sun Yat-sen* (Compiled by N. Genulee) (London: The Sylvan Press, 1945), pp. 39-40.

34. *Ibid.*, p. 41.

35. *Ibid.*, p. 42.

36. Sun Wen (Sun Yat-sen), *Chung-kuo ts'un-wang wen-t'i* [*The Question of China's Survival*] (Shanghai: Min-chih Bookstore, 1928), pp. 111-112.

37. Sun Yat-sen, *The International Development of China*, p. 236.

38. *Ibid.*, p. 237. A former Comintern agent severely criticizes Sun's project as follows: "The implication of his scheme was to deliver the country, body and soul, to the tender mercies of international imperialism, which, for more than half a century, had plundered, pillaged and partitioned it. . . . By making that fantastic scheme, Sun Yat-sen once again demonstrated his inability to understand the nature of imperialism." M. N. Roy, *Revolution and Counterrevolution in China* (Calcutta: Renaissance Publishers, 1946), pp. 265-267.

39. See letters from American Minister to China Paul S. Reinsch, General Caviglia of Italy, and others. Sun Yat-sen, *The International Development of China*, pp. 251-265.

40. Professor Paul M. A. Linebarger, in a talk with one of the authors, maintains that Dr. Sun, although a poor administrator, was very creative and farsighted in many ways. According to Linebarger, not only did Sun's project of "The International Development of China" contain ideas some thirty years ahead of his time, but the Kuomintang founder was also the first man to organize a popular front to include the Communists.

41. A Kuomintang leader says: "The May Fourth movement proves that the resistance of foreign aggression and the downfall of Peking's traitorous government have become the unanimous demand of the Chinese people. At the same time it proves that the principle of Nationalism of our party has been accepted by the people." Tsou Lu, *op. cit.*, p. 111. The Chinese Communists regard the May Fourth movement as the turning point of the Chinese revolution. Mao Tse-tung says: "After the May 4 movement, although the Chinese national bourgeoisie continued to participate in the revolution, the political leaders of China's bourgeois-democratic revolution belonged no longer to the Chinese bourgeoisie, but to the Chinese proletariat. . . . The slogan 'Down with Imperialism,' together with the thoroughgoing program of the entire bourgeois-democratic revolution, was proposed by the Chinese Communist Party, and the agrarian revolution was carried

out by the Chinese Communist Party alone." "On New Democracy," p. 116.
42. *Tsung-li ch'üan-chi, [Complete Collected Works of President Sun]* Vol. II, pp. 25-26; Department of State, *op. cit.,* 1921, Vol. I, p. 337.
43. Wang Ching-wei, *China and the Nations* (New York: Frederick A. Stokes Co., 1927), pp. 108-109, quoted by Harold R. Isaacs, *The Tragedy of the Chinese Revolution* (Stanford: Stanford University Press, 1951), p. 60.
44. Quoted from a manifesto issued by Dr. Sun on June 29, 1923. *Tsung-li ch'üan-shu, [Complete Writings of President Sun],* Vol. 6, pp. 85-86; Department of State, *op. cit.,* 1923, Vol. I, p. 513.
45. For Sun's relations to the Twenty-One Demands of 1915, see Marius B. Jansen, *The Japanese and Sun Yat-sen* (Cambridge: Harvard University Press, 1954), chapter 8. Citing two documents attributed to Sun, Mr. Jansen shows that the Kuomintang leader offered more favorable terms than Yüan Shih-k'ai was willing to grant in return for Japanese support.
46. *Tsung-li ch'üan-shu [Complete Writings of President Sun],* Vol. 10, part I, pp. 543-546, 573-575.
47. *Ibid.,* part II, pp. 776-782, 853-854.
48. At a banquet in 1924, he told the members of the First National Congress of the Kuomintang: "Once I met several Russians at a library in England while I was doing some reading. After an exchange of conversation we knew that we were all revolutionary comrades. The Russians asked me, 'How long will it take the Chinese Revolution to succeed?' . . . I gave them a very conservative estimation by saying, 'About thirty years.' The Russians were surprised and remarked 'In such a big country as yours, do you only need thirty years to achieve a revolution?' Then I asked the Russian, 'How long does it take your revolution to succeed?' They answered, 'If we can succeed in one hundred years, we shall be satisfied. At present we are struggling. Although success only comes after one hundred years, we must struggle now. If we do not, we shall not succeed even in one hundred years. Because we want to succeed in one hundred years, therefore we must struggle hard now.' . . . After I heard what they said, I knew that their program was many times surer and their spirit many times greater than mine." Woo, *op. cit.,* p. 130. Whether Sun had met Lenin in Europe during their exile is a matter of conjecture. Hsü, *op. cit.,* p. 34, describes Dr. Sun as an intimate friend of Lenin but gives no explanation or evidence. Nevertheless, there is a reason to believe that Sun had met a number of important Russian leaders while in Europe. For instance, he is said to have seen Chicherin often in Paris. See Lyon Sharman, *Sun Yat-sen: His Life and Its Meaning* (New York: John Day, 1934), p. 234.
49. Tsou Lu, *Chung-kuo Kuo-min-tang shih-kao [Draft History of the Kuomintang]* (Chungking: The Commercial Press, 1944), p. 304.
50. Ho Hsiang-ning, "Some Recollections about Dr. Sun Yat-sen," *Wei-ta ti Sun Chung-shan [The Great Sun Yat-sen]* (Hong Kong: Hsin-ti Publishing Co., 1957), p. 39.
51. Quoted by a letter from Chicherin to Sun Yat-sen on August 1, 1918. See Jane Degras (ed.), *Soviet Documents on Foreign Policy, 1917-1924* (London: Oxford University Press, 1951), Vol. I, p. 92.
52. Sun Fo, *Sino-Soviet Relations,* p. 3, quoted in Ts'ao Hsi-chên, *Chung-su wai-chiao shih [Sino-Soviet Diplomatic History]* (Peking: Shih-chieh chih-shih she, 1951), p. 40.

53. The three stages are: (1) a period of military operation, (2) a period of political tutelage, and (3) a period of constitutional government. They can be best explained as: (1) the acquisition of political power by the teachers of the new ideology, (2) the teaching of the new ideology, and (3) the practice of government by people in accord with the new ideology. Paul M. A. Linebarger, *The Political Doctrines of Sun Yat-sen* (Baltimore: Johns Hopkins Press, 1937), p. 207. A detailed comparison between this theory of revolution and the Communists' theory of the dictatorship of the proletariat is found in Tsui Shu-chin, *op. cit.,* pp. 177-209.
54. For the text of the Manifesto, see *Chung-shan ch'üan-shu [Complete Writings of Sun Yat-sen],* Vol. IV, pp. 1-3.
55. *Tsung-li ch'üan-chi [Complete Collected Works of President Sun],* Vol. IV, p. 31.
56. Sun Yat-sen, *Memoirs of a Chinese Revolutionary,* p. 146.
57. *Ibid.,* p. 137.
58. According to Wang Ching-wei, Sun was pleased to know that his three stages of revolution were similar to those of the Bolsheviks, and the latter also showed deep respect for Sun when they found out this fact. Tsui Shu-chin, *op. cit.,* p. 185.
59. T'ang leang-li, *op. cit.,* pp. 171-172.
60. Tsou Lu, *Chung-kuo Kuo-min-tang shih-kao [Draft History of the Kuomintang],* p. 304.
61. *The Current Digest of Soviet Press,* December 9, 1950, p. 21. The Chinese text of this letter is in *Sun Chung-shan hsüan-chi [Selected Works of Sun Yat-sen]* (Peking: Jen-ming Publishing Co., 1956), Vol. I, pp. 434-436.
62. *Tsung-li ch'üan-shu [Complete Writings of President Sun],* Vol. 8, pp. 131-134.
63. Sharman, *op. cit.,* p. 246. Shortly after reading this news, Chiang Kai-shek came to Sun's defense with the comment: "After the World War, to resume diplomatic relations with Russia and Germany, and to try and find what could be done by way of mutual help, has been the endeavour of all the countries such as England, America, France, Italy, and Japan. How could we alone afford to be left in a state of isolation by not trying to resume good relationship with these two countries." S. L. Hsiung, *The Life of Chiang Kai-shek* (London: P. Davies, 1948), pp. 173-174.
64. There is a great difference between the first declaration and the second one regarding the Chinese Eastern Railway. The first offered to return it to China without compensation, whereas the second implied the joint control of the Railway. The reason for the change was that the Soviet regime was stronger in 1920 than in 1919. For the discussion of the declarations, see Aitchen K. Wu, *China and the Soviet Union* (New York: John Day, 1950), pp. 134-140. For a detailed examination of the evolution of early Soviet policy in China, see Allen S. Whiting, *Soviet Policies in China, 1917-1924* (New York: Columbia University Press, 1954).
65. Throughout China, newspapers and various civic, student, and labor organizations joined to hail the Soviet offer as "unprecedented" and "righteous" and to urge the establishment of close ties between China and the new Russia. For documents on the response of the Chinese public to the Soviet declarations, see Hu Hua (ed.), *Chung-kuo hsin min-chu chu-i ko-ming shih ts'an-k'ao tzu-liao [Reference Materials for the History of the Chinese New*

Democratic Revolution] (Shanghai: The Commercial Press, 1951), pp. 38-55.
A Chinese author thinks that Soviet Russia's diplomacy was quite skillful in
her new approach to China. She actually lost little, but gained the general
sympathy of the Chinese people and an eventual legal recognition of the
Peking government. Ch'eng Shang-wen, *Chung-Su Kuan-hsi chien-shih* [*A
Brief History of Sino-Soviet Relations*] (Hong Kong: Tsu-yu Publishing Co.,
1951), p. 17.

66. Lenin's thesis was best stated in his reports on "national and colonial
questions" in June and July 1920, before the Second Congress of the Communist International. See V. I. Lenin, *Selected Works* (New York: International Publishers, 1943), Vol. X, pp. 231-244. For an excellent, brief
summary of the historic debate on Lenin's thesis in the preparatory commission which met prior to the Second Congress of the Comintern and during
the session of the Congress, see Whiting, *op. cit.,* pp. 42-58. Detailed reports of the proceedings of the Second Comintern Congress are also available. See, for example, *The Second Congress of the Communist International,
Stenographic Report* (Moscow, 1920), and *The Second Congress of the
Communist International as Reported and Interpreted by the Official Newspapers of Soviet Russia* (Washington, 1920).

67. Lenin, *op. cit.,* Vol. X, p. 237.

68. *Ibid.,* p. 241.

69. Edgar Snow, *Red Star Over China* (New York: Modern Library, Random House, 1938), pp. 140-141; Benjamin Schwartz, *Chinese Communism
and the Rise of Mao* (Cambridge: Harvard University Press, 1951), pp. 31-
34; C. Martin Wilbur and Julie L. Y. How (eds.), *Documents on Communism, Nationalism, and Soviet Advisers in China, 1918-1927* (New York:
Columbia University Press, 1956), pp. 79-80.

70. See *Izvestia* (Moscow), October 9, 1920 for V. Vilensky's article, which
also expected a Russian orientation of General Wu; quoted by Leo Pasvolsky,
Russia in the Far East (New York: Macmillan Co., 1922), p. 87.

71. This article was written by Lenin to comment on Sun's article, "The
Social Significance of the Chinese Revolution." For the text of Lenin's
article, see Lenin, *op. cit.,* Vol. IV, pp. 305-311.

72. *Ibid.,* p. 313.

73. Degras, *op. cit.,* Vol. I, p. 92.

74. *The Current Digest of Soviet Press,* December 9, 1950, p. 20.

75. The identity of the Kuomintang delegate is still obscure. The Communist International, *The First Congress of the Toilers of the Far East* (Petrograd: 1922) lists him as Tao. Mr. Whiting, in *op. cit.,* seems to accept this
identification with some reservation. Ernestine Evans, "Looking East from
Moscow," *Asia,* December 1922, p. 976, identifies the Kuomintang representative as Kuo Min-tao. Unless it is proved to the contrary, the authors
are inclined to go along with the Evans article, because of its general ac-
curacy in translating Oriental names.

76. *The First Congress of the Toilers of the Far East,* pp. 23-30.

77. *Ibid.,* p. 182.

78. Robert C. North, *Moscow and Chinese Communists* (Stanford: Stanford
University Press, 1953), pp. 69-70.

79. Ts'ao hsi-chên, *op. cit.,* p. 41; Tsui Shu-chin, *Sun Chung-shan yü Kung-*

ch'an chu-i [*Sun Yat-sen and Communism*] (Hong Kong: The Asia Press, Ltd., 1954), p. 21.

80. Tsou Lu, *Chung-kuo Kuo-min-tang shih-kao* [*Draft History of the Kuomintang*], p. 304.

81. Hu Hua, *Chung-kuo hsin min-chu chu-i ko-ming shih* [*History of the Chinese New Democratic Revolution*] (Canton: Hsin-hua Bookstore, 1951), p. 46.

82. Whiting, *op. cit.*, pp. 87-88.

83. *Ibid.*, p. 89.

84. In *Revolution and Counterrevolution in China*, p. 266, M. N. Roy writes: "A critical interpretation of the history of the Chinese nationalist movement reveals the fact that Sun Yat-sen became a half-hearted revolutionary when a quarter of a century of failures forced him to turn to the masses and establish an alliance with the working class. Under the pressure of the revolutionary masses, he discarded, rather laid aside, some of his old reactionary ideas and made a praiseworthy effort to come out of the dreary wilderness of illusion in which he had wasted the best part of his life."

85. For the differences that existed among Soviet leaders concerning China, see Whiting, *op. cit.*, chapters VI and VII.

86. The same document praised the Kuomintang as a revolutionary party but demanded that it "renounce once and for all every policy of vacillation, compromise, and endless zigzags." For the text of the Manifesto, see Conrad Brandt, Benjamin Schwartz, and John K. Fairbank, *A Documentary History of Chinese Communism* (Cambridge: Harvard University Press, 1952), pp. 54-63.

87. *Ibid.*, pp. 64-65. The Chinese text is available in Hu Hua (ed.), *Chung-kuo hsin min-chu chu-i ko-ming shih ts'an-k'ao tzu-liao* [*Reference Materials for the History of the Chinese New Democratic Revolution*], pp. 69-84.

88. Wilbur and How, *op. cit.*, p. 84.

89. Ch'en Tu-hsiu, *Kao ch'üan-tang t'ung-chih shu* [*A Letter to All Comrades of the Party*] (Shanghai, 1929), p. 2.

90. *Ibid.*, pp. 2-3. For excellent treatment of this meeting and other sources, see Schwartz, *op. cit.*, pp. 40-44; Wilbur and How, *op. cit.*, pp. 83-84; and Isaacs, *op. cit.*, pp. 58-59.

91. David J. Dallin, *The Rise of Russia in Asia* (New Haven: Yale University Press, 1949), p. 210; Ch'en Tu-hsiu, *op. cit.*, p. 2.

92. Tsou Lu, *Chung-kuo Kuo-min-tang shih-kao* [*Draft History of the Kuomintang*], p. 304.

93. *Tsung-li ch'üan-shu* [*Complete Writings of President Sun*], Vol. 10, part II, pp. 924-925.

94. Ch'en Tu-hsiu, *op. cit.*, p. 2.

95. Schwartz, *op. cit.*, pp. 44-45; T'ang Leang-li, *op. cit.*, p. 156.

96. Sun wrote this letter to encourage Chiang Kai-shek to defend Foochow firmly against Ch'en Ch'iung-ming. For the text, see *Tsung-li ch'üan-shu* [*Complete Writings of President Sun*], Vol. 10, part II, pp. 1009-1012.

97. For a discussion of the various Soviet missions to Peking, see Whiting, *op. cit.*, chapters IX and X.

98. Chiang Kai-shek, *Soviet Russia in China* (New York: Farrar, Straus and Cudahy, 1957), p. 17; T'ang Leang-li, *op. cit.*, p. 156.

Chapter 4: Sun Yat-sen's Alliance with Soviet Russia

1. *The China Year Book, 1928* (Tientsin: The Tientsin Press, 1928), p. 1318.
2. *The New York Times,* January 28, 1923.
3. Liao, one of the leaders of the Kuomintang's Left Wing, was assassinated on August 20, 1925.
4. T'ang Leang-li, *op. cit.,* p. 158.
5. Typed copy of original file of Sun-Karakhan correspondence in the personal collection of Louis Fischer, quoted in Allen Whiting, *Soviet Policies in China, 1917-1924* (New York: Columbia University Press, 1954), p. 243.
6. For Chiang's account of his trip to Russia, see Chiang Kai-shek, *Soviet Russia in China* (New York: Farrar, Straus and Cudahy, 1957), pp. 19-25; Shih-i Hsiung, *The Life of Chiang Kai-shek* (London: P. Davies, 1948), pp. 175-179.
7. Wu and Sun were previously considered potential allies by Moscow. The feeling of bitterness after the incident was recorded by Pavel Mif: "The shooting down of the workers dispersed all illusions concerning Wu Pei-fu, whom hitherto a number of workers' organizations regarded as a 'friend of the workers' and as 'being in favor of working-class legislation.' It became clear to every worker that Wu Pei-fu was the servant of the foreign capitalist." *Heroic China* (New York: Workers' Library Publishers, 1937), p. 20.
8. See the extract from a telegram, dated November 12, 1926, sent by the Commissariat of Foreign Affairs at Moscow to the Soviet representative at Peking, as disclosed in a *White Paper* issued by the British Foreign Office on May 26, 1927, following the raid on Arcos House. *The China Year Book, 1928,* pp. 823-824.
9. This was the letter Karakhan wrote to Sun on September 23, 1923. For the text, see Whiting, *op. cit.,* p. 244.
10. Louis Fischer, *The Soviets in World Affairs* (London: Jonathan Cape, 1930), Vol. II, p. 635.
11. *Ibid.,* pp. 635-636.
12. T'ang Leang-li, *op. cit.,* p. 160.
13. *The China Year Book, 1928,* p. 1321.
14. *Tsung-li ch'üan-shu [Complete Writings of President Sun],* (Taipeh: The China Culture Service, 1953), Vol. 7, part II, p. 752.
15. Radek warned: "You must understand, comrades, that neither the question of socialism nor of the Soviet republic are now the order of the day. . . . The immediate task is: (1) To organize the young working class. (2) To regulate its relations with the revolutionary bourgeoisie elements in order to organize the struggle against the European and Asiatic imperialism." Benjamin Schwartz, *Chinese Communism and the Rise of Mao* (Cambridge: Harvard University Press, 1951), p. 37.
16. Mif, *op. cit.,* pp. 21-22.
17. For the full text of the manifesto, see Conrad Brandt, Benjamin Schwartz, and John K. Fairbank, *A Documentary History of Chinese Communism* (Cambridge: Harvard University Press, 1952), pp. 71-72. It should be noted that interesting criticism of the Kuomintang's past mistakes was

also voiced by the Manifesto, which demanded that "the Kuomintang will resolutely discard its two old notions of reliance on foreign powers and concentration on military action, and that it will pay attention to political propaganda among the people."

18. C. Martin Wilbur and Julie L. Y. How (eds.), *Documents on Communism, Nationalism, and Soviet Advisers in China* (New York: Columbia University Press, 1956), pp. 148-149.

19. T'ang Leang-li, *op. cit.,* p. 178.

20. Chiang Kai-shek, *op. cit.,* p. 27.

21. Of the twenty-four Committee members, three were Communists, including Li Ta-chao and T'an P'ing-shan. Of the seventeen Reserve CEC members, six were Communists, including Chang Kuo-t'ao, Ch'ü Ch'iu-pai, and Mao Tse-tung. Probably more important, T'an P'ing-shan became the head of the Department of Organization of the Kuomintang.

22. *Protokoll des IV Kongresses der Kommunistischen Internationalis* (Hamburg: [publisher unknown], 1923), p. 615, quoted in Robert C. North, *Moscow and Chinese Communists* (Stanford: Stanford University Press, 1953), p. 70,

23. After Sun's death, these Right Wing leaders formed, in 1925, the Western Hills Conference group for an immediate purge of the Communists.

24. *Min-kuo shih-wu-nien i-ch'ien chih Chiang Chieh-shih hsien-sheng* [*Chiang Kai-shek before 1926*] ([Place and publisher unknown], 1936?), Vol. 6, pp. 28-29.

25. See *Tan-ho Kung-ch'an-tang liang-ta yao-an* [*Two Important Cases of Impeachment of the Communist Party*] (Nanking: Edited and published by the Central Supervisory Committee of the Kuomintang, 1927), pp. 13-23.

26. *Chang P'u-ch'üan hsien-sheng ch'üan-chi* [*Complete Collected Works of Mr. Chang Chi*], [Place, publisher, and date unknown], pp. 159-161, as cited in Tsui Shu-chin, *Sun Chung-shan yü Kung-ch'an chi-i* [*Sun Yat-sen and Communism*] (Hong Kong: The Asia Press, Ltd., 1954), p. 30.

27. Chiang Kai-shek, *op. cit.,* pp. 24-25.

28. In a speech on November 25, 1923, Sun said that the ideology of the Russian Communist Party actually coincided with the Three People's Principles. *Tsung-li ch'üan-shu* [*Complete Writings of President Sun*], Vol. 7, part II, p. 751. On January 20, 1924, speaking before the First National Congress of the Kuomintang, he declared that "the Russian revolution was in actual fact a *San Min Chu I* revolution." Sun Yat-sen *Fundamentals of National Reconstruction* (Chungking: Chinese Ministry of Information, 1945), p. 76. In his second lecture on the Principle of People's Livelihood in 1924, Sun stated: "It [the *Min-sheng* Principle] is communism and it is socialism. So not only should we not say that communism conflicts with the *Min-sheng* Principle, but we even should claim communism as a good friend." Sun Yat-sen, *San Min Chu I,* trans. Frank W. Price, ed. L. T. Chen. (Shanghai: The Commercial Press, 1928), p. 428.

29. *Tan-ho Kung-ch'an-tang liang-ta yao-an* [*Two Important Cases of Impeachment of the Communist Party*], pp. 3-4.

30. T. C. Woo, *The Kuomintang and the Future of the Chinese Revolution* (London: Allen & Unwin, 1928), pp. 165-166.

31. See *Chung-shan ch'üan-shu* [*Complete Writings of Sun Yat-sen*] (Shang-hai: Ming-li Bookstore, 1936), Vol. III, pp. 104-112.

32. *Ibid.*, p. 112.

33. *Min-kuo shih-wu-nien i-ch'ien chih Chiang Chieh-shih hsien-sheng* [*Chiang Kai-shek before 1926*], Vol. 8, p. 8 (italics added). Apparently be-cause of Chiang's influence, Wang Ching-wei was eventually included on the Committee. Hu Han-min, while excluded, continued to hold a high position in the Kuomintang.

34. In his marginal comments on the letter of Teng Tse-ju and others, Sun said: "The draft [of the Kuomintang constitution, etc.] was prepared by Mr. Borodin at my request and approved by myself. It was originally in English and was translated into Chinese by Liao Chung-k'ai." *Tan-ho Kung-ch'an-tang liang-ta yao-an* [*Two Important Cases of Impeachment of the Communist Party*], p. 2.

35. For an English translation of the Constitution of the Kuomintang, as amended by the subsequent Congresses of the Kuomintang, see Arthur N. Holcombe, *The Chinese Revolution* (Cambridge: Harvard University Press, 1930), pp. 356-370.

36. Woo, *op. cit.*, pp. 39-40. Slightly changed in accordance with the Chi-nese text in *Tsung-li ch'üan-chi* [*Complete Collected Works of President Sun*], ed. Hu Han-min (Shanghai: Min-chih Bookstore, 1930), Vol. II, pp. 372-373.

37. One Kuomintang member praised Soviet aid by saying: "Thus the result of the failure of Dr. Sun to obtain English and American instructors for the Kuomintang army was a blessing in disguise. For in a war of liberation political consciousness, on which the Russian instructors, fresh from their experience against Denikin and Kolchak, laid the greatest emphasis, was obviously of more importance than trench mortars, machine guns, and the like, the things which Anglo-Saxons would undoubtedly have concentrated on." T'ang Leang-li, *The Foundations of Modern China* (London: N. Doug-las, 1928), p. 166.

38. See *Tsung-li ch'üan-shu* [*Complete Writings of President Sun*], Vol. 7, part II, pp. 637-643, 734-754, 815-844, 1072-1079.

39. *Ibid.*, p. 896.

40. *Min-kuo shih-wu-nien i-ch'ien chih Chiang Chieh-shih hsien-sheng* [*Chiang Kai-shek before 1926*], Vol. 8, p. 9.

41. Hu Han-min, one of the Right Wing Kuomintang leaders, admitted that the Chinese did not have the slogan "Down with Imperialism" in the 1911 revolution, and gave much credit to the Bolsheviks for their anti-imperialist lesson or inspiration to the Chinese. *Hu Han-ming's Speeches in Russia* (Canton: [publisher unknown], 1927), Vol. I, pp. 1-5, as cited in Tsui Shu-chin, "The Influence of the Canton-Moscow Entente upon Sun Yat-sen's Political Philosophy," *The Chinese Social and Political Science Review* (Peiping) April-October 1934, p. 118, n. 63.

42. For the text of the letter, see *Sun Chung-shan hsüan-chi* [*Selected Works of Sun Yat-sen*] (Peking: Jen-ming Publishing Co., 1956), Vol. II, pp. 467-471.

43. Sun made this hint in an interview with a foreign reporter. *Tsung-li ch'üan-chi* [*Complete Collected Works of President Sun*], Vol. II, p. 599.

44. *Tsung-li ch'üan-shu* [*Complete Writings of President Sun*], Vol. 6, pp. 212-213.

45. For his six lectures on the Principle of Nationalism, see Sun Yat-sen, *San Min Chu I,* pp. 3-148.
46. The following passage of Sun's lecture illustrates this theme of international class war: "Yesterday a Russian said to me: 'Why has Lenin been attacked by all the powers? Because he dared to say that the people of the world were divided into two classes—the twelve hundred fifty millions and the two hundred fifty millions; the twelve hundred fifty millions are being oppressed by the two hundred fifty millions, and the oppressors are moving not in harmony with but in defiance of Nature. Only when we resist Might are we moving with Nature.' If we want to resist Might, we must unite our four hundred millions and join the twelve hundred fifty millions of the world. We must espouse nationalism and in the first instance attain our own unity; then we can consider others and help the weaker, smaller peoples to unite in a common struggle against the two hundred fifty millions." *Ibid.,* p. 76.
47. For the texts of the two Manifestoes, see *Tsung-li ch'üan-shu [Complete Writings of President Sun],* Vol. 6, pp. 104-112, 282-287.
48. *Ibid.,* p. 95.
49. "Hands off China!" *International Press Correspondence* (Vienna), September 11, 1924, p. 697.
50. The term "three great policies" was first used in 1927 by the Wuhan group to defend their pro-Communist policy and to attack Chiang Kai-shek's "betrayal." The Chinese Communists have frequently made use of it in their interpretation of Sun Yat-sen's doctrine. See chapter 5.
51. *Tsung-li ch'üan-shu [Complete Writings of President Sun],* Vol. 6, p. 226.
52. Sun maintained that the Chinese workers were as yet not oppressed by Chinese capitalists but were oppressed by foreign capitalists. Their liberation, therefore, lay in the successful struggle against foreign imperialism. *Chung-shan ch'üan-shu [Complete Writings of Sun Yat-sen],* Vol. III, pp. 36-42.
53. *Ibid.,* pp. 60-63.
54. *The New York Times,* May 24, 1925; also *Chung-shan ch'üan-shu [Complete Writings of Sun Yat-sen],* Vol. IV, pp. 23-24. This message was drafted by Eugen Ch'en, a prominent figure of the Left Wing of the Kuomintang, and was signed by Dr. Sun on March 11. It should be noted that with Dr. Sun in Peking in 1925 were such Left Wing leaders as Wang Ching-wei, Madame Sun Yat-sen, Sun Fo, and Ho Hsiang-ning (Madame Liao Chung-k'ai), who must have exerted considerable influence on Dr. Sun's thinking. Wang Ching-wei, in particular, was most influential and had a hand in drawing up the will for Dr. Sun. However, several important Right Wing leaders of the Kuomintang, Tsou Lu, Wu Chih-hui, Tai Chi-t'ao and Shao Yung-ch'ung, were also with Dr. Sun in Peking and witnessed the signing of important documents by Sun in his last days. Consequently, there is no reason to doubt the authenticity of the famous will and the message to Soviet Russia, both of which, in the authors' opinion, reflected the true feelings of the dying President of the Kuomintang. For some detailed account of Sun's trip to the North and of his death, see "Huang Ch'ang-ku's Report," *Chung-shan ch'üan-shu [Complete Writings of Sun Yat-sen],* Vol. IV, Appendix, pp. 1-17 and T'ang Leang-li, *The Inner History of the Chinese Revolution,* pp. 190-197.

55. For an excellent and detailed study of the Bolsheviks' influence on Sun's political philosophy, see Tsui Shu-chin, "The Influence of the Canton-Moscow Entente," in which the author shows that Sun was little affected ideologically by his alliance with Moscow. In *Sun Yat-sen Versus Communism* (Baltimore: Williams & Wilkins, 1932), Dr. Maurice William claims that his book *The Social Interpretation of History* (New York: Lipshitz Press, 1920) was responsible for making Dr. Sun reverse his previous "pro-Marxian" and "pro-Bolshevist" position. According to William's theory, Dr. Sun endorsed Marxism in his lectures on the Principles of Nationalism and Democracy, but the Chinese leader apparently read *The Social Interpretation of History* immediately after, and consequently changed his mind by taking an anti-Marxian stand in his lectures on the Principle of Livelihood. This theory, however, is generally discounted by qualified observers, although no one denies that William's book was quite useful to Dr. Sun. For one thing, there is no evidence to show that at any time in his life had Sun become converted to Marxism. For another, Dr. Sun actually had read *The Social Interpretation of History* before his first lecture on the *San Min Chu I*, because his first public reference to William's book was made as early as January 21, 1924. See Tsui Shu-chin, "The Influence of the Canton-Moscow Entente," pp. 121-123, n. 72 and Paul M. A. Linebarger, *The Political Doctrines of Sun Yat-sen* (Baltimore: Johns Hopkins Press, 1937), pp. 142-145.

56. Sun Yat-sen, *San Min Chu I,* pp. 382-383.

57. *Ibid.,* p. 391.

58. *Ibid.,* pp. 391-392.

59. *Ibid.,* p. 393.

60. *Ibid.,* pp. 401-402.

61. *Tsung-li ch'üan-shu* [*Complete Writings of President Sun*], Vol. 8, pp. 162-163.

62. Sun Yat-sen, *San Min Chu I,* pp. 417-418.

63. *Ibid.,* pp. 440-441.

64. Dr. Tsui Shu-chin maintains that Sun identified the *Min-sheng* Principle with Communism out of political motivations. See Tsui Shu-chin, *Sun Chung-shan yü Kung-ch'an chu-i* [Sun Yat-sen and Communism], pp. 139-149.

65. Sun Yat-sen, *San Min Chu I,* p. xii.

66. *Ibid.,* p. 416.

67. *Ibid.,* p. 434.

68. *Ibid.,* p. 444. For an excellent discussion of the relations of Sun's *Min-sheng* Principle and Confucius' Great Commonwealth, see Tsui Shu-chi, "The Influence of the Canton-Moscow Entente," pp. 365-369.

69. See Allen S. Whiting, "A New Version of *San Min Chu I*," *The Far Eastern Quarterly* (May 1955), pp. 389-391. This significant manuscript is kept by the Kuomintang in Taipeh, Formosa. Based on the same notes of Huang Ch'ang-ku as the published version, it was written by P'eng Ch'eng and Lo Lei-sheng and was personally corrected and revised in many places by Dr. Sun himself. As the corrections are clearly in the brush of Sun, there is little doubt about the authenticity of the manuscript.

70. Sun Yat-sen, *San Min Chu I,* p. 364.

71. Whiting, "A New Version of *San Min Chu I*," p. 391.

72. Tsou Lu, *Chung-kuo Kuo-min-tang shih-kao* [*Draft History of the Kuomintang*] (Chungking: The Commercial Press, 1944), p. 391, n. 4.

73. For the text of this letter, see *Tsung-li ch'üan-shu* [*Complete Writings of President Sun*], Vol. 10, part II, pp. 1133-1135.

74. *Ibid.*, Vol. 9, pp. 576-577.

75. Sun Yat-sen, *San Min Chu I*, pp. 442-443.

76. For Sun's speeches and interviews in Japan in 1924, see *Tsung-li ch'üan-shu* [*Complete Writings of President Sun*], Vol. 7, pp. 1184-1250 and Vol. 8, pp. 158-181.

77. Sun Yat-sen, *San Min Chu I*, p. vii.

78. One of the best illustrations of the contemptuous attitude with which the Western nations treated Sun is the following incident. In January 1924, Sun sent a telegram of congratulations to the new Labour government in England, but not even an acknowledgment was received from London. T'ang Leang-li, *The Inner History of the Chinese Revolution*, p. 180.

79. For instance, the Manifesto of the First National Kuomintang Congress declared that the Kuomintang "recognizes the right of self-determination of all races in China, will organize a free united Republic of China, based on the free union of various races, after the success of the revolution against imperialism and the militarists." *Tsung-li ch'üan-shu* [*Complete Writings of President Sun*], Vol. 6, p. 223.

80. Tsou Lu, *op. cit.*, p. 636, n. 9. The unequivocal support of the Chinese Communists for Outer Mongolia's independence was expressed in an article in their official organ, *Hsiang-tao* [*The Guide Weekly*], September 27, 1922. See Tsui shu-chin, "The Influence of the Canton-Moscow Entente," p. 130.

81. *Chung-shan ch'üan-shu* [*Complete Writings of Sun Yat-sen*], Vol. 3, p. 106. The Mongolian problem apparently was one of the topics under discussion during Chiang Kai-shek's visit to Russia, as evidenced by the following letter Chiang wrote to Soviet Foreign Minister Chicherin on October 26, 1923: ". . . The other day you told me that 'the Mongols are afraid of the Chinese.' It should be understood what the Mongols fear is the present Peking government and not the Kuomintang that is sponsoring nationalism. . . . If Soviet Russia is sincere, she ought to make the Mongols rid of such fear. Let it be known that the Kuomintang's nationalism does not mean the secession of each race; rather it means various races to work out a way of collaboration in a true national spirit and based on mutual love." *Min-kuo shih-wu-nien i-ch'ien chih Chiang Chieh-shih hsien-sheng* [*Chiang Kai-shek before 1926*], Vol. 5, pp. 61-62.

82. Ch'en Tu-hsiu, *Kao ch'üan-tang t'ung-chih shu* [*A Letter to all Comrades of the Party*], (Shanghai, 1929), p. 3.

83. *Tan-ho Kung-ch'an-tang liang-ta yao-an* [*Two Important Cases of Impeachment of the Communist Party*], p. 6.

84. Tsou Lu, *op. cit.*, p. 368.

85. T'sai Ho-shen "The Lesson of the Merchant Corps Incident," *Hsiang-tao* [*The Guide Weekly*], September, 10, 1924.

86. For the text, see Brandt, Schwartz, and Fairbank, *op. cit.*, pp. 74-77.

87. See article by Liu Lu-yin, a Right Wing Kuomintang leader, in Lang Hsing-shih (ed.), *Ko-ming yü fan-ko-ming* [*Revolution and Counterrevolution*] (Shanghai: Min-chih Bookstore, 1928), p. 467. Chiang Kai-shek also records that before Dr. Sun's departure for the North, Borodin forwarded

the Kuomintang president an invitation from Moscow for him to go to Russia for a visit. *Soviet Russia in China*, p. 35.

88. *Tsung-li ch'üan-shu* [*Complete Writings of President Sun*], Vol. 7, part II, pp. 879-880.

89. In the "Outline of National Reconstruction" of 1924, no provisional constitution was included in the period of political tutelage. *Ibid.*, Vol. 5, pp. 493-498.

90. A statement in the "Manifesto of the First National Congress of the Kuomintang." *Ibid.*, Vol. 6, p. 227.

91. *Ibid.*, Vol. 5, p. 493.

Chapter 5: The Chinese Communists' Interpretations of Sun Yat-sen's Doctrine

1. For instance, Liao Chung-k'ai, Sun's trusted aide and one of the chief architects of the Russian alliance, was assassinated in August 1925. This plot was traced to a Right Wing conspiracy with such senior Kuomintang members as Hu Han-min involved. Harold R. Isaacs, *The Tragedy of the Chinese Revolution*, (Stanford: Stanford University Press, 1951), p. 84. In November 1925, a group of Right Wing members led by Hsieh Ch'ih, Tsou Lu, Lin Shen and Chang Chi held a conference in the Western Hills, near Peking. The conference called for the expulsion of Communists from the Kuomintang and the dismissal of Borodin. For details of this conference, see Tsou Lu, *Tsou Lu wen-ts'un* [*Collected Essays of Tsou Lu*] (Peking: Pei-hua Bookstore, 1930), part III, pp. 96-98.

2. In January 1926, the Second National Congress of the Kuomintang declared in a special resolution: "The concentration of all revolutionary forces of the country is the only way to promote the success of the revolution. Therefore the Party reiterated its obedience to the policy of the dead leader in admitting the members of the Chinese Communist Party to the Kuomintang for the common task." T. C. Woo, *The Kuomintang and the Future of the Chinese Revolution* (London: Allen & Unwin, 1928), p. 170. Chiang Kai-shek, in an article written on December 5, 1929, also stated: "We cannot deny that the Chinese Revolution is part of the World Revolution. The realization of the Three People's Principles means the realization of Communism Knowing that we cannot separate the Chinese Revolution from the World Revolution, why should there be any quarrel amongst us about the Three People's Principles and Communism?" T'ang Leang-li, *The Inner History of the Chinese Revolution*, p. 232.

3. For details, see C. Martin Wilbur and Julie L. Y. How (eds.), *Documents on Communism, Nationalism, and Soviet Advisers in China, 1918-1927* (New York: Columbia University Press, 1956) parts IV-VII; Benjamin Schwartz, *Chinese Communism and the Rise of Mao* (Cambridge: Harvard University Press, 1951), chapters IV-VII; David J. Dallin, *The Rise of Russia in Asia*, (New Haven: Yale University Press, 1949) chapter 9; Isaacs, *op. cit.*, chapters 5-17; M. N. Roy, *Revolution and Counterrevolution in China* (Calcutta: Renaissance Publishers, 1946), chapters XIV-XX. The following writings by Trotsky and Stalin should also be consulted: Leon Trotsky, *Problems of the Chinese Revolution*, trans. Max Shachtman (New York:

Pioneer Publishers, 1932); Stalin, *Lun Chung-kuo ko-ming* [*On the Chinese Revolution*], ed. the Sino-Soviet Friendship Association (Peking: Hsin-hua Bookstore, 1949).

4. Chang Ch'i-yün, *Tang-shih kai-yao* [*Outline of the History of the Chinese Nationalist Party*] (Taipeh: Central Reform Committee, 1951), Vol. II, chapter 21. There are two books which specially compile some Kuomintang leaders' speeches and writings on the issue of the Party purge of 1927: *Ch'ing-tang yün-tung* [*The Party Purification Movement*] (Nanking: edited and published by the Association for the Promotion of the Party Purification Movement, 1927) and *Ko-ming yü fan-ko-ming* [*Revolution and Counterrevolution*], ed. Lang Hsing-shih (Shanghai: Min-chih Bookstore, 1928).

5. Donald G. Tewksbury (ed.), *Source Book on Far Eastern Political Ideologies: Modern Period, China, Japan* (New York: Columbia University Press, 1949), p. 56.

6. Madame Sun has continuously cooperated with the Communists since her husband's death and has held various important positions in the People's Republic of China.

7. Soong Ching Ling (Madame Sun Yat-sen), *The Struggle for New China* (Peking: Foreign Languages Press, 1953), pp. 1-6.

8. For the text of this statement, see *ibid.*, pp. 7-11.

9. Dallin, *op. cit.*, p. 229, n. 18.

10. J. V. Stalin, *Works* (Moscow: Foreign Languages Press, 1954), Vol. 9, p. 229.

11. Conrad Brandt, Benjamin Schwartz, and John K. Fairbank, *A Documentary History of Chinese Communism* (Cambridge: Harvard University Press, 1952), p. 95. Mao Tse-tung, in his report to the Seventh National Congress of the Chinese Communist Party in 1945, commented on Chiang's purge of 1927: "The allies of yesterday—the Kungchantang and the people —were now regarded as enemies, while the enemies of yesterday—the imperialists and feudalists—were now regarded as allies of the Kuomintang. This sudden and treacherous attack on the Kungchantang and the Chinese people killed the glowing Revolution," Mao Tse-tung, "On Coalition Government," in Stuart Gelder (trans.) *The Chinese Communists* (London: Victor Gollancz Ltd., 1946), p. 7. There are several English translations of Mao's "On Coalition Government." The authors are satisfied with the translation in Mr. Gelder's book after checking with the Chinese text, Mao Tse-tung, *Lun lien-ho cheng-fu* (Yenan: chieh-fang she, 1945).

12. Brandt, Schwartz, and Fairbank, *op. cit.*, p. 102.

13. Mao Tse-tung, "On Coalition Government," p. 8.

14. For instance, the Resolution of the Sixth National Congress of the Chinese Communist Party on the Peasant Movement (September 1928) approved the slogan of equal distribution of land which Sun had long advocated. But the Resolution also called this slogan an "illusion of petty-bourgeois socialism," and instructed: "The Party must criticize it in order to make the peasants understand fully that under the present capitalist system real equality is absolutely impossible. Only after the victory of the proletarian revolution will a truly socialistic reconstruction be feasible." Brandt, Schwartz, and Fairbank, *op. cit.*, p. 158.

15. As early as 1932, following the Japanese invasion of Manchuria on

September 18, 1931, the Chinese Communists had declared "war" against
Japan and expressed the willingness to cooperate with all anti-Japanese
groups. Since the Kuomintang was still the target to overthrow, it was
obviously not included in any contemplated united front. It was only after
1935 that the offer of a united front was made to the Kuomintang by the
Communists. For the background of the second united front between the
Kuomintang and the Communists, see *United States Relations with China*
(Washington, 1949), pp. 45-48.
16. Edgar Snow, *Red Star over China* (New York: Modern Library, Random House, 1938), p. 388.
17. See *United States Relations with China,* pp. 47-51.
18. Mao Tse-tung, *Selected Works* (New York: International Publishers,
1954), Vol. I, p. 266.
19. *Ibid.,* pp. 266-267.
20. Stalin, *Works,* p. 205.
21. The manifesto was handed to the Kuomintang in July 1937, but its
publication was delayed because of the outbreak of hostilities with Japan
in that month. Full text is given in Lawrence K. Rosinger, *China's Wartime
Politics, 1937-1944* (Princeton: Princeton University Press, 1944), pp. 96-97.
The Chinese text is in Hu Hua (ed.), *Chung-kuo hsin min-chu chu-i ko-ming
shih ts'an-k'ao tzu-liao* [*Reference Materials for the History of the Chinese
New Democratic Revolution*], (Shanghai: The Commercial Press, 1951),
pp. 354-356.
22. For the text, see Mao Tse-tung, *Selected Works,* Vol. II, pp. 77-88.
23. *Ibid.,* p. 94.
24. The wartime cooperation between the Kuomintang and the Communists
was, like their first alliance in 1923-1927, based on expediency and characterized, particularly, by suspicion and friction as a result of the bitter
memories of many years of civil war. The united front began to crack in
1939 and 1940 as Japanese pressure on China lessened, and the war became
a stalemate. Later, it became an open secret that the Kuomintang and the
Communists were more interested in preparing for the postwar showdown
than cooperating to fight the Japanese. There is an unconfirmed comment
on the war attributed to Mao Tse-tung as follows: "The war between China
and Japan is an excellent opportunity for the development of our party.
Our determined policy is 70 per cent self-development, 20 per cent compromise, and 10 per cent fight Japanese." Quoted in *The Strategy and Tactics
of World Communism,* Supplement III (H. Doc. 154, part 3, 81st Cong.,
1st sess.), (Washington, 1949), p. 24.
25. Mao Tse-tung's "On New Democracy" was published early in 1940 for
the theoretical framework of the new Party line. Interesting comments on
Mao's "New Democracy" are found in John King Fairbank, *The United
States and China* (Cambridge: Harvard University Press, 1948), pp. 259-
274; Brandt, Schwartz, and Fairbank, *op. cit.,* pp. 260-263; *The Strategy and
Tactics of World Communism,* Supplement III, pp. 27-34.
26. Ch'en Po-ta, *San-min chu-i kai-lun* [Survey of the Three People's Prin-
ciples], p. 1.
27. *Ibid.,* pp. 17-18. Another Communist writer attributes the development
of the Three People's Principles in this period to the combined influence
of the May Fourth Movement, the October Revolution, and the Chinese

Communist Party. Yang K'ang-hua, "A Brief Study of the Three People's Principles," Chao Yüan-ming (ed.), *Lun San-min chu-i* (Concerning the Three People's Principles) (Dairen: Ta-chung Bookstore, 1946), p. 119.

28. Ch'en Po-ta, *op. cit.*, p. 122.

29. Mao Tse-tung, *The Chinese Revolution and the Communist Party of China* (New York, 1949), p. 18. Published in Chinese in 1939, this booklet was translated into English by the *China Digest* in Hong Kong and distributed by the Committee for a Democratic Far Eastern Policy in New York in 1949. Checked with the Chinese Text, Mao Tse-tung, *Chung-kuo ko-ming yü Chung-kuo Kung-ch'an-tang* (Hong Kong: Hsin min-chu Publishing Co., 1949).

30. Mao Tse-tung, "On New Democracy," *Selected Works* (New York: International Publishers, 1954), pp. 132-141.

31. He meant after the founding of the Soviet Regime in Russia, after the establishment of the Chinese Communist Party, and after the workers and peasants had already awakened and shown their political consciousness.

32. At the same time Mao also pointed out the *differences* between the Three People's Principles and Communism. We shall discuss them later.

33. "Propaganda outline issued by the Central Committee on the seventeenth anniversary of the Chinese Communist Party (June 24, 1939)," Brandt, Schwartz, and Fairbank, *op. cit.*, pp. 258-259.

34. Mao Tse-tung, *Selected Works*, Vol. III, p. 16.

35. *Ibid.*, p. 181.

36. *Ibid.*, p. 202. (Italics added.)

37. In the Communist-controlled areas direct elections were fostered in the "three-thirds" system which restricted the Communists' own representation to one-third and gave two-thirds of the offices to other parties and independents. As to their land policy, the Communists temporarily abandoned their program of land confiscation in favor of one of rent reduction. This merely carried out the Kuomintang law of 1930 which limited rent to 37½ per cent of the crop. Fairbank, *op. cit,* p. 206. The Communists' wartime land policy not only reduced rent and interest rates, but also gave the landlords the guarantee for the actual payment of reduced rent and interest. It further guaranteed the civil, political, and property rights of the landlords, as well as those of the peasants. For details, see "Decision of the Central Committee [of the Chinese Communist Party] on land policy in the anti-Japanese base areas (January 28, 1942)," Brandt, Schwartz, and Fairbank, *op. cit.*, pp. 276-285.

38. Gunther Stein, *The Challenge of Red China* (New York:McGraw-Hill, 1945), pp. 111-113.

39. Kao Kang, "Move Forward to Develop Production in Commemoration of the Sixth Anniversary of the Resistance War," Chao Yüan-ming, *op. cit.*, p. 91.

40. See its editorial on October 10, 1943, commemorating the 32nd anniversary of the Chinese Republic and another editorial on March 12, 1945, for the 20th anniversary of the death of Sun Yat-sen.

41. Harrison Forman, *Report from Red China* (New York: Henry Holt and Co., 1945), p. 180 (italics added).

42. Mao Tse-tung, "On Coalition Government," p. 28.

43. *Ibid.*, p. 24.

44. *Ibid.*, p. 25. In pp. 40-42, Mao claimed that the Chinese Communists had long been fighting for the realization of Sun's policy of "land to the tiller."

45. *Ibid.*, pp. 38, 41, 50.

46. See statements by Mao Tse-tung, Ch'en Po-ta, and Chou En-lai cited above.

47. V. I. Lenin, *Selected Works* (New York: International Publishers, 1943), Vol. IV, pp. 305-311.

48. Wang Chia-hsiang, "Concerning the Three People's Principles and Communism," Chao Yüan-ming, *op. cit.*, pp. 22-23.

49. *Ibid.*, pp. 23-24.

50. Ah Tou was a stupid and incompetent ruler during the period of the Three Kingdoms (122-265 A.D.), but he turned the affairs of state over to Chu-ko Liang, a very capable statesman, to administer.

51. Mao Tse-tung, "On New Democracy," pp. 130-131.

52. *Ibid.*, p. 133.

53. In the same year a leading Kuomintang theoretician, T'ao Pai-ch'uan, also published in Chungking a book titled *San-min chu-i yü Kung-ch'an chu-i* [*The Three People's Principles and Communism*] (Chungking: Pai-li Publishing Co., 1946), to refute the Communists' "fallacious interpretation" of Sun Yat-sen.

54. Ch'en Po-ta, *Lun Sun Chung-shan chu-i* [*On Sun Yat-senism*] ([place of publication unknown]: Tso-chê Publishing Co., 1946), pp. 135-164.

55. For Ch'en's criticism of Sun's Principle of Nationalism, see *ibid.*, pp. 88-93.

56. In his letter Sun suggested that Britain and other powers help overthrow the Manchu court and reform China. For the text, see *Tsung-li ch'üan-chi* [*Complete Collected Works of President Sun*] ed. Hu Han-min (Shanghai: Min-chih Bookstore, 1930), Vol. III, pp. 107-109.

57. This refers to Sun's speech of November 28, 1924, given in Kobe, Japan, in which he advocated a Pan-Asiatic movement based on the Oriental culture of the rule of Right, against European oppression and the Western civilization of the rule of Might. Japan was urged to join hands with China to lead the oppressed people in Asia to fight for their liberation and to seek a civilization of peace for all. For the text of this speech, see *Tsung-li ch'üan-shu* [*Complete Writings of President Sun*] (Taipeh: The China Culture Service, 1953), Vol. 7, part II, pp. 1221-1241.

58. The Chinese Communists have criticized Sun for the idea of "Pan-Hanism" or "the Chinese supremacy," but T'ao Pai-ch'uan, in *op. cit.*, pp. 11-12, cites evidence to show that Sun never entertained such an idea. Actually, Sun's position on this issue was rather ambiguous. Although "Drive away the Tartars" was one of the objectives of T'ung Meng Hui, Sun stated, in 1907, that "we have no hate against Manchus as such." (N. Gangulee (comp.), *The Teachings of Sun Yat-sen*, [London: The Sylvan Press, 1945], p. 32.) When the Republic was established, the first national flag had five stripes representing the five constituent races of China. In 1912, in his proclamation as well as speeches, Sun talked about the equality and unity of the five races. (See *Tsung-li ch'üan-chi* [*Complete Collected Works of President Sun*], Vol. II, pp. 6, 81-84.) Yet in a speech in 1921, while endorsing the principle of self-determination, he nevertheless main-

tained that the other four races should be assimilated to the Hans (Chinese) to form a Chung-hua nation. (*Ibid.*, pp. 204-205.) Probably Sun meant to give political equality to the other four races, but at the same time he would keep the position of the Hans as the cultural center around which the others should revolve.

59. For Ch'en's comments on Sun's Principle of Democracy, see Ch'en Po-ta, *Lun Sun Chung-shan chu-i* [*On Sun Yat-senism*], pp. 106-119.

60. According to Sun, the first group are those who see and perceive first; the second group those who see and perceive later; the third group those who do not see or perceive. Sun Yat-sen, *San Min Chu I*, trans. Frank W. Price, ed. L. T. Chen (Shanghai: The Commercial Press, 1928), p. 297.

61. In his lecture on the Principle of Democracy Sun stated: "The foundation of the government of the nation must be built upon the rights of the people, but the administration of government must be entrusted to experts." To make this idea work he suggested four "political powers" (suffrage, recall, initiative, and referendum) for the people to control the government, and five "governing powers" (legislative, judicial, executive, examination, and control) for the government to run the country. See *ibid.*, pp. 318-319; 350-360.

62. Actually Sun was concerned only with the liberty of the nation, for which individual liberty should be sacrificed. For a further discussion of this point, see the next chapter.

63. Sun's "Five-Power Constitution," a rather ingenious combination of the classical Western political system and the Chinese tradition of government, divided governmental powers into five, namely, legislative, executive, judicial, examination, and control. It was designed to rectify the defeats of the three-power constitution and to meet the special requirements of China. For Sun's own explanations, see *Tsung-li ch'üan-chi* [*Complete Collected Works of President Sun*], Vol. I, pp. 830-847. An impartial commentary on the five powers is found in Paul M. A. Linebarger, *The Political Doctrines of Sun Yat-sen* (Baltimore: Johns Hopkins Press, 1937), pp. 221-227.

64. For Ch'en's criticism of the Principle of the People's Livelihood, see Ch'en Po-ta, *Lun Sun Chung-shan chu-i* [*On Sun Yat-senism*], pp. 129-131.

65. According to Sun, the "inequalities between rich and poor" were merely differences between the fairly poor and the extremely poor. Sun Yat-sen, *San Min Chu I*, pp. 417-418. For a discussion of Sun's controversial Principle of People's Livelihood, see both the preceding and the following chapters.

66. Differences should be noted between the international class war of which Sun approved and the intranational class war within China of which he disapproved.

67. Ch'en Po-ta, *Lun Sun Chung-shan chu-i* [*On Sun Yat-senism*], p. 133.

68. *Ibid.*, pp. 133-134.

69. *Ibid.*, p. 134.

70. Liu Shao-chi, "Internationalism and Nationalism," *Soviet Press Translations*, July 15, 1949, p. 436. Liu is Chairman of the People's Republic of China today and generally is considered the leading Chinese Communist theoretician with the possible exception of Mao Tse-tung himself. This article was designed to denounce Titoism and appeared in *Pravda* from June 7 to 9, 1949.

71. *Ibid.*, p. 437.

72. Mao Tse-tung, *On People's Democratic Dictatorship* (Peking: Foreign Languages Press, 1951), p. 10. This English translation by Communist China's Foreign Languages Press proves to be most satisfactory as checked with the Chinese text, Mao Tse-tung, *Lun jen-min min-chu chuan-cheng* (Hong Kong: Hsin-hua Book Co., 1950).

73. Mao Tse-tung, *On People's Democratic Dictatorship,* pp. 10-11.

74. *Ibid.*, p. 15.

75. *Ibid.*, p. 24.

76. The Political Consultative Conference approved three basic documents of the People's Republic of China: (1) the Common Program of the People's Political Consultative Conference; (2) the Organic Law of the Central People's Government; (3) the Organic Law of the People's Political Consultative Conference. The texts of these documents are given in *The China Weekly Review,* October 8, 15, and 22, 1949.

77. "The Organic Law of the Central People's Government," *The China Weekly Review,* October 15, 1949, p. 104.

78. Since the reorganization of the government of Communist China, based on a new Constitution adopted in September 1954, both of them have become Vice-Chairmen of the Standing Committee of the National People's Congress.

79. Article 27 of the Common Program. *The China Weekly Review,* October 8, 1949, p. 86.

80. *New China News Agency* (NCNA) (Peking), September 21, 1949.

81. *Ibid.*, September 22, 1949. Li Chi-shen's address was to the effect that the basic spirit of the Common Program corresponded to the revolutionary ideals of Sun Yat-sen. *Ibid.*, September 24, 1949.

82. *Ibid.*, September 22, 1949. Her husband was one of Sun's closest aides and the leader of the Kuomintang Left Wing. He strongly supported Sun's alliance with Soviet Russia and was assassinated in August 1925.

83. According to a report of the educational transformation getting under way in East China in 1949, among the "reactionary" courses dropped was "the Kuomintang's Three People's Principles." The *China Weekly Review,* October 29, 1949, p. 133.

84. Liu Shao-chi, "Sino-Soviet Friendship," *The China Weekly Review,* October 29, 1949, p. 141.

85. Liu Shao-chi, "On the Agrarian Reform Law," *People's China,* July 1, 1950, p. 7.

86. *People's China,* April 1, 1955, p. 6.

87. For instance, see Chou Chê, *Sun Chung-shan* [*Sun Yat-sen*] (Peking: San-lien Bookstore, 1950). *Jen-min shou t'se* [*People's Handbook*] (Shanghai: Ta-kung pao, 1951), Vol. I also includes a brief account of Sun Yat-sen in the section "Important Memorable Days." All stress Sun's alliance with the Communists. Personal relations between Sun and Wu Yü-chang, a Communist leader, are related by some newspapers in such a way as to emphasize the "treachery" and "renegade" character of Chiang Kai-shek. (H. Arthur Steiner, "Recent Literature on Chinese Communists Party History," *The American Political Science Review,* June 1952, p. 546.)

88. According to China News Service, Nanking, March 12, 1955, the num-

ber of visitors to the Sun Yat-sen Mausoleum has increased each year: in 1950, there were 300,000 visitors; in 1954, one million visitors.

89. Madame Sun is at present Vice-Chairman of the People's Republic of China and Vice-Chairman of the Sino-Soviet Friendship Association. In 1951, she was awarded the International Stalin Prize for the "Promotion of Peace Among Nations." During the winter of 1955-1956 she visited India, Burma, and Pakistan on a good-will tour. She was welcomed warmly in all the three countries, and did much to promote the interests of Communist China.

90. *Jen-min jih-pao* [*The People's Daily*], November 12, 1956.

91. *New China News Agency,* November 11, 1956.

92. The book includes some of Sun's correspondence with the Russians not to be found in other Chinese collections, but it omits the Sun-Joffe joint statement in 1923 which openly declared the inapplicability of Communism to China.

93. Frank Moraes, *Report on Mao's China* (New York: Macmillan Co., 1953), p. 110.

94. The full text of the report is given in *Kuang-ming jih-pao* (Peking), January 21, 1953.

95. *New China News Agency,* March 12, 1955.

96. Soong Ching-ling, "In Memory of Sun Yat-sen," *Wei-ta ti Sun Chung-shan* [*The Great Sun Yat-sen*] (Hong Kong: Hsin-ti Publishing Co., 1957), p. 23.

97. It should be noted that in spite of their criticism of Confucianism as "feudal" and "outmoded," the Chinese Communists treat Confucius as a historical figure with considerable respect. According to Frank Moraes' account, on a visit to the grave of Confucius in Shantung, his Communist guide remarked: "The sage of feudal China, but worthy of our esteem." Moraes, *op. cit.,* p. 124. Both Liu Shao-chi and Kuo Mo-jo, now a Vice-Premier of Communist China, at times have quoted Confucius to bolster their arguments. H. G. Creel, *Chinese Thought: From Confucius to Mao Tse-tung* (Chicago: University of Chicago Press, 1953), pp. 256-257.

Chapter 6: Comparison of Sun Yat-senism and Chinese Communism

1. "History of the Chinese Revolution," *Tsung-li ch'üan-chi* [*Complete Collected Works of President Sun*] ed. Hu Han-min (Shanghai: Min-chih Bookstore, 1930), Vol. I, p. 915.

2. For some information about the various Western thinkers to whom Dr. Sun referred, see Lin Tse-hsuen, *Kuo-fu hsüeh-shuo yü Hsi-fang wen-hua* [*Dr. Sun's Theory and Western Culture*] (Taipeh: The China Cultural Publishing Committee, 1953). This book, however, is only a useful reference book; it contains no analysis of how far Dr. Sun was substantially influenced by Western thinkers.

3. Sun Yat-sen, *Memoirs of a Chinese Revolutionary* (London: Hutchinson & Co., 1927), p. 227.

4. "The Constitution of the Chinese Communist Party," Liu Shao-chi, *On the Party* (Peking: Foreign Language Press, 1950), p. 157.

5. Mao Tse-tung, "On New Democracy," *Selected Works* (New York:

International Publishers, 1954), p. 154. For similar statements of Mao and other Chinese Communists leaders, see *Mao's China: Party Reform Documents, 1942-44*, trans. Boyd Compton (Seattle: University of Washington Press, 1952). The "unorthodoxy" of Mao—the Sinonization of Marxism—can find its justification in Lenin's statement that "subsequent revolutions in Eastern countries, which possess vastly more numerous populations, and are distinguished by a vastly greater diversity of social conditions, will undoubtedly display even greater peculiarities than the Russian revolution." V. I. Lenin, *Selected Works* (New York: International Publishers, 1943), Vol. VI, p. 512. However, some writers maintain that Mao Tse-tung, like Lenin, has perverted Marxism. For this type of view, see Benjamin Schwartz, "On the 'Originality' of Mao Tse-tung," *Foreign Affairs*, October 1955.

6. Sun Yat-sen, *San Min Chu I*, trans. Frank W. Price, ed. L. T. Chen (Shanghai: The Commercial Press, 1928), pp. 406-407.

7. *Ibid.*, p. 391.

8. Mao Tse-tung, "On New Democracy," p. 107.

9. *Ibid.*, p. 133.

10. Two of Sun's admirers, Tai Chi-t'ao in "The Philosophical Foundation of Sun Yat-senism" (*Chung-shan ch'üan shu* [Complete Writings of Sun Yat-sen], Vol. IV, pp. 56-84) and Sun Ching-ya in "A Discussion of 'The Philosophical Foundation of Sun Yat-senism'" (*Ibid.*, pp. 84-103), link The Three People's Principles to Confucianism, particularly to such virtues as sincerity (*ch'eng*) benevolence (*jen*), and universal love (*po-ai*). M. N. Roy, former Comintern agent in China and one of Sun's severe critics, says that Sun accepted the Confucian culture and on that foundation constructed his ideological system. *Revolution and Counterrevolution in China* (Calcutta: Renaissance Publishers, 1946), p. 253.

11. Paul M. A. Linebarger, *The Political Doctrines of Sun Yat-sen* (Baltimore: Johns Hopkins Press, 1937), p. 68.

12. Sun Yat-sen, *San Min Chu I*, pp. 122-148.

13. *Ibid.*, pp. 126-133.

14. *Ibid.*, p. 134.

15. *Ibid.*, p. 444.

16. Linebarger, *op. cit.*, p. 75.

17. Robert Payne, *Mao Tse-tung: Ruler of Red China* (New York: Henry Schuman, 1950), pp. 61-62, 171-172, 265-267. Payne says: "Later, he was to destroy Confucianism root and branch; it is inconceivable that he would have been able to destroy it without having submitted to its power, without, in fact, being a Confucian himself." *Ibid.*, p. 62. H. G. Creel, in *Chinese Thought: From Confucius to Mao Tse-tung* (Chicago: University of Chicago Press, 1953), pp. 252-257, also tries to show some connection between Confucianism and Chinese Communism. Frank Moraes in *Report on Mao's China* (New York: Macmillan Co., 1953), pp. 196-197, points out Mao's frequent use of Confucian sayings.

18. For example, to stress the importance of training and self-cultivation, Liu cites the following words of the two sages for his Party members. Confucius: "At fifteen, I had my mind bent on learning. At thirty, I stood firm. At forty, I had no doubt. At fifty, I knew the decrees of Heaven. At sixty, my ear was an obedient organ for the reception of truth. At

seventy, I could follow what my heart desired, without transgressing what was right." Mencius: "Thus, when Heaven is about to confer a great office on any man, it first exercises his mind with suffering, and his sinews and bones with toil. It exposes his body to hunger, and subjects him to extreme poverty. It confounds his undertakings. By all these methods it stimulates his mind, hardens his nature, and supplies his incompetencies." Also, in urging the Party members to have the determination to follow the footsteps of Marx, Engles, Lenin, and Stalin, Liu quotes Mencius' statement that all men may become Yaous and Shuns (Yaou and Shun were two model sovereigns of ancient China). Liu Shao-chi, *Lun Kung-ch'an-tang-yüan ti hsiu-yang* [*On the Training of a Communist Party Member*] (Hong Kong: Hsin min-chu Publishing Co., 1949), pp. 5, 10.

19. *Ibid.,* pp. 13-14.

20. Mao Tse-tung, "On New Democracy," p. 141.

21. *Ibid.*

22. *Ibid.,* p. 145.

23. *Ibid.,* pp. 153-154.

24. As provided by Article 42 of "The Common Program of the Chinese People's Political Consultative Conference," *China Weekly Review,* October 8, 1949, p. 87.

25. Sun Yat-sen, *San Min Chu I,* pp. 8-11.

26. Ch'en Po-ta, *Lun Sun Chung-shan chu-i* [*On Sun Yat-senism*], pp. 88-89.

27. Chen Pai-ta (Ch'en Po-ta), "Criticism of Chiang Kai-shek's 'China's Destiny,'" in Stuart Gelder (trans.), *The Chinese Communists* (London: Victor Gollancz Ltd., 1946), p. 260.

28. Sun Yat-sen, *San Min Chu I,* pp. 113-121.

29. *Ibid.,* p. 114.

30. See his speeches delivered in 1912 on the subject, *Tsung-li chüan-chi* [*Complete Collected Works of President Sun*], Vol. II, pp. 81-84. The Manifesto of the First National Congress of the Kuomintang in 1924 stated: "The Kuomintang's Principle of Nationalism has a two-fold meaning: the self-emancipation of the Chinese nation, and the equality of all races within China." *Tsung-li ch'üan-shu* [*Complete Writings of President Sun*] (Taipeh: The China Culture Service, 1953), Vol. 6, p. 220.

31. *Ibid.,* Vol. 7, part I, pp. 434-439. A similar statement was made in an article Sun wrote in 1919. *Ibid.,* Vol. 5, pp. 389-393.

32. *Ibid.,* Vol. 6, p. 223.

33. For the discussion of Sun's attitude toward Outer Mongolia and Tibet, see Tsui Shu-chin, *Sun Chung-shan yü Kung-ch'an chu-i* [*Sun Yat-sen and Communism*] (Hong Kong: The Asia Press, Ltd., 1954), pp. 71-72.

34. Quoted from the Declaration of the Kuomintang in 1923. *Tsung-li ch'üan-shu* [*Complete Writings of President Sun*], Vol. 6, p. 196.

35. Sun Yat-sen, *San Min Chu I,* pp. 122-148. This lecture was delivered in March 1924.

36. Mao Tse-tung, "On Coalition Government," Stuart Gelder (trans.) *The Chinese Communists* (London: Victor Gollancz Ltd., 1946), p. 48; Chen pai-ta (Ch'en Po-ta), "Criticism of Chiang Kai-shek's 'China's Destiny,'" pp. 257-261.

37. A simple list of the national minorities is given by Weng Tu-shien,

a member of the Nationalities Affairs Commission, in "China's Policy on National Minorities," *People's China,* April 1, 1950, p. 6.

38. See articles 9, 50, 51, 52, 53 in "Common Program of the CPPCC," *The China Weekly Review,* October 6, 1949, pp. 85, 88; also Articles 3, pp. 67-72 in "Constitution of the People's Republic of China," *People's China,* October 1, 1954, supplement.

39. John De Francis, "National and Minority Policies," *The Annals of the American Academy of Political and Social Science,* September 1951, p. 149.

40. *Jen-min jih-pao,* April 25, 1959.

41. The Preamble of the Constitution.

42. Liu Shao-chi, "Report on the Draft Constitution of the People's Republic of China," American Consulate General, Hong Kong, *Current Background,* No. 294 (September 20, 1954).

43. Wang Feng's report to the 5th meeting of the Nationalities Committee of the First National People's Congress on February 9, 1958. *New China News Agency* (Peking), February 28, 1958.

44. For details, see Chapter 4.

45. Mao Tse-tung, *The Chinese Revolution and the Communist Party of China* (New York: Committee for a Democratic Far Eastern Policy, 1949), p. 5.

46. Tsui Shu-chin, "The Influence of the Canton-Moscow Entente upon Sun Yat-sen's Political Philosophy," *The Chinese Social and Political Science Review* (Peiping), April-October 1934, p. 139.

47. For the analysis of Sun's alliance with Moscow, see chapters 3 and 4.

48. Sun Yat-sen, *San Min Chu I,* p. 20; Sun's speech on "The Correct Attitude in Our Diplomacy," *Tsung-li ch'üan-shu* [*Complete Writings of President Sun*], Vol. 8, pp. 131-134.

49. In November 1924, Sun made a trip to the North by way of Japan. When interviewed by Japanese reporters, he suggested that China and Japan should cooperate to resist foreign aggression and that Japan should help China to abolish unequal treaties. *Ibid.,* pp. 158-159, 164-172.

50. His main idea of using foreign capital to build China's economy was incorporated in *The International Development of China* (New York: G. P. Putnam's Sons, 1922).

51. See his interview with an American correspondent, Mr. Ford, on January 13, 1924. *Tsung-li ch'üan-shu* [*Complete Writings of President Sun*], Vol. 8, pp. 148-150.

52. Sun Yat-sen, *San Min Chu I,* pp. 442-443.

53. Mao Tse-tung, "On New Democracy," p. 124.

54. Mao Tse-tung, *On People's Democratic Dictatorship* (Peking: Foreign Languages Press, 1951), pp. 8-10; Liu Shao-chi, "Internationalism and Nationalism," *Soviet Press Translations,* July 15, 1949, p. 433.

55. Mao Tse-tung, *On People's Democratic Dictatorship,* p. 11.

56. *Ibid,* p. 12.

57. *Ibid.,* p. 15.

58. Sun Yat-sen, *San Min Chu I,* p. 147.

59. For the text of his famous Pan-Asian Speech of November 28, 1924, delivered in Kobe, Japan, see *Chung-shan ch'üan-shu* [*Complete Writings of Sun Yat-sen*], Vol. III, pp. 80-88.

60. *Sun Yat-sen, San Min Chu I*, p. 148.

61. *Ibid.*, pp. 68-69, 89-90.

62. *Ibid.*, pp. 99-100.

63. Professor Linebarger thinks that Sun's program of nationalism involved "use of China resurgence of national power to restore the benevolent hegemony which the Chinese had exercised over Eastern Asia, and possibly to extend it over the whole world." Linebarger, *op. cit.*, p. 203.

64. Sun Yat-sen, *San Min Chu I*, p. 148.

65. See the joint declaration by the "democratic" parties of China on November 4, 1950, in *People's China*, November 16, 1950, pp. 4-5.

66. Gunther Stein, *The Challenge of Red China* (New York: McGraw-Hill, 1945), p. 118.

67. For instance, Liu Shao-chi, in *Lun Kung-ch'an-tang-yüan ti hsiu-yang* [*On the Training of a Communist Party Member*], p. 47, calls his Party one of the best Communist Parties in the world. He is also quoted as saying: "The Chinese Communist Party has experienced more great events in these twenty-two years than any other Communist Party in the world and has gained richer experiences in the revolutionary struggle." Compton (trans.) *Mao's China*, p. xiv. Lu Ting-yi, a Central Committee member, maintains that Mao's theory of the Chinese revolution "has significance not only for China and Asia—it is of a universal significance for the world Communist movement." *People's China*, July 1, 1951, p. 11.

68. Mao Tse-tung, *The Chinese Revolution and the Communist Party of China*, p. 2.

69. Liu Shao-chi, *Lun Kung-ch'an-tang-yüan ti hsiu-yang* [*On the Training of a Communist Party Member*], p. 47.

70. American Consulate General, Hong Kong, *Chinese Communist Propaganda Review* No. 43 (July 1, 1953); *People's China*, January 1, 1954, p. 39.

71. Mao Tse-tung, *The Chinese Revolution and the Communist Party of China*, p. 5.

72. For the complete text of the poem, see Payne, *op. cit.*, p. 229.

73. Mao Tse-tung, "On New Democracy," pp. 110-111; Mao Tse-tung, *On People's Democratic Dictatorship*, pp. 7-8.

74. He made this remark when interviewed by a correspondent of *The New China Daily*. Mao Tse-tung, *Selected Works*, Vol. 3, p. 31.

75. *Ibid.*, Vol. 2, p. 245.

76. Liu Shao-chi, "Internationalism and Nationalism," p. 424. He pointed out that in some oppressed countries the bourgeoisie may participate in the struggle for national liberation. "But as soon as the bourgeoisie of any nation comes to power and becomes capable of oppressing nations," he warned, "it immediately makes a radical change in its policy, and becomes an oppressor of other nations." *Ibid.*, pp. 424-425.

77. *Ibid.*, pp. 426, 438-439.

78. *Ibid.*, p. 425.

79. *Ibid.*, p. 434.

80. For instance, in October 1951, the Sino-Soviet Friendship Association decided to begin this education, the purpose of which was to be to "absolutely liquidate all vestiges of anti-Soviet thoughts, rebut the viewpoint of narrow nationalism in relation to Sino-Soviet relations, and eliminate the masses' misgivings and worries with regard to Soviet Union and questions of

Sino-Soviet friendship." American Consulate General, Hong Kong, *Survey of China Mainland Press,* No. 195 (October 16, 1951).

81. See the editorial of *Jen-min jih-pao* on February 14, 1954.

82. Published in *Jan-min jih-pao on* December 29, 1956, this document was prepared by the editorial department of the paper on the basis of discussions of the Political Bureau of the Chinese Communist Central Committee. An English version of the full text was released by the *New China News Agency* on December 28, 1956.

83. See Mao Tse-tung's speech in Moscow on November 6, 1957. *New China News Agency,* November 6, 1957.

84. For Communist China's latest condemnation of Titoism, see "Modern Revisionism Must Be Criticized," *Jen-min jih-pao,* May 5, 1958, and "The More Evil Is Covered Up, the More It Is Obvious," *ibid.,* June 26, 1958.

85. For a clear exposition of Sun's three-stage revolution, see "The Fundamentals of National Reconstruction" (issued on April 24, 1924), *Tsung-li ch'üan-shu* [*Complete Writings of President Sun*], Vol. 5, pp. 493-498.

86. Mao Tse-tung, "On New Democracy," p. 128.

87. Sun Yat-sen, *San Min Chu I,* pp. 244-245, 297-299.

88. *Ibid.,* pp. 302-310.

89. *Ibid.,* p. 318.

90. *Ibid.,* p. 345.

91. Sun Yat-sen, *Memoirs of a Chinese Revolutionary,* pp. 133, 136. An excellent treatment of Sun's theory of political tutelage is given by Dr. Tsui, who lists three grounds on which Sun justified his stand: the necessity of training the Chinese people in citizenship, the necessity of "revolutionary construction" after the extraordinary destruction of the revolution, and the prevention of the use of the name of democracy by counterrevolutionaries when they were actually practicing autocracy. Tsui Shu-chin, "The Influence of the Canton-Moscow Entente," pp. 192-193.

92. Sun Yat-sen, *Memoirs of a Chinese Revolutionary,* p. 137.

93. The bureaucratic capitalists are defined by the Chinese Communists as those former Kuomintang elements who ran state-controlled economic facilities to further personal gains, the national bourgeoisie as those capitalists who have shown their vigor in the struggle against imperialism and feudalism, and the petty bourgeoisie as a collective name for the intelligentsia, poor people in the cities, employees, and handicraftsmen, free professional men, and small businessmen. For some detailed discussion of the various social classes by the Chinese Communists, see Mao Tse-tung, *The Chinese Revolution and the Communist Party of China,* pp. 8-16; "Decisions Concerning the Differentiation of Class Status in the Countryside," *People's China,* October 16, 1950, Supplement.

94. Mao Tse-tung, *On People's Democratic Dictatorship,* p. 22.

95. *Ibid.;* Mao Tse-tung, "On New Democracy," p. 131; Mao Tse-tung, *The Chinese Revolution and the Communist Party of China,* pp. 19-20.

96. Mao Tse-tung, "On Coalition Government," pp. 58-59.

97. Liu Shao-chi, *On the Party,* p. 59.

98. Liu Shao-chi, *Ibid.,* pp. 45-46, 58-59.

99. A resolution of the Central Committee of the Chinese Communist Party on methods of leadership, passed on June 1, 1943, stated: "In all our Party's actual work, correct leadership must come from the masses and go

to the masses. This means taking the views of the masses (unintegrated, unrelated views) and subjecting them to concentration (they are transformed through research into concentrated, systematized views), then going to the masses with propaganda and explanation in order to transform the views of the masses, and seeing that these [views] are maintained by the masses and carried over into their activities. It also means an examination of mass activities to ascertain the correctness of these views." *Mao's China,* p. 179. Concerning the relationships between the Party and the people, Mao Tse-tung, in an address on April 1, 1948, said that "it should be understood that any suggestions of the people that are correct should be appreciated by the Party leading the people in accordance with existing conditions, while those which are incorrect should be rectified by educating the people." H. Arthur Steiner, "Current 'Mass Line' Tactics in Communist China," *The American Political Science Review,* June 1951, p. 428.

100. For Sun's discussion of liberty, see his second lecture on the Principle of Democracy (Sun Yat-sen, *San Min Chu I,* pp. 187-214) and his speech of January 3, 1924, entitled "For the Success of the Revolution, the Organization but Not the Individual Should Have Freedom" (*Chung-shan ch'üan-shu* [*Complete Writings of Sun Yat-sen*], Vol. III, pp. 63-71).

101. Sun Yat-sen, *San Min Chu I,* pp. 212-214.

102. Liu Shao-chi, *Lun kung-ch'an-tang-yüan ti hsiu-yang* [*On the Training of a Communist Party Member*], pp. 30-36; Ch'en Yün, "How To Be a Communist Party Member," *Mao's China,* pp. 100-101.

103. Mao Tse-tung, "In Opposition to Liberalism," *ibid.,* p. 186.

104. Sun Yat-sen, *Memoirs of a Chinese Revolutionary,* p. 134. A Chinese liberal scholar also stresses the more positive aspect of Sun's Second Principle: "In the whole scheme of his Second Principle, strong government certainly occupies only an auxiliary place, whereas the enjoyment of full political powers by the people was his main concern." Ch'ien Tuan-sheng, *The Government and Politics of China* (Cambridge: Harvard University Press, 1950), p. 114.

105. See Sun's first lecture on the Principle of Democracy in *San Min Chu I,* pp. 151-188.

106. *Ibid.,* p. 318.

107. For Sun's explanation of the superiority of this formula, see his sixth lecture on the Principle of Democracy in *ibid.,* pp. 320-360, and his speech on the "Five-Power Constitution" in 1921, in *Tsung-li ch'üan-shu* [*Complete Writings of President Sun*], Vol. 7, part II, pp. 460-492.

108. Sun Yat-sen, *San Min Chu I,* p. 358.

109. Article 1 of the Constitution.

110. Article 2 of the Constitution.

111. Mao Tse-tung, *On People's Democratic Dictatorship,* pp. 15-16. Although there have been some changes in the class structure and relationships since 1949, the fiction of a multiclass dictatorship is still being kept in China. (See the 1954 Constitution.) The bourgeoisie have been undergoing a re-molding process in the rectification campaign to resolve their "contradictions" with the proletariat and to make themselves "socialist-minded."

112. According to Chou En-lai, "absolute democracy" is impossible in Communist China, and under no circumstances will the Communists abandon

centralized leadership in favor of democracy. "Report on the Work of the Government," *People's China,* July 16, 1957, Supplement, p. 31.
113. Mao makes it clear that the dictatorship is only benevolent to the "people" but oppressive to the "reactionaries." In a true Marxist tone, he stresses the oppressive nature of the state: "Such state apparatus as the army, the police, and the courts are instruments with which one class oppresses another. As far as the hostile classes are concerned, these are instruments of oppression. They are violent and certainly not 'benevolent' things." *On People's Democratic Dictatorship,* p. 17. Article 19 of the 1954 Constitution reads: "The People's Republic of China safeguards the people's democratic system, suppresses all treasonable and counterrevolutionary activities and punishes all traitors and counterrevolutionaries. The state deprives feudal landlords and bureaucrat-capitalists of political rights for a specific period of time according to law; at the same time it provides them with a way to live, in order to enable them to reform through work and become citizens who earn their livelihood by their own labor."
114. Raja Hutheesing, *The Great Peace* (New York: Harper and Brothers, 1953), pp. 239-240.
115. For Sun's first lecture on the Principle of Livelihood, see Sun Yat-sen, *San Min Chu I,* pp. 363-407.
116. *Chung-shan ch'üan-shu [Complete Writings of Sun Yat-sen],* Vol. III, pp. 60-61.
117. Sun Yat-sen, *San Min Chu I,* pp. 457-458.
118. *Tsung-li ch'üan-shu [Complete Writings of President Sun],* Vol. 6, p. 225.
119. Mao Tse-tung, "On New Democracy," p. 122.
120. Article I of "The Agrarian Reform Law," *People's China,* July 16, 1950, Supplement. Article 30 also provides: "After agrarian reform is completed, the people's government shall issue title deeds and shall recognize the right of all land owners to manage, buy, sell, or rent out land freely."
121. Chang Lin-chih, "A Five-Year Plan for Increasing Agricultural Output," *People's China,* September 16, 1955, pp. 8-11. In a report before the Eighth National Congress of the Chinese Communist Party on May 17, 1958, Tan Chen-lin, a member of the Central Committee, summarized the development of certain agricultural projects from October 1957 to April 1958: "We estimate that the new water conservancy projects built throughout the country will increase the irrigated area by 350 million *mow* and improve irrigation facilities on another 140 million *mow.* More than 200 million *mow* of low-lying and easily waterlogged farmland and more than 100 million *mow* of hitherto unfertile land have been transformed; 290 million *mow* of land were afforested and the loss of water and soil was brought under control over an area of 160,000 square kilometers. . . . In the meantime, a mass movement to improve farm implements has been launched in rural areas throughout the country. The peasants have invented or improved several thousand kinds of agricultural implements, processing tools, and means of transport." *New China News Agency,* May 27, 1958.
122. Sun Yat-sen, *San Min Chu I,* p. 456.
123. *Tsung-li ch'üan-shu [Complete Writings of President Sun],* Vol. 6, p. 225.
124. Liu Shao-chi, "On the Agrarian Reform Law," *People's China,* July

16, 1950, p. 7.

125. Article 1 of the "The Agrarian Reform Law."

126. Theodore H. E. Chen, "China: Communist Reform," *Current History,* November 1953, p. 277.

127. *Chung-shan ch'üan-shu* [*Complete Writings of Sun Yat-sen*], Vol. II, pp. 60-63 (full text).

128. *Tsung-li ch'üan-shu* [*Complete Writings of President Sun*], Vol. 6, pp. 225-226.

129. Mao Tse-tung, *The Chinese Revolution and the Communist Party of China,* p. 15. He has also referred to the peasants as a powerful factor in China's industry, the source of China's armies, and the main foundation for China's democracy and cultural movement. Mao Tse-tung, "On Coalition Government," pp. 42-43.

130. Edgar Snow, "Mao Tse-tung as I Know Him," *The Reporter,* January 1950, p. 14.

131. For some brief discussion of the significant changes in the Communist land program, see C. M. Chang, "Mao's Stratagem of Land Reform," *Foreign Affairs,* July 1951, pp. 553-555; T. H. E. Chen, *op. cit.,* pp. 275-276.

132. Mao Tse-tung, "Report to the Central Committee of the Communist Party of China, June 6, 1950," American Consulate General, Hong Kong, *Current Background,* No. 1 (June 13, 1950).

133. Liu Shao-chi, "Report on the Draft Constitution of the People's Republic of China," *ibid.,* No. 294 (September 20, 1954).

134. On various occasions Sun stated that the two policies of his *Min-sheng* Principle (equalization of land ownership and regulation of capital) would enable China to achieve the social revolution peacefully or to avoid it altogether. *Tsung-li ch'üan-chi* [*Complete Collected Works of President Sun*], Vol. II, pp. 74-78, 123-124, 351.

135. Sun Yat-sen, *San Min Chu I,* pp. 418-419, 431.

136. *Ibid.,* pp. 431-434. Here shows the strong influence of the thought of Henry George, but Sun did not accept the orthodox single-tax theory, as he also looked into other sources of revenue for the state. *Tsung-li ch'üan-shu* [*Complete Writings of President Sun*], Vol. 8, p. 139.

137. Sun Yat-sen, *San Min Chu I,* pp. 434-435.

138. *Chung-shan ch'üan-shu* [*Complete Writings of Sun Yat-sen*], Vol. III, pp. 61-62.

139. *Ibid.,* p. 63.

140. Liu Shao-chi, "On the Agrarian Reform Law," p. 30.

141. Articles 2, 4, 6, 7, and 10 of the Agrarian Law.

142. The text of "Decisions Concerning the Differentiation of Class Status in the Countryside" appears in *People's China,* October 16, 1950, Supplement.

143. "Resolution on Agricultural Cooperation" (adopted at the Sixth Plenary Session of the Seventh Central Committee of the Communist Party of China), *New China News Agency,* October 17, 1955.

144. For a critical study of the Chinese Communist land reform, see Chang, "Mao's Stratagem of Land Reform," and Tung Shih-chin, *Jên-shih Chung-kung ti t'u-kai* [*Understand the Chinese Communist Land Reform*] (Kowloon: Yu-lien Publishing Co., 1953).

145. Sun Yat-sen, *San Min Chu I,* p. 456.

146. "CCP Central Committee Decision on Development of Agricultural Producer Cooperatives," American Consulate General, Hong Kong, *Current Background*, No. 278 (February 15, 1954).

147. The text of Mao's report appears in *People's China*, November 1, 1955, pp. 3-16.

148. Chou En-lai, "Report on the Work of the Government," *People's China*, July 16, 1957, Supplement, p. 3.

149. *New China News Agency*, December 18, 1958.

150. The uncomfortable feeling of Eastern European Communists about the Chinese is reportedly reflected in a joke going around Warsaw's coffee houses and clubs: "Thank God for the Soviet Union. We are lucky to have a buffer state between us and the Chinese." A. M. Rosenthal, "China's Communes Stun Europe Reds," *The New York Times*, October 21, 1958.

151. Sun Yat-sen, *San Min Chu I*, pp. 387, 437; *Tsung-li ch'üan-chi [Complete Collected Works of President Sun]*, Vol. II, pp. 127, 140.

152. Sun Yat-sen, *The International Development of China*, p. 11.

153. "The Manifesto of the First National Congress of the Kuomintang," *Tsung-li ch'üan-shu [Complete Writings of President Sun]*, Vol. 6, pp. 224-225; "How to Develop China's Industry," *Chung-shan ch'üan-shu [Complete Writings of Sun Yat-sen]*, Vol. IV, p. 8.

154. Sun Yat-sen, *San Min Chu I*, p. 443.

155. Sun Yat-sen, *Fundamentals of National Reconstruction* (Chungking: Chinese Ministry of Information, 1945), p. 5.

156. Sun Yat-sen, *San Min Chu I*, pp. 388-389, 403.

157. "The Manifesto of the First National Congress of the Kuomintang," *op. cit.*, p. 225; "How to Develop China's Industry," *op. cit.*, p. 8.

158. Mao Tse-tung, "On New Democracy," p. 122.

159. *Ibid.*

160. Mao Tse-tung, "On Coalition Government," p. 25.

161. Sun Yat-sen, *San Min Chu I*, pp. 434-435.

162. *Ibid.*, pp. 386-389, 410.

163. *Ibid.*, pp. 417-418, 440-441.

164. Sun Yat-sen, *The International Development of China*, p. 236.

165. *Tsung-li ch'üan-shu [Complete Writings of President Sun]*, Vol. 8, p. 139.

166. *Chung-shan ch'üan-shu [Complete Writings of Sun Yat-sen]*, Vol. III, pp. 38-41.

167. Mao Tse-tung, *The Chinese Revolution and the Communist Party of China*, p. 20.

168. Mao Tse-tung, *On People's Democratic Dictatorship*, p. 23.

169. For a discussion of these two campaigns, see T. H. E. Chen and W. H. C. Chen, "The 'Three-Anti' and 'Five-Anti' Movements in Communist China," *Pacific Affairs*, March 1953.

170. Chou En-lai, "Report on the Work of the Government," pp. 3-4.

171. Liu Shao-chi, "The Present Situation, the Party's General Line for Socialist Construction and Its Future Tasks," *New China News Agency*, May 26, 1958.

172. Sun Yat-sen, *The International Development of China*, pp. 6-8, 11-13, 30, 77, 129, 197-199, 222-223.

173. *Ibid.*, 237. In his *San Min Chu I*, p. 442, Sun said: "If we use existing

foreign capital to build up a future Communist society in China, 'half the work will bring double the results.' "

174. Tseng Wen-ching, "The Socialist Industrialization of China," *People's China,* March 1, 1954, p. 4.

175. For Communist China's official sources on the Five-Year Plans, see *First Five-Year Plan for Development of the National Economy of the People's Republic of China in 1953-1957* (Peking, 1956) and "Proposals for the Second Five-Year Plan for the Development of the National Economy (1958-1962)," *Eighth National Congress of the Communist Party of China* (Peking, 1956), Vol. I, pp. 229-328. Objective and interesting studies of Peking's economic planning by non-Communist scholars are available in Yuan-li Wu, *An Economic Survey of Communist China* (New York: Bookman Associates, 1956) and Solomon Adler, *The Chinese Economy* (London: Routledge & Paul, 1957).

BIBLIOGRAPHY

Sources in Oriental Languages

Chang Ch'i-yün. *Tang-shih kai-yao* [*Outline of the History of the Chinese Nationalist Party*]. 2 vols. Taipeh: Central Reform Committee, 1951.

Chang Chung-fu. *Chung-hua min-kuo wai-chiao shih* [*Diplomatic History of Republic of China*]. Vol. I. Peking: National University of Peking, 1936.

Chao Yüan-ming (ed.). *Lun San-min chu-i* [*Concerning the Three People's Principles*]. Dairen: Ta-chung Bookstore, 1946.

Ch'en Po-ta. *Lun Mao Tse-tung ssu-hsiang* [*On Mao Tse-tung's Thought*]. Peking: Jen-min Publishing Company, 1951.

––––––. *Lun Sun Chung-shan chu-i* [*On Sun Yat-senism*]. [Place of publication unknown]: Tso-chê Publishing Co., 1946.

––––––. *San-min chu-i kai-lun* [*Survey of the Three People's Principles*]. Chungking: Sheng-huo Bookstore, 1939.

Ch'en Tu-hsiu. *Kao ch'üan-tang t'ung-chih shu* [*A Letter to All Comrades of the Party*]. Shanghai: 1929.

Ch'eng Shang-wen. *Chung-Su kuan-hsi chien-shih* [*A Brief History of Sino-Soviet Relations*]. Hong Kong: Tsu-yu Publishing Co., 1951.

Ch'ing-tang yün-tung [*The Party Purification Movement*]. Nanking: Edited and published by the Association for the Promotion of the Party Purification Movement, 1927.

Chou chê. *Sun Chung-shan* [*Sun Yat-sen*]. Peking: San-lien Bookstore, 1950.

Chou Fu-hai. *San-min chu-i li-lun ti t'i-hsi* [*The Theoretical System of the Three People's Principles*]. Shanghai: Hsin sheng-ming yueh-k'an she, 1928.

Chung-shan ch'üan-shu [*Complete Writings of Sun Yat-sen*]. 4 vols. Shanghai: Ming-li Bookstore, 1936.

Committee for Research on Chinese Modern History. *Chung-kuo hsien-tai ko-ming yün-tung shih* [*A History of the Modern Chinese Revolutionary Movement*]. Kiaotung: Hsin-hua Bookstore, 1946.

Hu Han-min. *San-min chu-i che chih shih-ming* [*The Mission of the Followers of the Three People's Principles*]. Shanghai: Min-chih Bookstore, 1927.

————. *San-min chu-i ti lien-huan hsing* [*The Interdependent Nature of the Three People's Principles*]. Shanghai: Hsin sheng-ming Bookstore, 1928.

Hu Hua. *Chung-kuo hsin min-chu chu-i ko-ming shih* [*History of the Chinese New Democratic Revolution*]. Canton: Hsin-hua Bookstore, 1951.

———— (ed). *Chung-kuo hsin min-chu chu-i ko-ming shih ts'an-k'ao tzu-liao* [*Reference Materials for the History of the Chinese New Democratic Revolution*]. Shanghai: The Commercial Press, 1951.

Hua Kang. *I-chiu-erh-wu chih i-chiu-erh-ch'i nien ti Chung-kuo ta ko-ming shih* [*History of the Great Chinese Revolution, 1925-1927*]. Shanghai: Ch'un-keng Bookstore, 1932.

Hua Lin-i. *Chung-kuo Kuo-min-tang shih* [*History of the Chinese Kuomintang*]. Shanghai: The Commercial Press, 1928.

Iwamura Michio. *Sammin shigi to gendai Chūgoku* [*The Three People's Principles and Contemporary China*]. Tokyo: Iwanami Bookstore, 1950.

Jen-min jih-pao [*The People's Daily*]. Published in Peking.

Kao Liang-tso. *Sun Chung-san hsien-sheng ch'uan* [*Biography of Sun Yat-sen*]. [Place unknown]: Chin-fen Bookstore, 1945.

Lang Hsing-shih (ed.). *Ko-ming yü fan-ko-ming* [*Revolution and Counterrevolution*]. Shanghai: Min-chih Bookstore, 1928.

Lin Tse-hsuen. *Kuo-fu hsüeh-shuo yü Hsi-fang wen-hua* [*Dr. Sun's Theory and Western Culture*]. Taipeh: The China Cultural Publishing Committee, 1953.

Liu Shao-chi. *Lun ch'un-chung lu-hsien* [*On the Mass Line*]. Hong Kong: Hsin min-chu Publishing Company, 1949.

————. *Lun Kung-ch'an-tang-yüan ti hsiu-yang* [*On the Training of a Communist Party Member*]. Hong Kong: Hsin min-chu Publishing Co., 1949.

Mao Tse-tung. *Chung-kuo ko-ming yü Chung-kuo Kung-ch'an-tang* [*The Chinese Revolution and the Chinese Communist Party*]. Hong Kong: Hsin min-chu Publishing Co., 1949.

————. *Hsin min-chu chu-i lun* [*On the New Democracy*]. Yenan: Chieh-fang she, 1946.

————. *Lun jen-min min-chu chuan-cheng* [*On the People's Democratic Dictatorship*]. Hong Kong: Hsin-hua Book Co., 1950.

————. *Lun lien-ho cheng-fu* [*On Coalition Government*]. Yenan: Chieh-fang she, 1945.

Min-kuo jih-pao [*Republican Daily News*]. Published in Shanghai and Canton.

Min-kuo shih-wu-nien i-ch'ien chih Chiang Chieh-shih hsien-sheng [*Chiang Kai-shek before 1926*]. 20 vols. ca. 1936.

Miyazawa Toshiyoshi. "Sun Yat-senism and Communism," *Kaizō*, Tokyo: January 1940.

Satō Shunzō. *Shina no kokunai tōsō-Kyōsantō to Kokuminto no Sōkoku* [*Internal Struggle in China between the Communists and the Kuomintang*]. Tokyo: Osakayago Bookstore, 1941.

Shao Yuan-ch'ung. *Sun Wen chu-i tsung-lun* [*Summary of Sun Yat-senism*]. Shanghai: Min-chih Bookstore, 1927.

Shen Pao [*Shanghai Daily*].

Stalin. *Lun Chung-kuo ko-ming* [*On the Chinese Revolution*]. Edited by the Sino-Soviet Friendship Association. Peking: Hsin-hua Bookstore, 1949.

Sun Chung-shan hsüan-chi [*Selected Works of Sun Yat-sen*]. 2 vols. Peking: Jen-ming Publishing Co., 1956.

Sun K'o hsien-sheng tsui-chin chih yen-lun [*Recent Speeches of Mr. Sun Fo*]. Published by the Ministry of Youth, Central Executive Committee of the Kuomintang, 1927.

Sun Wen (Sun Yat-sen). *Chung-kuo ts'un-wang wen-t'i* [*The Question of China's Survival*]. Shanghai: Min-chih Bookstore, 1928.

Ta-kung Pao [*L'Impartial*]. Published in Tientsin.

Tai Chi-t'ao. *Kuo-min ko-ming yü Chung-kuo Kuomintang* [*The National Revolution and the Kuomintang*]. Shanghai, 1925.

————. *Sun-wen chu-i chih che-hsüeh chi-ch'u* [*The Philosophical Foundation of Sun Yat-senism*]. Canton: Min-chih Bookstores, 1925.

Takahashi Yūji. *Chūgoku Kokuminto to Chūgoku Kyōsantō* [*The*

Kuomintang and the Chinese Communists]. Tokyo: Hakujitsu Bookstore, 1948.

Tan-ho Kung-ch'an-tang liang-ta yao-an [*Two Important Cases of Impeachment of the Communist Party*]. Nanking: Edited and published by the Central Supervisory Committee of the Kuomintang, 1927.

T'ao Pai-ch'uan. *San-min chu-i yü Kung-ch'an chu-i* [*The Three People's Principles and Communism*]. Chungking: Pai-lu Publishing Co., 1946.

Teng Tse-ju. *Chung-kuo Kuo-min-tang erh-shih-nien shih-chih* [*Historical Records of the Kuomintang during the Last Twenty Years*]. Shanghai: Cheng-chung Bookstore, 1948.

Ts'ao Hsi-chên. *Chung-su wai-chiao shih* [*Sino-Soviet Diplomatic History*]. Peking: Shih-chieh chih-shih she, 1951.

Tsou Lu. *Chung-kuo Kuo-min-tang shih-kao* [*Draft History of the Kuomintang*]. Chungking: The Commercial Press, 1944.

———. *Chung-kuo Kuo-min-tang shih-lüeh* [*A Brief History of the Kuomintang*]. Chungking: The Commercial Press, 1945.

———. *Hui-ku-lu* (Memoirs). 2 vols. Nanking: Tu-li Publishing Company, 1946.

———. *Tsou Lu wen-ts'un* [*Collected Essays of Tsou Lu*]. Peking: Pei-hua Bookstore, 1930.

Tsui Chu-chin. *Sun Chung-shan yü Kung-ch'an chu-i* [*Sun Yat-sen and Communism*]. Hong Kong: The Asia Press, Ltd., 1954.

Tsung-li ch'üan-chi [*Complete Collected Works of President Sun*]. 4 vols. Edited by Hu Han-min. Shanghai: Min-chih Bookstore, 1930.

Tsung-li ch'üan-shu [*Complete Writings of President Sun*]. 10 vols. Taipeh: The China Culture Service, 1953.

Tung Shih-chin. *Jên-shih Chung-kung ti t'u-kai* [*Understand the Chinese Communist Land Reform*]. Kowloon: Yu-lien Publishing Co., 1953.

Yeh Hu-shêng. *Hsien-tai Chung-kuo ko-ming shih-hua* [*A History of the Modern Chinese Revolution*]. Peking: K'ai-ming Bookstore, 1951.

Wei-ta ti Sun Chung-shan [*The Great Sun Yat-sen*]. Hong Kong: Hsin-ti Publishing Co., 1957.

Sources in Western Languages

American Consulate General, Hong Kong, *Current Background, Survey of the China Mainland Press,* and *Review of the Hongkong China Press.*

Band, Claire and William. *Two Years with the Chinese Communists.* New Haven: Yale University, 1948.

Boorman, Howard L., and others. *Moscow-Peking Axis.* New York: Harper and Brothers, 1957.

Brandt, Conrad, Benjamin Schwartz, and John K. Fairbank. *A Documentary History of Chinese Communism.* Cambridge: Harvard University Press, 1952.

Cantlie, Sir James, and C. Sheridan Jones. *Sun Yat-sen and the Awakening of China.* New York: Fleming H. Revell, 1912.

Chang, Carsun. *The Third Force in China.* New York: Bookman Associates, 1952.

Chang Kuo-tao. "Mao—A New Portrait by an Old Colleague," *The New York Times Magazine,* August 2, 1953.

Chen, Stephen, and Robert Payne. *Sun Yat-sen: A Portrait.* New York: John Day, 1946.

Chen, Tien-fong. *A History of Sino-Russian Relations.* Washington: Public Affairs Press, 1957.

Chiang Kai-shek. *China's Destiny.* Authorized translation by Wang Chung-hui. New York: Macmillan Co., 1947.

——. *Soviet Russia in China.* New York: Farrar, Straus and Cudahy, 1957.

Ch'ien Tuan-sheng. *The Government and Politics of China.* Cambridge: Harvard University Press, 1948.

China Weekly Review. Shanghai.

The China Year Book. Tientsin: The Tientsin Press, 1923-1928.

The Communist International. *The First Congress of the Toilers of the Far East.* Petrograd, 1922.

Compton, Boyd (trans.). *Mao's China: Party Reform Documents, 1942-1944.* Seattle: University of Washington Press, 1952.

Creel, H. G. *Chinese Thought: From Confucius to Mao Tse-tung.* Chicago: University of Chicago Press, 1953.

Dallin, David J. *The Rise of Russia in Asia.* New Haven: Yale University Press, 1949.

Degras, Jane (ed.). *Soviet Documents on Foreign Policy, 1917-1924.* London: Oxford University Press, 1951.

Department of State. *Papers Relating to the Foreign Relations of the United States, 1911-1925.* Washington: Government Printing Office, 1918-1940.

Eighth National Congress of the Communist Party of China. 3 vols. Peking: Foreign Languages Press, 1956.

d'Elia, Paschal M. (ed. and tr.). *Le Triple Démisme de Suen Wên.* Shanghai, 1930. Translated as *The Triple Demism of Sun Yat-sen,* Wuchang, Franciscan Press, 1931.

Fairbank, John King. *The United States and China.* Cambridge: Harvard University Press, 1948.

Fischer, Louis. *The Soviets in World Affairs.* 2 vols. London: Jonathan Cape, 1930.

Fitzgerald, Charles P. *Revolution in China.* New York: Frederick A. Praeger, 1952.

Forman, Harrison: *Report from Red China.* New York: Henry Holt and Co., 1945.

Gluckstein, Ygael. *Mao's China: Economic and Political Survey.* Boston: Beacon Press, 1957.

Holcombe, Arthur N. *The Chinese Revolution.* Cambridge: Harvard University Press, 1931.

Hsiung Shih-i. *The Life of Chiang Kai-shek.* London: P. Davies, 1948.

Hsü, Leonard Shihlien. *Sun Yat-sen: His Political and Social Ideals.* Los Angeles: University of Southern California Press, 1933.

Hu Ch'iao-mu. *Thirty Years of the Communist Party of China.* Peking: Foreign Languages Press, 1951.

Hutheesing, Raja. *The Great Peace.* New York: Harper and Brothers, 1953.

International Press Correspondence. Organ of the ECCI. Vienna, 1921-1926.

Isaacs, Harold R. *The Tragedy of the Chinese Revolution.* Stanford: Stanford University Press, 1951.

Jansen, Marius B. *The Japanese and Sun Yat-sen.* Cambridge: Harvard University Press, 1954.

Kuo Ping-chia. *China: New Age and New Outlook.* New York: Alfred A. Knopf, 1956.

Lenin, V. I. *Selected Works.* 12 vols. New York: International Publishers, 1943.

Li Tien-yi. *Woodrow Wilson's China Policy, 1913-1917.* New York: Twayne Publishers, 1952.

Linebarger, Paul. *The Gospel of Sun Chung-shan.* Paris, 1932.

———. *Sun Yat-sen and the Chinese Republic.* New York: The

Century Co., 1925.

Linebarger, Paul M. A. *The China of Chiang Kai-shek.* Boston: World Peace Foundation, 1941.

―――. *The Political Doctrines of Sun Yat-sen.* Baltimore: Johns Hopkins Press, 1937.

Liu Shao-chi, "Internationalism and Nationalism," *Soviet Press Translations,* July 15, 1949.

―――. *On the Party.* Peking: Foreign Languages Press, 1950.

MacNair, Harley Farnsworth. *China in Revolution.* Chicago: University of Chicago Press, 1931.

Mao Tse-tung. *The Chinese Revolution and the Communist Party of China.* New York: Committee for a Democratic Far Eastern Policy, 1949.

―――. *On People's Democratic Dictatorship.* Peking: Foreign Languages Press, 1951.

―――. "On Coalition Government," translated in Stuart Gelder, *The Chinese Communists,* pp. 1-60. London: Victor Gollancz Ltd., 1946.

―――. *Selected Works.* 3 vols. New York: International Publishers, 1954.

Mif, Pavel. *Heroic China.* New York: Workers' Library Publishers, 1937.

Moraes, Frank. *Report on Mao's China.* New York: Macmillan Co., 1953.

"More on the Historical Experience of Proletarian Dictatorship," (A *Jen min jih-pao's* editorial), *New China News Agency* (Peking), December 28, 1956.

The New York Times.

North, Robert C. *Kuomintang and Chinese Communist Elites.* Stanford: Stanford University Press, 1952.

―――. *Moscow and Chinese Communists.* Stanford: Stanford University Press, 1953.

Pasvolsky, Leo, *Russia in the Far East.* New York: Macmillan Co., 1922.

Payne, Robert. *Mao Tse-tung: Ruler of Red China.* New York: Henry Schuman, 1950.

People's China. (Peking) 1950-1957.

Rosinger, Lawrence K. *China's Wartime Politics, 1937-1944.* Princeton: Princeton University Press, 1944.

Rostow, W. W. *The Prospects for Communist China.* New York: John Wiley & Sons, 1954.

Roy, M. N. *Revolution and Counterrevolution in China.* Calcutta: Renaissance Publishers, 1946.

Schiffrin, Harold. "Sun Yat-sen's Early Land Policy," *The Journal of Asian Studies,* August 1957.

Schwartz, Benjamin. *Chinese Communism and the Rise of Mao,* Cambridge: Harvard University Press, 1951.

Sharman, Lyon. *Sun Yat-sen: His Life and Its Meaning.* New York: John Day, 1934.

Snow, Egar. *Red Star over China.* New York: Modern Library, Random House, 1938.

Soong Ching-ling (Madame Sun Yat-sen). *The Struggle for New China.* Peking: Foreign Languages Press, 1953.

Stalin, J. V. *Works.* 13 vols. Moscow: Foreign Languages Press, 1952-1955.

Stein, Gunther. *The Challenge of Red China.* New York: McGraw-Hill, 1945.

Steiner, H. Arthur (ed.). "Report on China," *The Annals of the American Academy of Political and Social Science,* September 1951.

Sun Yat-sen, "China's Next Step," *The Independent* (New York), June 13, 1912.

———. *Fundamentals of National Reconstruction.* Chungking: Chinese Ministry of Information, 1945.

———. *The International Development of China.* New York: G. P. Putnam's Sons, 1922.

———. "A Letter to Georgi Chicherin, August 28, 1921," *The Current Digest of the Soviet Press,* December 9, 1950.

———. *Memoirs of a Chinese Revolutionary.* London: Hutchinson & Co., 1927.

———. *San Min Chu I.* Translated by Frank W. Price and edited by L. T. Chen. Shanghai: The Commercial Press, 1928.

T'ang Leang-li. *The Foundations of Modern China.* London: N. Douglas, 1928.

———. *The Inner History of the Chinese Revolution.* New York: E. P. Dutton & Co., 1930.

Tcheng Chao-yuen. *L'Evolution de la Vie Constitutionelle de la Chine sous l'Influence de Sun Yat-sen et de sa Doctrine.* Paris: Librairie Générale de Droit et de Jurisprudence, 1937.

The Teachings of Sun Yat-sen: Selections from His Writings. Compiled by N. Gangulee. London: The Sylvan Press, 1945.

Teng, Ssu-yü, and John K. Fairbank. *China's Response to the West.* Cambridge: Harvard University Press, 1954.

Tewksbury, Donald G. (ed.). *Source Book on Far Eastern Political Ideologies: Modern Period, China, Japan.* New York: Columbia University Press, 1949.

Thomas, S. B. *Government and Administration in Communist China.* New York: Institute of Pacific Relations, 1953.

Trotsky, Leon. *Problems of the Chinese Revolution.* Translated by Max Shachtman. New York: Pioneer Publishers, 1932.

Tsui Shu-chin. "The Influence of the Canton-Moscow Entente upon Sun Yat-sen's Political Philosophy," *The Chinese Social and Political Science Review.* (Peiping), April-October 1934.

Walker, Richard L. *China under Communism.* New Haven: Yale University Press, 1955.

Wei, Henry. *China and Soviet Russia.* Princeton: Van Nostrand, 1956.

Whiting, Allen S. "A New Version of *San Min Chu I,*" *The Far Eastern Quarterly,* May 1955.

———. *Soviet Policies in China, 1917-1924.* New York: Columbia University Press, 1954.

Wilbur, C. Martin, and Julie L. Y. How (eds.). *Documents on Communism, Nationalism, and Soviet Advisers in China, 1918-1927.* New York: Columbia University Press, 1956.

William, Maurice. *Sun Yat-sen Versus Communism.* Baltimore: Williams & Wilkins, 1932.

Wittfogel, Karl A. *Sun Yat Sen, Aufzeichnungen eines chinesischen Revolutionärs.* Wien: Agis-Verlag, ca. 1927.

Woo, T. C. *The Kuomintang and the Future of the Chinese Revolution.* London: Allen & Unwin, 1928.

Wu, Aitchen K. *China and the Soviet Union.* New York: John Day, 1950.

Wu, Yuan-li. *An Economic Survey of Communist China.* New York: Bookman Associates, 1956.

Yakhontoff, Victor A. *The Chinese Soviets.* New York: Coward-McCann, 1934.

Index

Agrarian policy:
  of Chinese Communists, 154-5, 156-8, 159-62
  of Sun Yat-sen, 21, 117-8, 154, 155, 156, 157, 158-9, 160
Agrarian Reform Law of 1950, 155, 156, 159
Alexieff (Comintern agent), 55
Asia:
  Communist China and, 146
  Sun Yat-sen and, 89, 141
  Western policy toward, 175-7

Bismarck, 25-6
Bluecher, Gen. Galen, 77
Borodin, Michael:
  and Sun Yat-sen, 68-9, 88, 91
  mission to Canton, 67-8
  reorganizes Kuomintang, 69, 76-7
Britain:
  policy toward China, 44
  Sun Yat-sen and, 44, 80, 88-9

Cantlie, Dr. James, 18
Canton-Moscow alliance; see Kuomintang-Communist alliance; Sun Yat-sen
Chang, Carsun, 11
Chang Chi, 72, 73

Ch'en Ch'iung-ming:
  revolt in 1922, 40, 43, 51
Ch'en, Eugene, 64-5
Ch'en Po-ta:
  on Chinese bourgeoisie, 119
  on nation, 115, 135
  on Sun Yat-sen's doctrine, 105, 114-20
Ch'en Tu-hsiu, 98
  and Sun Yat-sen, 90
  opposition to Kuomingtang-Communist alliance, 58
Chiang Kai-shek:
  and Sun Yat-sen, 59, 60-1, 66, 73, 75-6, 78
  heads Whampoa Academy, 77
  in Russia, 66-7
  on Communist objectives in China, 72-3
  purges Communists in 1927, 97-9
  Sian incident, 101
Chicherin, 66, 67
  and Sun Yat-sen, 51, 54, 68
China, 14, 170, 171
  between 1912 and 1922, 39-40, 44-7
  old and new, 1, 119
  under the Manchus, 38
  see also People's Republic of China; Nationalist China